Books should be returned or renewed by the
last date stamped above

_____

_____

_____

MARCHING TO THE SOUND OF GUNFIRE

MARCHING TO THE SOUND OF GUNFIRE

PATRICK DELAFORCE

CHANCELLOR
PRESS

CIS 2174801

First published in 1996 by
Sutton Publishing Limited
Phoenix Mill · Far Thrupp · Stroud · Gloucestershire

This edition published in 2000 by Chancellor Press,
an imprint of Bounty Books,
a division of Octopus Publishing Group Limited,
2–4 Heron Quays, London, E14 4JP.

British Library Cataloguing in Publication Data

A catalogue record for this book is available from the British Library.

ISBN 0-75370-379-3

940·5421

Typeset in 10/12 Plantin Light
Typesetting and origination by
Sutton Publishing Limited.
Printed and bound in Great Britain by
J. H. Haynes & Co., Sparkford.

Contents

Acknowledgements

I would like to express my thanks and appreciation to the many 'sharp end' contributors to this book, some alas no longer present or able to 'march to the sound of gunfire'.

Major Bill Apsey MC, 'Chuck' Baldwin, A.J.M. Bannerman, Les Baynton, J. Bell, Major Noel Bell MC, Bill Bellamy MC, Major W.R. Birt, Geoffrey Bishop MC, Major Bindon Blood, 'Snatch' Boardman, Robert Boulton, Wally Brereton, R.N.B. Brett-Smith, Lieutenant Colonel Steel Brownlie MC, J.A. Brymer, Hedley Bunce, Major B.E.L. Burton, Wally Caines, Jim Caswell, Major Bill Close MC, Eric Codling, Ron Cookson, Major Arthur Cuckmay, Bernard Cuttiford, D. Davies, Bob Day, Edward K. Deeming, Stanley Dickinson, 'Nipper' Dutton, Lieutenant Colonel Hart Dyke DSO, Raymond Ellis, Major John Evans DSO, Rex Flower, N.L. Francis, Simon Frazer, Major Creagh Gibson, Major H.S. Gillies, Major Mickey Gold, William Gould, Richard Greenwood, Phil Grimmet, Major 'Algy' Grubb, Norman Habertin, 'Henry' Hall MC, Ernie Hamilton, Lieutenant Colonel C.D. Hamilton, Ian Hammerton, Lieutenant Colonel Godfrey Barker Harland MC, Stuart Hills MC, Major J.J. How MC, Major S. Jacobson MC, Sydney Jary MC, Anthony Jeans, Roland Jefferson BEM, H. Jobson, Lieutenant Colonel Eddie Jones, Major Harry Jones MC, Albert J. Kings, G.H. Kingsmill, Jim Kuipers MC, Revd John du B. Lance, John Lappin MC, Barrett Leonard, Major John Leytham, Lieutenant Colonel Martin Lindsay DSO, John Longfield, Major D.W. McCaffrey, George Marsden, Brigadier G.G. Mears, John Meredith, Albert Mitchell, Major Robert Moberley, Major L. Moody MC, Frank Moppett, W.R. Moseley, Roy Nash, D. O'Donnell, Roden Orde, Major Harry Parker, Major A.D. Parsons, Albert Pattison, Clifford Payne, Geoffrey Picot, John Pilborough, Doug Proctor, Hedley Prole, Guy Radcliffe, Lieutenant Colonel Ivor Rees DSO, Peter Reeve, Major W.N. Richardson MC, Peter Roach, Lionel Robertson MC, Graham Roe, Lionel Roebuck, Reg Romain, S. Rosenbaum, Major Sandy Saunders, Robert Sheldrake, Revd Leslie Skinner, Norman Smith, Reg Spittles, Geoffrey Steer, Lieutenant Colonel John Stirling MC, Len Stokes, Lieutenant Colonel David Swiney, Lieutenant Colonel George Taylor DSO, John Thorpe, Michael Trasenster, George Upton, Major Derrick Watson, Bill Wellings, Kenneth West, Major Mike Whittle MC, Michael Wilford, George Wilson, Major Humphrey Wilson, Revd Iain Wilson, Rex Wingfield, Revd Jim Wisewell.

Introduction

'Nobody enjoys fighting. Yet the forward area in any theatre of war, the sharp end of the battle, as we used to call it, is inhabited by young men with a gleam in their eye, who actually *do* the fighting. They are comparatively few in number and they are nearly always the same people.' Those were the memorable words of a great Corps Commander – perhaps the best in the Second World War – Lieutenant General Brian Horrocks.

This book is about the 'young men with a gleam in their eye who actually did the fighting', told by themselves, in that fantastic and dangerous eleven months of bloody warfare in North-west Europe after D-Day. It is written by a 'young man' (at that time) who had a 'gleam in his eye' and like thousands of others who fought their way from the Normandy bridgehead, took part in many actions: Operation Bluecoat in the break-out; The Great Swan to liberate northern France, Belgium and Holland; the capture of Antwerp, and right-flanking for Market Garden. He was blown up in the Peel Country in the bleak midwinter of 1944–5, fought in the Reichwald and at the Rhine crossing, and took part quite vigorously in the five canal and river battles in Germany before his Armoured Division smashed its way to the Baltic.

Marching to the Sound of Gunfire has stories by the PBI, the tough, solid, mortar-swept infantry who plodded forward from slit to slit – the Brengunners, riflemen, mortarmen, stretcher-bearers and signallers; stories from the Tankies in their out-gunned Shermans, Cromwells and Churchills tackling Mk IVs with some relish, Panthers with trepidation and Tigers with fear in their hearts, and tales of the brave assault troops – Dragoons and Hussars – who bashed their way ashore on D-Day with AVREs and Flails. Also here are the intrepid Recce types in their thin-skinned armoured cars, pushing and prodding round dangerous corners, always radioing back their vital information to the 'management'; the various kinds of gunners, led by their devoted FOOs with self-propelled or towed guns bringing down fast, furious, close support barrages to protect their 'little friends'; sappers building bridges under fire, clearing minefields, 'delousing' booby traps – all the nasty battlefield jobs; padres seeking dead young men burnt alive in tanks or lying in ditches and giving them a decent burial; RAMC doctors and orderlies in the front line tending their wounded with their RAP under fire, and all the support services – RASC bringing up food, ammo and mail and the REME repairing armoured vehicles for the morrow.

Marching to the Sound of Gunfire depicts not only victories, but also bloody defeats, attacks and withdrawals, the shock of being wounded in action, the trauma of being surrounded and captured, 'friendly' fire and grim accidents in the field. It brings back the magic moments of the break-out from Normandy, the exhilaration of the chase called The Great Swan, and the delirious welcomes in the liberated villages and towns on the centre lines. It recalls the tragedy of Market Garden, the tedium of the winter months, watching and guarding the Maas, the dash south to act as longstop in the Ardennes and the ferocious little rearguard battles fought by the SS and paratroopers in Germany on the way to seizing Bremen and Hamburg. But interspersed with the grim and sometimes frightening incidents are many comical interludes, as Tommy Atkins has always been renowned for his sense of humour.

Grateful thanks are owed to the hundred or so front-line soldiers whose stories are included in this book, and specially to Donald Green, the young Queen's Rifleman with the Desert Rats in Normandy for his marvellous 'live' pencil drawings. Thanks also to Birkin Haward OBE, the AVRE sapper whose drawings of the major battlefields enhance this book, and to Random House for permission to use extracts from Martin Lindsay's *So Few Got Through* (Hutchinson).

This book is dedicated to the memory of the young men who fought so bravely and are now buried in the many peaceful War Cemeteries, so well tended by the War Graves Commission – 'the privates and the bombardiers, the riflemen and tank drivers, the signalmen and sappers, the stretcher-bearers and doctors – who all, one way or another, "marched to the sound of gunfire".'

CHAPTER ONE

Overlord

The Great Adventure

The years of training and exercises had honed the British Army – Burger, Grab, Smash, Crown, Anchor, Leap Year, Baron, Kilbride, Millhouse, Blindman, Euclid, Fabius and scores of others. HM King George VI and Winston Churchill had visited most units and Monty had stood on the bonnet of his jeep a hundred times – 'Gather round, I want to talk to you.' In schoolboy language, with cricketing terms, he reduced the complexities of war to its simplest ingredients – 'We have trained, we are fit, we are well-led, we will win.' The troops loved it.

Undoubtedly in May–June 1944 morale was extremely high. Long-lasting partnerships were made between the gunner regiments and 'their' infantry battalions which they supported. In the armoured divisions, but rarely elsewhere, the partnership between motorized infantry and the tank regiments proved itself time and again in battle. Over six hundred young Canadian officers under the codename Canloan volunteered, and were gratefully integrated into British county infantry battalions. Every British infantry division received about forty Canloan officers. For instance, 3rd British Division received thirty-nine, of whom ten were killed in action and five were awarded the Military Cross. Monty had chosen his old division, 3rd British, and his desert faithful, 50th Tyne/Tees, to spearhead the invasion.

Padre Iain Wilson, chaplain to 1 KOSB wrote:

It is difficult to resist the temptation to dwell upon the years between 1940 and 1944 when we trained and journeyed together, leading a curiously self-contained life from the Sussex Downs to the Moray Firth. The winter snows on Salisbury Plain, the gentle Devonshire valleys, the woods and gardens of Buckinghamshire, the cliffs above Dover, the wild lands and seas of Moidart and Morar, the ancient peace and simplicity of our Borderland – in these settings we lived, worked and played together, sharing all things that men can share, from our very uniform and food, to our worship of God. It had greatly changed us from the exhausted men who had staggered off destroyers and minesweepers and countless 'little ships' in June 1940.

Jackie's 'Boys'

Captain John Stirling 2 i/c 'A' Sqn, 4/7 Royal Dragoon Guards, whose Sherman tanks landed on D-Day, described his fellow officers waiting for the 'off':

Jackie Goldsmid was the father of the family in a very real sense [Sqn CO]. Ten to fifteen years older than the rest, a regular soldier in the best sense of the word. A big, dark man with eyebrows that could beetle his eyes out of sight on occasion. He commanded respect, endowed with a very keen brain and a conscience, gifted with a great sense of humour, sympathy and considerable charm. He could possess a worse liver in the morning than most people. David Richards was the other captain. Twenty-eight, medium height, black curly hair and eyes as full of life as a mountain stream when the fish are rising. Hunting, horses, farming and the country were in his blood. He was an invaluable link between Jackie and the 'boys' – the troopleaders. It is still true as ever that it is the officers who make or mar. There was not a bad troop in 'A' Sqn, and the 'boys' were the reason. Peter Aizlewood led 1st Troop. A boyish, twenty-year-old Wykehamist with a superiority of manner and a wisdom that sat strangely on such young shoulders. 2nd Troop, Mike Trasenster, another Wykehamist, but tall and blond, temperamental as a racehorse, with a magnificent predilection for arguments. He expected to give orders and take the lead and his men expected it too. Charles Pillman ran 3rd Troop. Widely travelled, older than the others, both in years and appearance. Tall and dark, with a lithe, strong body, he looked the athlete he was. Full of fun, always ready to take everything that was coming. Garth Alastair Morrison, 4th Troop, was short, thickset, red-faced with tousled hair. He lacked the superiority of manner of the others – but he was the leader of an excellent troop. Geoffrey Mitchell, 5th Troop, with a simple nature, babyish face, tall, slim, almost frail figure with perfect manners – quiet and efficient.

These were John Stirling's companions-in-arms – Jackie's 'Boys'. On D-Day Pillman and Mitchell were killed, and Aizlewood badly wounded.

Grubby is Mad

Private Albert J. Kings, 1 Worcesters with the 'green' 43rd Wessex Wyvern Division, described his officer.

We joined the 43rd Div, our training was stepped up. We were being whipped into a real fighting unit. Our officer and NCOs did their job well, we were really good and we knew it. We were brimming over with confidence in ourselves and our ability. I reckoned I was the best

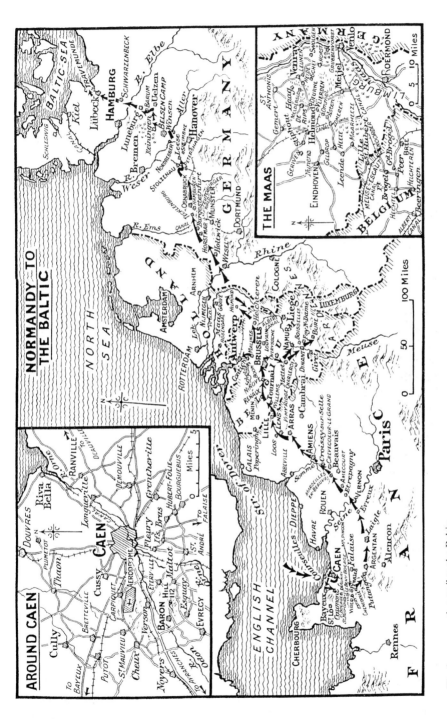

AROUND CAEN

Douvres · Plumetot · Riva Bella · R. Orne · RANVILLE · DEAUVILLE · DIVES · CABOURG · Cully · Bretteville · Thaon · Longueville · DEMOUVILLE · Grentheville · To Bayeux · Putot · St. Mauvieu · Carpiquet · AERODROME · CAEN · Verson · Maltot · Eterville · Fleury · Ifs Bras · St. André · HUBERT-FOLIE · BOURGUEBUS · To Falaise · Cheux · Noyers · Esquay · Baron Hill 112 · Evrecy · Hill 113 · R. Odon · To Avranches

Miles 0 5

NORMANDY TO THE BALTIC

NORTH SEA · BALTIC SEA · Schleswig · Kiel · CANAL · Lübeck · TRAVEMÜNDE · HAMBURG · Schwarzenbeck · R. Elbe · Bremen · Lüneburg · Winsen · BELSEN CAMP · Barum · Uelzen · Reininger · R. Aller · Nordheide · Soltau · Leese · Hanover · STOLZENAU · Weser · NIENBURG · R. Ems · FRIESLAND · CANAL · OSNABRÜCK · Burgsteinfurt · Rheine · HORSTMAR · Holdwick · Wesel · Munster · DORTMUND · GERMANY · Rhine · Cologne

HOLLAND · AMSTERDAM · ROTTERDAM · Lek · Arnhem · NIJMEGEN · Maas · Grave · Hertogenbosch

Antwerp · Heichteren · MALINES · BRUSSELS · Louvain · ALBERT CANAL · Liège · Namur · LUXEMBURG · Meuse · A R D E N N E S

BELGIUM · Menin · WYTSCHAETE · RENAIX · TOURNAI · St. WILLEMS · Charleroi · Dinant · Givet · FOY-NOTRE · BUR · Bastogne · LUXEMBURG

LILLE · LOOS · LENS · VIMY RIDGE · ARRAS · Cambrai · CATEAU-LE-GRAND

Calais · Poperinghe · ABBEVILLE · MARCELLES-EN-BEAUVAIS · Somme · AMIENS · Croixsey-sur-Scie · BEAUVAIS · AMECOURT

St. of Dover · ENGLISH CHANNEL · CHERBOURG · HAVRE · Yvetot-Dieppe · ROUEN · Seine · VERNON · EVREUX · Etrepagny

Bayeux · St. Lô · CAEN · Falaise · MT. PINCON · ARGENTAN · Alençon · Laigle · Putanges

Rennes · Paris

F R A N C E

NORTH SEA

0 50 100 Miles

THE MAAS

GERMANY · Venlo · ROERMOND · St. ANTHONIS · Gemert · Gennep · Reichswald · Helmond · Venraij · MEUSE ESCAUT CANAL · Meijel · Eindhoven · Leende · St. Hubert · BELGIUM · Peer · Bree · Bocholt · ALBERT CANAL

N

0 5 10 Miles

The long campaign trail to the Baltic

Brengunner there was, my reflexes were quick, my work rate was high and I was very fleet of foot. That may sound conceited but this was the sort of confidence we possessed. There was a certain rapport between all ranks which is difficult to describe. We were behind Freddie Henry [12 Platoon OC] to a man, and the same for Major [Algy] Grubb, our Coy Co. [Later in France] a batch of reinforcements arrived. One said to one of my mates, 'They tell me the Major of "B" Coy is mad.' The reply came back in the best soldiers' language. 'Grubby, he is mad, mad as an effing hatter, but his company will follow him anywhere. If you're not prepared to do that, piss off to some other company.'

Comradeship

Private Bob Day, a veteran of Salerno, served with the East Surreys and 2/6 Queen's in the Italian campaign where he was wounded by a mortar fragment. Having recovered in England from his 'blighty' wound he wrote:

I began to miss the comradeship of men in danger, a comradeship I have never quite found since. I missed simple pleasures such as brewing tea in the shelter of a slit trench or deserted farmhouse which can mean so much more than luxurious living. Such were the thoughts of a brash 20-year-old and when D-Day came on June 6th and the first flying bombs, V-1s, came over our barracks one night, I resolved to rejoin a fighting unit. I became part of a reinforcement draft which set sail from Dover.

Bob joined the 1st Leicesters and celebrated his twenty-first birthday in a Dutch barn on the way to Nijmegen in November 1944.

The Tank Crew

Of all the close-knit 'families' going to war, the four or five individuals in a Sherman, Cromwell or Churchill tank have to live with each other at very close quarters under awful stress. John Stirling, 4/7 Royal Dragoon Guards, describes his Sherman tank crew:

Except for myself they all came from the North. Nixon was the driver from Northumberland. An older man, about 35, quiet, patient and utterly reliable. Vallance as his mate, the co-driver also from Northumberland. Tall and quiet, an ex-policeman with a cool, sound head, a great worker with the strength for the many jobs in a tank with big weights to be lifted, strains to be borne. Up in the turret with me the loader-wireless operator Tarran, a Geordie, a thin-faced, slight, little man, as sharp as he looked and as quick. For both those jobs you need to be quick to do them well. Murphy was the gunner, a little, dark man from Glasgow, a bit older, who had been a miner, with great resolution and sense of humour. I could never understand that terrible brogue!

This was my tank crew. I never hope to have a gamer, more willing, more reliable set of friends in any walk of life.

Keep them Guessing

Secrecy was of course paramount and the British Army went to extraordinary pains to ensure that the enemy was kept guessing. Lieutenant Raymond Ellis, with his 82 Assault Squadron Royal Engineers and their AVREs (Churchill engineer tanks), Arks (bridging tanks) and tanks bearing fascines for filling in trenches or bomb craters, were due to land on D-Day on the well-defended beaches – but where?

I was to command No. 5 Beach Breaching Lane. About two days before we loaded the tanks on Q2 Hard on to the LCT an 'Information tent' was set up guarded night and day as it was 'Top Secret' Plus. In it tables were laid out on which were displayed large-scale maps of the landing area with the exact positions of the six 'Beach breaching lanes'. It was our task to make our way through the beach obstacles, through the low sandhills for about 120 yards, which were mined, on to the lateral road. The steel tetrahedra, minefields, gun positions and emplacements and tracks were marked. There were also excellent aerial photographs taken coming in from the sea. A prominent sanatorium was an outstanding feature and a large blockhouse near by. All of us wondered where exactly this beach was, which had been illustrated in so much detail. Perhaps Calais or was it Normandy? At the top of the photographs was a broad black streak which obviously concealed the name of the key places. Some inquisitive soldiers soon discovered that by wetting your handkerchief and giving the photo a rub, the name of the coastal village was clearly decipherable. But names like Le Hamel and Arromanches meant nothing to us, so we were not much the wiser!

Waiting for the 'Off'

For weeks the British Army was held captive in scores of camps. Lionel Roebuck of the East Yorkshires recalls:

On the last pay day before leaving camp each man was given 200 French francs mostly in 5-franc notes. They were blue-green in colour, square and had a picture of the French Flag on the reverse side. In addition we all had a tin of Taverner & Rutledge quality boiled sweets and two FLs [condoms]. The latter were used to protect rifle barrels from the sand and seawater during the landing and by some as waterproof containers for watches and other valuables. Although the game of Housey-Housey run by the NCOs, who were on to a good thing, was the only officially allowed gambling game, additional gambling schools on the results of card games, using a mixture of the new issue money and English money, were soon started. Pitch and Toss using any flat secluded area to toss up two half pennies, became a popular way to gamble, betting on two heads or two tails, one of each resulting in a new throw. Lectures were given on the correct behaviour and attitude towards the French civilians and unofficially the problems of taking too many prisoners!

Eventually, for security reasons, all the camps were turned into 'concentration' laagers.

Moving Up

Major W.R. Birt's Flail tanks of 22 Dragoons were to lead the beach attack in front of 3rd Division:

0215 hrs June 2. The wait has prolonged itself. We are eight hours behind programme. Heavy with rum-laced tea we doze in the back of the car. Under the green balconies a group of soldiers have been singing for hours to the tinkle of an RAF man's ukelele. A strong tenor leads a drowsy bee-contented hum. They sing over and over again, 'Roll me over, love'. Then the mood changes. With notes long-drawn they turn to 'Home, Sweet Home' and 'Love's Old Sweet Song'. From the balconies close above us in the darkness, girls' voices join in sweetly, strongly. There is a sudden move ahead of us. The ukelele and the tenor voice tumble into a truck and above the growl of the lorries we hear the lilt of 'Goodbye, ladies'. We jerk forward and are on the loading dock. There under the arc-lamps is the great gaping mouth of our landing ship, its monstrous belly lamp-lit and up whose throat there crawls a procession of tiny men in tiny vehicles.

Long-awaited Journey

Harry Jones, No. 10 Platoon Commander, 'X' Company 2 KSLI recalls:

On the morning of 4th June 1944, my Platoon consisting of myself and 36 infantry soldiers, climbed into lorries and began the long-awaited journey to the South Coast. It was a warm sunny day and I was amazed at the sight of hundreds of tanks, guns, ammunition stacks and stores, lining the roads nose-to-tail. The whole countryside appeared to be one massive depot.

Harry sailed from Newhaven in a LSI. After the famous twenty-four hour delay caused by adverse weather, 'Ike' bravely unleashed his Anglo-Saxon armies. The troops were each issued with 200 French francs, a small booklet of French phrases, blurb about France and the French, Mae West lifebelts, chewing gum, tommy cookers, META fuel, water-sterilizing tablets, tins of twenty cigarettes, biscuits, chocolate, bullybeef, two twenty-four hour ration packs, three bags of 'vomit', small bottles of anti-seasick pills, compo packs, water-cans, self-heating soups and cocoa. Some lucky men who went in US-built LSIs had a luxury voyage watching Mickey Rooney and Judy Garland films in the cafeteria.

After the issue of a special assault jerkin, a light gas respirator, a new steel helmet, a brand-new battledress, BAFVs, spare underwear and boots, plus all the above, each infantryman carried a load of about 65 lb. Brengunners and the mortar platoons carried rather more. The entrenching tool/spade also was a vital 'accessory'. Operation Overlord went active as the Liberty ships, LCTs, LCIs and craft of all kinds were filled up, despite the lacklustre working habits of the London dockers.

On Board Ship and Seasick

Corporal Clifford Arthur Payne of 2 East Yorkshires writes:

A Padre gave us a sermon on board ship and at the finish we sang the hymn 'For those in peril on the sea'. After that we began to move again and overhead there was a terrible noise of plane engines. Of course it was dark about one or two o'clock. We learned later that it was the Airborne boys going over. I tried to sleep but it just wouldn't come to me. Anyway I was seasick and I didn't care if the first shell hit us, I was so bad.

The Shropshires – 'All at Sea'

Guy Radcliffe, adjutant 2 KSLI, wrote:

Landing craft are not the ideal ships in which to make a rough Channel crossing. Their blunt bows sent cascades of spume over the ship, the quarters on LCIs are cramped and in LCTs non-existent. Most men felt none too well and on the LCTs especially it was difficult to keep dry. But the cheerfulness was amazing! Two hundred troops of 2 KSLI set sail from Portsmouth in a LSI, via Spithead to the lea of the Isle of Wight for the fleet RV at 'Piccadilly Circus'.

Hugh Gunning, journalist and observer: '1st KOSB had a wretched time in their crossing of the Channel. LCTs roll like a porpoise but they have plenty of weight throbbing their way through the sea. It is a trim little vessel, functional in its design with its two ramps at the bow and every modern facility for pouring men off a ship on to a beach.'

Major H.S. Gillies was CO of 'C' Company:

> The sea was very high – great green troughs of waves, other craft plunging and rolling as they made their way onwards. Ahead lay the coast of France, then quiet and expressionless, puffs of smoke here and there. The skies were full of aircraft circling over the fleet for its protection. Above the wind could be heard the dull thudding from the heavy guns of the battleships and cruisers [*Warspite, Ramillies, Roberts, Dragon, Frobisher* and *Danae* had guns deployed on Sword beach defences]. One of the most heartening sights was a tank landing craft from which the artillery were firing salvo after salvo of rockets onto the enemy defences.

Prayers and Confidence

Despite the issuing of anti-seasick tablets the majority of the invasion force suffered from *mal de mer* and some were so ill they could not fight on arrival, but the sense of confidence was awe-inspiring, as Albert J. Kings, 1 Worcesters, recalls:

> At last the balloon went up and we moved to Newhaven on the LCIs. I felt excited and eager to get going. I remember standing on deck, watching the shores of home disappearing. Suddenly someone somewhere knelt down to pray and everyone joined in. How many knew in their heart that they would not be coming back. I felt sorry for those who had families, their tears were unashamed. My thoughts turned to my young wife who I had married only three months before. I thought to myself I must have been mad. She could be a widow before the year was out. I tried to look ahead to better times but I knew it would only be brought about by our efforts. I was determined to do my best. Thoughts of my death didn't occur to me. *I* was going to be alright.

Albert was wounded in the foot during Market Garden and was flown back to Nottingham Hospital.

The Suffolk on Battleaxe

'It was the worst 48 hours in my life on that landing craft,' recalls Albert Pattison, then Platoon Sergeant of the 6-pdr A/Tank guns with 1 Suffolk. Worse than swimming 2 miles off the Dunkirk beaches in 1940, aged seventeen. 'Isn't it marvellous what fear can make you do!'

Private Stanley Gardner, 1 Suffolk, kept a journal:

> On board the *Empire Battleaxe*, a converted American freighter, the boys were playing cards gambling away their last English money and starting on their new French money. At 8.45 the decks were crowded with troops

– hundreds of sun-burned fit young men in khaki with their safety belts on and everyone with a black triangle on their arms. [Later] dawn was just breaking and as we looked out over the rough sea we could see a huge red glow on the horizon. This must be France. A destroyer speeding by about eight miles from us struck a mine and blew up, scattering wreckage in all directions. At 3.30 we queued up with our trays for breakfast of porridge, two hard-boiled eggs, four rounds of white bread and butter and jam and a mug of tea. We gave our rifles the once-over, filled the magazines and made sure our ammunition and grenades were ready for use. At 4.45 the word came over the loud-speaker for us to get dressed [for battle]. At 4.50 the captain told us he could see the French coast – a blazing inferno with the Navy shelling it and the RAF bombing it. Then came the order 'Marines of ALC 23 lower away'. Slowly the winches began to turn and we slid down the ship's side and bumped into the stormy sea. We were then seven miles from shore. We made ourselves as comfortable as possible, some sitting, some standing but all singing. New songs and old – sentimental – patriotic and ballads but we all sang.'

Stanley was twenty and destined to be taken prisoner in three weeks' time.

A Million Trumpets Blow

'And when the vast invasion fleets moved out silently into the windy English Channel, it was as if a million trumpets began to blow again, a great heartful chorus of sanity and freedom, heavy with menace for the Nazis, thrilling with hope for those whom they had enslaved,' wrote Padre Iain Wilson, 1 KOSB.

CHAPTER TWO

Beachhead Assault

It is impossible to do justice in a few pages to the planning, the dedication, the astonishing bravery and the ultimate great success of the Allied landings on the beaches as part of Overlord. The British Army was mainly concerned with Sword beach in the eastern sector and Gold beach in the western sector, with the Canadian 3rd Infantry Division tackling Juno beach in the centre.

From west to east, Sword beach consisted of four 'sub' beaches, Oboe, Peter, Queen and Roger, and was known to be defended by 716 Coast Defences Infantry Division. The probability was that 21 Panzer Division was close to Caen, perhaps near the south-west suburbs. Queen beach had two small resort villages to contend with, River Bella and La Brèche to the left (east) and the rather larger Lion-sur-Mer to the right (west), 2 miles apart. All the houses had been turned into fortresses and the flat countryside behind heavily mined. The open beaches were mined, with many underwater obstacles, including 'hedgehogs'(three strong metal girders lashed together at the centre and splayed out) in overlapping rows, only exposed at low tide, backed by pillboxes and concrete emplacements whose guns commanded the beaches. Inland there were the objectives with codenames 'cars': Rover, Hillman and Morris, and 'fish': Cod, Sole, and Trout. Rommel had had plenty of time to strengthen his Atlantic Wall defences. It was hoped that the naval big guns and RAF bombers would have destroyed them in the preliminary huge supporting barrages.

The enemy defending Queen beach was the 736th Regiment. In their pillboxes and fortified villas they covered the beach defences with machine guns, 75 mm guns and mortars. They had been drenched with fire from the Royal Navy, RAF and seaborne artillery. The beaches had been well marked by the Royal Naval midget submarine crews of X20 and X23. Brigadier Lord Lovat's Commando Brigade were in support of the 8th Infantry Brigade. 4 Commando were to take Ouistreham and 41 Marine Commando were to advance westwards to Lion-sur-Mer and link up with the Canadian 3rd Division. The rest of Lord Lovat's command would link up with the airborne troops who had dropped 6 miles inland at Benouville.

The landing plan called for four LCTs each carrying four DD tanks apiece to be put 'ashore' at H–5 minutes, followed at H-Hour by another four LCTs carrying Hobart's unique 'Funnies', Flail tanks of the 22nd Dragoons, flame-throwing Crocodiles and Petards throwing drum-bombs.

82nd Assault Squadron RE lead assault on D-Day, Le Hamel, Arromanches, 6 June 1944, 0730 hrs. (Birkin Haward)

RE assault groups would begin work clearing the deadly beach obstacles. At H+7 came eight assault landing craft bearing the two leading infantry companies, and at H+20 another eight LCAs with two more infantry companies. At H+25 there followed two LCAs with more beach group backup teams, and at H+35 more backup 'Funny' tank support and bulldozers. At H+60 came nine LCTs with SP guns, at H+90 ten LCTs with more tanks, and the tenth wave was twenty-one DUKWs loaded with ammunition, stores and more gunner support. COSSAC, the Army Group planners, had forecast losses of 10 per cent of the landing craft sunk and a further 20 per cent damaged.

The beach obstacles consisted of a ramp of balks of timber about 15–16 ft long and about 8 ft high with the lower end facing seaward, plus vertical posts about 6–8 ft high and 'hedgehogs'. In most cases Teller mines or other explosives were fastened to the top of each of the obstacles which were half-covered at half tide and fully exposed at low tide. The immediate task of the Beach Group was to get the beach marker signs up – red and green banners to guide the follow-up waves of craft through lanes cleared of mines and obstacles. Their second task was to make the beach a working, functional area, clear remaining mines and barbed wire, mark beach exits through the dunes and seafront houses, develop lateral roads running along the beachhead, recover 'drowned' vehicles and – vitally – keep everybody moving. The Beachmasters were kings of the beaches and quite rightly brooked no arguments from anyone, including senior officers. H-Hour was 0725.

Composite Breaching Teams

Lieutenant Raymond Ellis describes the sapper role on the beaches:

The Assault Squadron, Royal Engineers with their 'Funny' armoured vehicles had a key role in the D-Day beach onslaught. The 1st Assault Brigade RE, commanded by Brigadier Clausen, consisted of the 5th, 6th and 42nd Assault Regts RE. The AVREs were normal Mk IV Churchill tanks with their turret gun replaced either by a 29 mm Spigot mortar known as the 'Petard' which fired a 'Dustbin' of 26 lbs of high explosive at the beach concrete defences at a range of 50–80 yards or the assault bridge mounted on the front of the tank capable of bridging a 30 foot gap or the 'Fascine', a 40 ton bundle of chest-paling, 12–14 feet wide designed to fill in large bomb craters or anti-tank ditches. And the special Sherman tanks fitted with flails (known as Crabs) which thrashed and flogged their way through minefields.

Six composite breaching teams of Flails and AVREs had the difficult task of creating lanes on each beach through or over high sea walls impassable to tanks, steel obstructions set in the beaches and often booby-trapped, ubiquitous minefields, barbed wire and road block defences.

From west to east 82 and 81 squadrons led 50th Northumbrian Division ashore, 26 and 80 squadrons the 3rd Canadian Infantry Division and 77 and 79 squadrons 3rd British Infantry Division.

The Flails

Major Raymond Birt, 22nd Dragoons, described the role of his 'Flail' tanks:

Our breaching teams were composed according to the nature of the defences to be attacked. First the sweep through minefields and barbed wire by Flail tanks, 'shot in' by whatever fire support was available. Secondly, the advance up the swept lane of the assault engineers to fill in or bridge a defensive ditch and given fire support by the now stationary Flails. Thirdly – if necessary – a further sweep over the obstacle by Flails. Fourthly, the movement through the completed lane of assault infantry and supporting arms.

On the right – Queen White beach – 'A' squadron of 22nd Dragoons Flails with AVREs of 77 squadron 5 ARE provided four breaching teams directed on the holiday villas of the small seaside resort of Lion-sur-Mer. On the left – Queen Red beach – 'C' squadron 22nd Dragoons Flails with AVREs of 79 squadron 5 ARE were to breach on the more open beach at La Brèche. The casino at Riva Bella was a particularly difficult strongpoint. The Queen sector guarded the entrance to the Caen canal, was heavily fortified and was within range of the long-range guns from the promontory of Le Havre to the east.

Queen Red beach was tougher still. Stretches of 'Fortress Europe' on 2nd British Army's front were held on the coastal perimeter by garrison troops with little stomach for fighting: renegades, some of them, from Russian POW camps or mean-spirited men from 'punishment' battalions stiffened with a sprinkling of tough Nazi officers and NCOs. But on Queen beach the defence was grim and fanatical. The Germans fought the irresistible wave of tanks and men that was flung upon them until it was seen to be engulfing them. Then firing their useless rifles and shouting perhaps their final salute to the Fuehrer who had willed their deaths, they ran out into the fire of the tank guns – men thirsty for the privilege of destruction in battle.

There was fierce shooting at close range: like so much of the fighting on Queen beaches tanks ran for the gun emplacements in a grim race to put their shells almost point blank through the mouths of the concrete 'boxes' before they themselves were put out of action. The team was thus able to complete its breach and shoot in the assault infantry before moving up to sweep [with Flail tanks] its lateral communications. In spite of this intense opposition on the beaches all eight lanes on the beaches themselves were through before 0800 and infantry of the East Yorks and South Lancs were passing through to the first lateral under very heavy mortar and small arms fire.

On D-Day the assault engineers of 5 ARE suffered 117 casualties including their CO, Lieutenant Colonel Cocks, who was killed, and 22nd Dragoons had 42 casualties. Fifteen of their twenty-six Sherman Flails were knocked out or damaged that day.

DD *Tanks*

Trooper Bernard Cuttiford had joined the Staffordshire Yeomanry, part of 27th Armoured Brigade commanded by Brigadier Prior Palmer. The other two Sherman tank regiments were 13/18th Hussars (QMO) and the East Riding Yeomanry. He wrote: 'First ashore on the White Area of Sword beach were the 13/18th with their DD tanks, who were dropped off at about 800 yards [in fact further out], and then swam ashore under their own steam. We were next with our ordinary land Shermans with wading equipment.' Twenty-four tanks of A and B squadrons 13/18th Hussars 'swam' for shore. En route two were rammed by the AVRE 'fleet' and sank immediately, four were disabled by enemy fire on the beach and five more were swamped by breakers. So only five were effective on White beach and eight on Red beach, but they were soon joined by five unable to launch at sea.

The Canloan Officer's Story: 'Swarm of Angry Bees'

The East Yorkshires and South Lancs arrived off the beaches in the *Empire Battleaxe* and *Glencarn* between 0430 and 0600 7 miles offshore. The East Yorks had to attack on the extreme left section of Sword beach called Queen Red, with objectives called Cod, Sole and Daimler – all formidable strongpoints. Lieutenant Leonard Robertson was a Canloan Platoon Commander and gave a vivid account of their landing under fire.

The East Yorkshires were in. As C Coy moved in to land behind A Coy and to the right, we discovered that all the wire entanglements and beach obstacles which were to be cleared by the sappers hadn't been. Major Barrow spotted an opening and made for it with 13 and 14 Platoons following in their LCAs. Not for me it wasn't. I figured that one or two might get through and not be spotted by the Jerries but certainly not four craft. Gave the order for full speed ahead . . . as I wanted to hit the wire hard and crash the entanglement with the mines without them going off. It was a chance to take but we didn't have all day to figure it out. The Marine corporal in charge of the LCA hesitated, and I really didn't blame him, but when I went to take the wheel he gave her the gun. Heads down! Here we go! The first wire parted like a string. The second wire jarred us and really gave us a scare as we just missed hitting an iron rail with a tellermine on top. Shells were falling all around us; a craft on our left received a direct hit and started to settle but on we went. . . . On the third wire we stuck and stayed. The corporal of the Marines thought we had hit the beach so he dropped the ramp and away I went with two of my men right behind me before we realized we were hooked on the wire. The three of us had gone right over our heads in water but we bobbed right up. I gave a yell to pull up the ramp and gun her while we got out of the way. The LCA broke loose and followed us and touched down and my men poured out. Bullets, shrapnel and what have you was flying around like a swarm of angry bees. Private Woodhead was the first hit in our Pl, stopping one in the arm. He was the one who the night before had said, 'If you will lead I will follow you anywhere.' Blood was flowing and bodies of other Pls from A and B Companies were floating face down in the water here and there. Things were moving so fast that one had hardly time to think or be scared. Our main thought was to get the hell off the beach. While the rest of the Pl made for dry land I grabbed Woodhead and his PIAT bombs and literally dragged him ashore. While doing so he was hit for the second time. Private Herbert simply disappeared – we never saw him again. . . . We were on the beach and soon organized and on the move, 15 Platoon was the first in the Coy to get moving as a unit and with the least casualties . . . two killed and two wounded, the lightest in the battalion, I believe. We felt very lucky indeed. My men were just grand all the way, even finding time to joke now and then.

A Lancashire Cup of Tea

Two waves, 'A' and 'C' companies of the South Lancs under Major
J.F. Harwood and Major E.F. Johnson, touched down from the LSIs at 0720
on a strip of sandy beach with dunes, in front of the village of Colville-sur-
Orne. Despite heavy MG and mortar fire they made good progress and the
second wave landed 25 minutes later – Battalion HQ, HQ Companies 'B'
and 'D' – and at once took casualties from small arms, mortars and 88 mm
gunfire. This wave landed opposite Cod, which was jointly attacked by 'C'
Company. The CO, Lieutenant Colonel R.P.H. Burbery, was killed by a
sniper. Three regimental flags with the Roman numeral XL in silver (40th
Regiment of Foot) were used as markers. One held by the battalion landing
officer was easily spotted by incoming craft and another was held by the
CO. The 2 i/c, Major Jack Stone, took over while 'B' helped deal with Cod.
Their CO, Major R.H. Harrison, and his immediate successor, Lieutenant
Bob Bell-Walker, were killed in action, but by 0830 the opposition was
overcome. The 1st Battalion South Lancashires (Prince of Wales Volunteer)
claim in their regimental history (by Colonel B.R. Mullaly) they were the
first British unit to brew tea on French soil!

A Bad State, Cold, Wet and Sick

Bill Wellings was with 'A' Company South Lancashires:

At 0725 hrs our assault craft dumped us on the landing beach Sword
Queen White. We were in a bad state, cold, wet, sick, glad to get off that
bloody LCA. Our first hold-up after landing was the wire. It must have
been 8 ft high and 12 ft deep so our Bangalore team went into action. The
first 6 ft length was slid under, then the second length was locked in and
pushed under and the third length was connected. The third man ran
back and I think he forgot to light the fuse for it didn't go off. Our OC
Major 'Spook' Harwood told us to keep our heads down while he went off
to investigate. On his way he caught a burst of Spandau fire. He crawled
forward and managed to light the fuse. He must have been in acute agony.
As I ran through the gap in the wire he looked at me with a half smile on
his face and I heard him say, 'Carry on Wellings, I'll catch up later.' He
died of his wounds about 0315 hrs on 7th June. We managed to get to the
safety of the seaside villas. To my left CSM Murphy stood beckoning the
next wave to come forward, the Coy runner Dickie Dallow by his side.
Suddenly there was a fierce explosion and they were both killed instantly.

No Time for a Drunken Orgy

Sole and Daimler were codenames for two of the strongpoints Private
Lionel Roebuck and the 2nd Battalion East Yorkshire Regiment had to

storm on D-Day. His mate Cliff Milnes, a boxer, had both his legs shattered and died of his wounds. When shell splinters hit the CO, Lieutenant Colonel C.P. Hutchinson, in the arm and side, Lionel was in a ditch on the opposite side of the track and some bits of shrapnel thwacked into his pack. Lionel described Daimler: 'Behind the wire fence there was a system of interlocking and overlapping cover of cross-fire MG positions. A deep open trench network linked all the pillboxes. Partly below ground level, blockhouses with a central domed shelter and ammo store bunker, in which the four 75 mm guns were housed standing out on a large concrete base, along with a stack of shells, their fire directed towards the beach and the vital crossings from it.' Although Lionel was caught temporarily on the fence, he and the rest of 'C' Company were throwing Mills 36 grenades into every pillbox (although by now some were empty). In one 'a picture of Hitler gazed down at me from the wall. Without hesitation, and in acute anger, I smashed the glass with a blow from my rifle butt and put two fountain pens on a desk into my pocket.' The Rhodesian Lieutenant Dickson, 13 Platoon Commander, fell down wounded. 'He had fallen over on his left side with his back arched, writhing, straining and twisting to try and ease away from the pain of his wound.' Lionel went back into the blockhouse for blankets and returned to make his officer more comfortable. Captain Cranford with his Sten gun and CSM Pullen with his revolver led the charge into the 75 mm gun site. Soon seventy prisoners were taken. One said in English, 'Only a raid, hey?', to which came the instant chorus, 'This is the invasion.' Another trying to curry favour showed his prized pornographic pictures. The victors soon found cases of wine and beer. CSM Pullen had to read the riot act. 'Not the time for a drunken orgy.' Lionel's share of the booty was a bottle of dry red wine. 'Not at all to my taste.'

Juno Beach

H-Hour had been delayed to 0745 and many landing craft were late and the first units ashore landed right in the midst of the German beach obstacles. Twenty out of the leading twenty-four craft were lost or damaged, and by midday ninety out of over three hundred were lost. Scores of RM Centaur tanks with 95 mm howitzers capsized and the infantry landed almost alone on the beaches *followed* by their DD swimming tanks. But by mid-afternoon, after heavy street fighting, the Canadians had taken Courseulles. The assault company attacking Bernières lost half its strength and the capture of St Aubin took three hours. Nevertheless, the 22nd Dragoons Flails supporting 2nd Canadian Armoured Brigade had a good day. By 0900 1st Troop had cleared their lanes and had opened their tins of self-heating soup and were discussing the weather and the political situation with three Frenchmen while their 'compo' tea brewed on a petrol fire. They discovered later on that they had chosen to light their fire on top of a Teller mine. The Troop spent the rest of the day under orders from 8 Beach Group until midnight.

On the left of Nan beach (eastern sector) Lieutenant P. Burbidge with 4th Troop had an uneventful landing on the dunes west of St Aubin. Snipers in seaside villas were blown out by 75 mm and Petard fire. The lanes were cleared of wire, Belgian box and Teller mines by 0830. By midday they set out from Bernières and moved inland 2 miles and harboured north of Villons-les-Buissons. 22nd Dragoons had made eight clear penetrations off the beaches for 3rd Canadian Division for the loss of only one trooper wounded and seven wrecked tanks. However, the intrepid 'C' Squadron of the Inns of Court – known as Bing Force – were almost the first troops ashore on Juno.

The Parson's Tale – 'A Glorious Failure'

On the landing craft, the Revd John du B. Lance, Inns of Court padre, celebrated Holy Communion and played a violent game on board called Stigger, a cross between rugger and soccer played with a piece of wood instead of a ball.

Our landing place was a mile west of Graye-sur-Mer on Juno beach. We [Bing Force] landed with the 3rd Canadian Division at 0745 (H+45 minutes). We were the first wheeled vehicles to land after the swimming DD tanks. One craft landed safely, ours struck a mine and my scout car was damaged and tipped into the sea. The landing ramp was damaged and two of the halftracks could not make the sea at that depth. Two scout cars went up on mines, another armoured car was shot up by an anti-tank gun, bypassed by the infantry. Another was destroyed by a well-defended road block on the lateral road. It was a costly start for such a small force. The remainder pushed steadily on through opposition from infantry, anti-tank guns and even tanks were eventually joined by the half-troops from a second landing craft.

They reached Tierceville five miles inland and in the evening four half-troops got as far as the railway between Bayeux and Caen, eleven miles from the beach. Another group pushed south across the river Seulles and met infantry and armour. Unfortunately one armoured car was hit by mistake by a Canadian tank, scored a direct hit killing driver and commander. By the end of D-Day the Inns of Court had lost three armoured cars, three scout cars and two halftracks. During the second day considerable advances were made but US Thunderbolts obliterated two half-troops at Jerusalem crossroads five miles south of Bayeux. There were other adventures: the destruction of a German artillery RHQ and capture of a colonel. On the fourth day the survivors were withdrawn. Their wireless drill had been excellent. They reported back the course of various battles to Corps HQ. Of the twelve young officers and sergeants who commanded the half-troops, six were killed and another severely wounded. One of the glorious failures of the war.

Gold Beach – 'A Krunnch not a Bang'

Raymond Ellis, then Lieutenant with 82 Assault Squadron RE, arrived in LCT 2029 off Gold beach to support the Hampshires' landing. Several of his engineers were so ill with seasickness that they had to be slapped into consciousness. His task was to clear lane No. 5 with his three AVREs and two Flail tanks under command:

> The skipper drove the LCT hard on to the sand, the ramp lowered and I went ashore without difficulty and blew off the waterproofing air inlet extensions and drove up the beach, steering between the barbed wire, tetrahedra, wooden poles with mines facing out to sea. The peat and clay composition of the beach caused little trouble. One steered by pulling the tiller bar once and then travel the length of the tank and then pull again. The enemy shells were falling fast by this time as the leading AVREs roughly in line abreast reached the top of the beach near the low sandhills. I sent forward the first Flail tank into the minefield to beat and explode the mines with its revolving chains. Many of the Hampshires were now waiting to get through the minefield. I regret to say many were killed and were lying blazing on fire – a rather horrifying sight. They were dead. The shrapnel had ignited the mortar ammunition they were carrying on their backs. The noise of the shells landing was terrific, many landing within 10–15 yards and made a Krunnch not a Bang. Captain H.P. Stanyon of 'B' Sqn Westminster Dragoons, commanding the Flails and in overall charge of lanes 4, 5 and 6, was about 15 yards behind me when his tank was hit on the engine hatches and set on fire.

The first Flail tank had progressed 50 yds into the minefield, had a track blown off and was stuck, so Raymond ordered forward a second Flail tank which flogged its way up to the lateral road beyond the sandhill. Next a huge bomb crater in the road had to be filled up by four AVRE fascines (named Lion, Leopard, Lurcher, etc.). Only then could the gun tanks, DDs and other armour queueing up behind nose-to-tail on the beaches between high and low tide, surge up and forward to secure Gold beach.

The fortified bunkers and strongpoints at Le Hamel manned by the 1st Battalion of the German 716 Division gave the beaching groups in front of 50th Tyne/Tees Division all sorts of trouble. The 1st Dorsets and 1st Hampshires landed under furious fire supported by Flail tanks of the Westminster Dragoons. Lieutenant Colonel Nelson Smith, CO of the Hampshires, was wounded almost immediately as was his FOO, Major Dick Gosling, 147th Field Regiment. The 47 RM Commando arrived two hours late and had to march 10 miles to attack Port-en-Bessin from the landward side. The 5th East Yorkshires of 69th Brigade were pinned down on the beach opposite La Rivière.

'Wooden Crosses' – 'Hedging our Bets'

Captain John Leytham was 2 i/c 82 Assault Squadron RE and landed on Gold Jig Green beach near Le Hamel at H–10, i.e. 0720. When his CO, Major H.G.H. Elphinstone, was killed an hour after the landing, John was promoted to command. He recalled the number of wooden crosses that had been made and taken with his squadron which sailed in Flotilla 28. Pink gin and cigarettes were available on LCT 808 – not Navy Woodbines but 'Passing Cloud'. Assault Force 'K' would bombard Gold beach with the cruisers HMS *Orion*, *Ajax*, *Argonaut* and *Emerald*, plus the Dutch gunboat HNMS *Flores* and thirteen destroyers. Jig beach was protected by fortified buildings dominated by a fortified sanatorium and pillboxes backed by mortars, machine guns, anti-tank guns and a field gun housed in a concrete bunker. Strongly defended positions covered the beach from Le Hamel to Asnelles-sur-Mer. Leytham recalled the various chaplains working overtime 'for the first time in their lives to deliver the last sacrament. An amazing number, including myself, took advantage of it. Hedging our bets you might say.' His escape gear consisted of a beautiful silk map of Europe, a file, a small compass and a concentrated ration pack with some Benzedrine. The RAF photographs of Gold beach clearly showed an anti-tank gun opposite where his LCT planned to touch down. 'The waiting is probably the worst time before any set-piece operation such as Overlord . . . for myself it was not so

Jig Green Sector Assault RE support 50th Tyne/Tees division clearing Le Hamel and Asnelles. (Birkin Haward)

much fear of death (though that in itself is not an attractive prospect) but more fear of possible mutilation. Far worse than either of these possibilities was the uncertainty as to how one will react to one's baptism of fire . . . the operation was to be the most traumatic experience of my life.' Leytham's tank had a new innovation called a 'roly-poly', a large roll of coir matting which was to be pushed up the muddy beach, travelling along the path it pounded, while behind was a 'bobbin' designed to lay metal tracking where the coir matting ended. The Assault Squadron spent three days aboard their pitching, tossing LCT with a foot of seawater sloshing over the deck.

D-Day: The Padre's Story

The Revd Leslie Skinner RAChD was chaplain to the Sherwood Rangers Yeomanry Regiment, part of 8th Armoured Brigade who landed on Gold beach. He kept a superb diary entitled 'The Man who worked on Sundays'.

As we beached at 0725 our LCT hit a mine. Men either side of me wounded – one lost leg. I was blown backwards on to Bren Carrier, but OK. Landing doors jammed. Gave morphine injections and rough dressings to injured men. Water about six feet deep – sea rough – coconut matting would not sink. Shellfire pretty hot. Infantry carriers/jeeps baling but left us to matting as tanks revved up. Chaos ashore. Germans firing everything they had. Road mined – great hole. Bulldozer unable to get through because of mines. Spent an hour with some Engineers demolishing remains of pillbox to make another exit from beach. Heavy work with pickaxe and chest hurting like hell. Finally got halftrack into queue. Along line on foot, saw CO and A Sqdn waiting to get on faster and further. No RAMC landed as yet on our part beach. Some casualties. Got Sgt Leader to bring halftrack back to beach, hull down behind sand dune. Start gathering wounded, mostly infantry. More as day went on from further down beach. No news yet of any Beach Dressing Station. Saw skipper of large LST waiting for evening tide to float him off. Persuaded him to take more seriously wounded when he left. By 1430 hrs got 43 on board – all carried by hand up 'Jacob's ladder'. Terribly tiring. Our Doctor came about 1530. Saw them all. OK except one likely to die before reaching England. CO wounded. Saw him off on DUKW en route UK. Comfortable. Told me Monty Horley had been killed. Set off after Regt. Caught up with them at Ryes. One Sqn had 'reccied' Sommervieu and taken it while other two Sqns approaching outskirts of Bayeux – shooting two infantry [Essex] companies into suburbs and railway station. Bed on ground 0130. Dead beat.

'D-Day Had a Certain Unreality'

Another Sherman regiment with 8th Armoured Brigade was 4/7 Royal Dragoon Guards. Lieutenant Michael Trasenster's diary reads:

On landing the tanks seemed to continue to roll and pitch from the motion one had got used to from the rough LCT crossing of the Channel. D-Day had a certain unreality that I found not too conducive to the sort of fear one felt later. It seemed like an unpleasant dream and one took part almost more as an observer than a participant. This was enhanced by an unwarranted trust in the [Sherman] armour against battlefield hazards outside, and an isolation caused by being deaf to most external noise from wearing radio headsets and the general noise of tanks. This made tank commanders very vulnerable to a sniper's bullet through the head. A great friend was killed early on like this at La Rivière. A timely warning to wear headsets round the neck or over one ear with a minimum of head showing. The beach was confused with spasmodic shelling. The war was quickly over for many. Our own wounded and dead, and 'bomb happy' or wounded German POWs sheltered under the sea wall to be taken back across the Channel. No personal animosity. In tank fighting, if you were shooting at the enemy close enough to recognise them as individuals, they were too close for safety! By good luck, my, by then, two tanks slipped behind the Mount Fleury Battery [where Sergeant Major Hollis got the only D-Day VC] and remained hidden from the other gun positions. We then over-ran Crepon, the HQ of the 'Eastern Bn' of Balts and Russians with German officers and NCOs who *all* seemed pleased to surrender! 'A' Sqn followed behind 'B' and 'C' who had landed an hour before and had a very rough time getting off the beach. But Captain John Stirling's Sherman sank into a quicksand or shell hole and had to be abandoned.

The Gunners on D-Day

Brigadier G.G. Mears was Commander Royal Artillery of 3rd Division. The three field regiments were a vital supporting factor in the landings on Sword beach.

Air photographs both vertical and oblique were studied by all ranks and everything possible was done to make them familiar with the bit of France on which they were to land. The embarkation began and units broke up into their shiploads. Guns were in their LCTs. COs were with their Brigadiers, and BCs and FOOs were with their Bns. 2 i/cs and their recce parties were in their allocated craft. Wireless sets after most careful netting were sealed, not to be opened until the battle was on. Packets of orders and crates of maps were on board all craft to be distributed when at sea. Everything that imagination, forethought and care could do, had been done. Now it all depended on the weather. The sea was rough. Some LCTs carrying the assault guns of the Royal Marines were swamped. The bombardment increased in intensity as the three field regiments of each division [50th Tyne/Tees and 3 Canadian] opened fire from their LCTs on the run in. . . . Not one had been fired at by any enemy weapon.

A Fearsome Sight

Lieutenant S. Rosenbaum was a young officer with 113/114 Field Battery, 33 Field Regiment RA:

> Major Wise's [the FOO] launch was sunk by the rough seas and transferred to that used by the FOO of 7th Field Reg. RA. 76 Field Reg's launch was also sunk and its FOO killed. At 0655 we opened fire at 11,000 yards – the rounds falling between the beach and 400 yards inland. The rate of fire was 3 rounds per minute for each of the Div's 72 guns (4 tons of HE every minute on our immediate front). Also HE filled rockets were being fired from LCTs. A fearsome sight as they launched their missiles simultaneously. John Humphries having given the first orders to fire then handed over to me. The range dropping by 200 yards a time every minute or so. The houses on the foreshore looked like the English seaside.

The D-Day VC

The 6th Green Howards landed 1,000 yd from the La Rivière strongpoint. Sergeant Major Stan Hollis advanced with 'D' Company several hundred yards inland which suffered casualties. His CO, Major Lofthouse, pointed out a pillbox to the right of the road. Hollis stormed the enemy post, ran 30 yds towards it firing his Sten gun, climbed on the roof and dropped a grenade through the slit. He returned in triumph with no fewer than twenty-five prisoners. Shortly after this and other amazing deeds, he was awarded the Victoria Cross.

By the end of D-Day in the British and Canadian sectors, Sword, Juno and Gold beaches, a stunning victory had been won. The casualties had been high, but not nearly as high as COSSAC had predicted. It was true that Caen – a very ambitious objective – had not been taken but a most substantial bridgehead had been established. And Der Fuehrer still thought that the major attack would still come – on the Calais front!

OUR TURN
TO BEACH (What I think
it would
have looked
like if I had
turned to look)
I was more
interested in
where I was
going than
what I'd just
left here as
we are just off
our L.C.P. JOHNNY
GREENAWAY is in
front with *L. to R. behind*
Choff. Myself, Tich. Coppins
is just going for b off the
top of left hand gang plank.

THE ABOVE HAVE ARRIVED....

Under water shell holes, obstacles and mines were the nuisance. Here the first
Assault troops — 50 DIV here (on GREEN BEACH! just East of ARROMANCHES) Our tanks
of 8TH Hussars have already gone in GOLD. supported by 3RD R.T.R. One of their tanks
is on left Gun and Turret just showing — one of the first tanks knocked out. Our
TANKS ARE coming in on L.S.T.'s CENTRE. IN THE FOREGROUND ARE OBSTACLES STICKING
OUT OF THE WATER. BARRAGE BALLOONS are over head. Warspite, RAMILLIES, RODNEY AND
NELSON WERE HERE, WITH WARSPITE JUST ON RIGHT OF SKETCH. SCRAMBLING and stumbling

Sketches by Donald Green, 1/5th Queens Regt, 7th Armoured Division

We made the beach and started the
business of invading the joint. One
TANK PUT IT PRETTY WELL SITTING in
his turret with water above the driver
visor he hollered "I feel more like a B—
Submarine than a tank." A Sgt Major near
a flame thrower CHURCHILL TANK CALLED
"PUT THAT B-Cigerette lighter out - we know
it works" On the left we are going
inland while a
Sherman of 3RD RTR
is having a goat
some snipers
I can't do any sketches
of the FIGHTING coming off
it looked like to draw the beaches — I don't know what
dead tired we dig in at ST VIGOR. our First
stopping place - in HEDGEROWS here
known as "HYACINTH DRIVE"
Notice on left was kindly left
just off the beach by the kind
GERMANS who didn't want us to
get hurt — much. THESE notices
were usually fakes. A platoon of GREEN HOWARDS
who followed us over a minefield got blown up - we never had a
casualty until JUNE 13TH — D+7. We had quite a lot of fun herewith—

5 miles inland soaking wet and

Achtung!
Minen!
Attention mines

3 DIVS. MET US HERE.
21ST PANZER.
12TH PANZER GREN.
AND THE HITLER YOUTH FANATICS —
PANZER LEHR.
WE KNOCKED THEM OUT OF THE WAR HERE.

TUES JUNE 13TH

BATTLE FOR THE MAIN STREET.
2 TIGERS were here in this Street and the first fired though corner of house (LEFT) hoping to hit something - he didn't. instead a 5TH R.T.R. Cromwell came up fired through the hole and knocked the TIGER out. PADDY SINGLETERRY "A" Car is firing PIAT from ROOF on RIGHT. TANK OFFICER on corner - RIGHT, had umbrella and was singing "Hold that TIGER!"

Sketches by Donald Green

Our only Armour DEFENCE while we were cut off were 2 knocked out CROMWELLS whose guns still worked. Here 2 8TH HUSSARS of the crew are spotting for Enemy TANKS. Cromwell is a Cruiser TANK with 7.5 gun, and two Beza's M'C guns.

June 14TH

Sketches by Donald Green

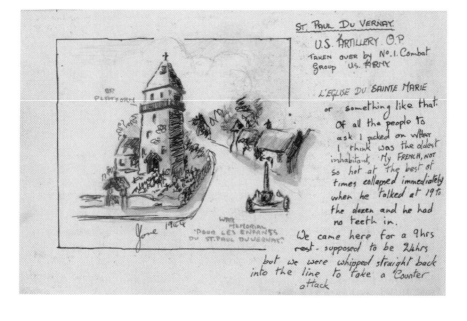

CHAPTER THREE

Attritional Battles in the Bridgehead – June

June was a month of massive battles. The Allies battled their way inland and tried in vain in a series of attacks to take, or at least envelop, the key city of Caen *and* its dominating feature across the river Odon, called Hill 112. Monty sent his trusted African divisions, 50th Tyne Tees and the Desert Rats, south-east towards Villers-Bocage. This was only partly successful.

Operation Martlet was to be a substantial attack mainly by the 49th Polar Bear Division of 30 Corps with the objective of capturing Fontenay-le-Pesnil and if possible Tessel Wood and Rauray. It would start on 25 June and act as the right flank protection for the much larger Operation Epsom in which the 15th Scottish, 11th Armoured Division and 43rd Wessex Wyverns would envelop Caen from the south-west, cross the river Odon and seize and retain possession of the vital Hill 112.

On 28 June 3rd British Division would pinch out the salient of Le Landel, La Londe, Chateau de la Londe and La Bigude held by 22 Panzer Division in Operation Mitten.

Disasters at Sea

On Sunday 18 June the 5th Glosters, the RAC Recce regiment of the 43rd Wessex Wyverns, embarked on the ill-fated ship *Derry Cunihy*. Six days later, early in the morning the engines were restarted after a day or so waiting off the beachhead for permission to disembark. A magnetic mine blew the ship up. The stern half sank rapidly. An ammunition lorry on the well deck was in flames and contents were exploding. Within seconds No. 5 hold was under water. The men of 'A' Squadron and HQ Squadron in No. 5 hold had little chance of escape. The sea was soon full of struggling figures and floating debris and patches of oil began to spread. A large motor gunboat came alongside and one by one the wounded were taken aboard. SSM Barr of 'A' Squadron plunged into the sea from the bows and towed a number of rafts to safety. Sergeant Drake of 'C' Squadron found a rope and towed several men out of the water. Trooper Greener of 'C' Squadron rescued his comrades and was later awarded the George Medal. 180 men were missing and a further 150 wounded. It was a disaster for the Glosters.

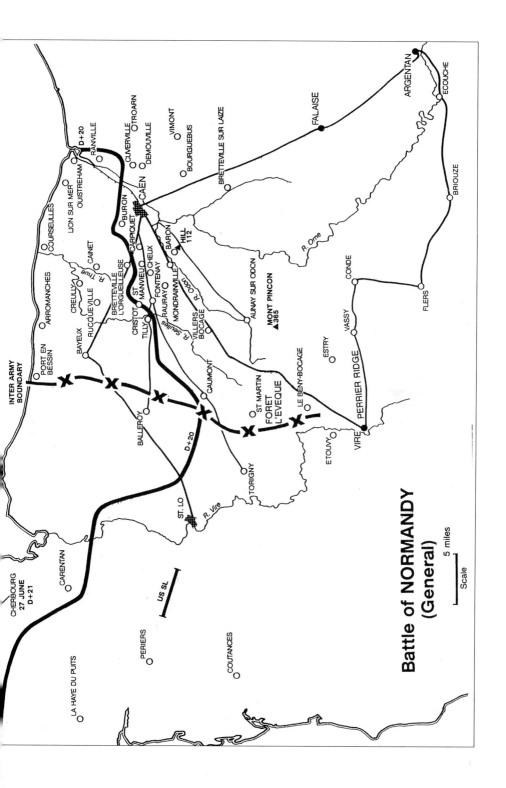

Battle of NORMANDY
(General)

Scale

5 miles

US SL

CHERBOURG
27 JUNE
D+21

LA HAYE DU PUITS

CARENTAN

PERIERS

COUTANCES

ST. LO

R. Vire

TORIGNY

BALLEROY

D+20

CAUMONT

ST MARTIN

FORET
L'EVEQUE

LE BENY-BOCAGE

ETOUVY

VIRE

PERRIER RIDGE

ESTRY

VASSY

CONDE

FLERS

BRIOUZE

ECOUCHE

ARGENTAN

FALAISE

BRETTEVILLE SUR LAZE

R. Orne

MONT PINCON
▲365

AUNAY SUR ODON

BOURGUEBUS

DEMOUVILLE

VIMONT

CUVERVILLE

TROARN

RANVILLE

D+20

OUISTREHAM

LION SUR MER

COURSEULLES

ARROMANCHES

PORT EN
BESSIN

INTER ARMY
BOUNDARY

BAYEUX

RUCQUEVILLE

CREULLY

R. Thue

CAINET

BRETTEVILLE
L'ORGUEILLEUSE

CRISTOT

TILLY

ST
MANVIEU

FONTENAY

CHEUX

CARPIQUET

BURON

CAEN

BARON

HILL
112

RAURAY

MONDRAINVILLE

VILLERS
BOCAGE

R. Odon

R. Seulles

R. Odon

The liberty ship SS *Sambut*, carrying 500 troops, was struck by two 16 in shells fired from German coastal batteries. After an hour the master abandoned ship. Among the many casualties were twenty-two members of 92 LAA of 3rd British Division.

Serious Trouble for the Warwicks at Lebisey

The village and wood of Lebisey, along the Breville–Caen road, was held by a formidable and fresh battalion of the 125th Panzer Grenadiers of 21st Panzer Division. Lieutenant Colonel 'Jumbo' Herdon, CO 2nd Battalion Warwickshire Regiment, was ordered on D+1 to take first the wood, then the village. Practically everything went wrong. 'B' and 'C' companies were caught in the open. Colonel Herdon was shot through the head and killed, and during the long day ten officers and 144 other ranks became casualties. The three lead companies hung on under continuous mortar and machine gun fire. The brigadier of 185 Brigade told Captain A.J.M. Bannerman, waiting at Breville with his six carrier-towed anti-tank guns, that Lebisey had been captured [patently untrue], that enemy tanks were in the vicinity [true] and that he was to take his anti-tank troop up, quickly, to his forward companies and consolidate.

> We had gone for about half a mile when all hell let loose. The noise was fantastic, cracking and humming past us. Luckily the banks were high. Somehow we weren't hit [but the five carriers and their anti-tank guns behind him were all knocked out]. We couldn't turn round. We pressed up the hill. I felt to stop was fatal, so we accelerated madly and fired our Bren and our Stens at either side of the road as we passed. Suddenly appeared a low bridge and a mass of rubble and broken houses that was Lebisey. Worse still was the sight of scurrying Germans – darting behind the houses as we careered forlornly into the middle of them. We passed a Mk IV tank whose crew was as surprised to see us as we were to see them.

The Warwick carrier got through the village and deployed their gun 'Action Rear'. 'The gun was soon firing and joy, we hit and holed the tank which had poked out from a house. We got off about eight rounds. I remember the loader quite imperturbable and another Birmingham lad firing the gun with a gleaming smile and a flood of obscenity. Suddenly an 88 got our range and up went our carrier in a deafening explosion with all our ammunition, knocking us all sideways.' The Warwicks were captured. Bannerman escaped but was captured again by a German officer. The Warwicks' adjutant, carrier and mortar officers were also captured. A very bad day indeed.

'Don't Shoot – We're the Paddies'

The most notorious feature on 9th Brigade front (3rd British Division) was Cambes Wood. Its trees had been splintered by furious bombardments and it smelt of death. The battalions who lived there during the weeks that followed loathed the place. It was surrounded by wheatfields in which the British and Germans fought bitterly for patrol superiority. At first the wood was isolated during daylight by enemy artillery fire, but the sappers working at night pushed their bulldozers through the soft soil and excavated a road which linked Cambes Wood with Le Mesnil. It lies on the right of the Delivrande–Caen road and the first attack was made on 7 June against the 12th SS Hitler Youth Division holding it. Initially the 2nd Battalion Royal Ulster Rifles made their attack, and again two days later supported by armour. The 1st King's Own Scottish Borderers put in a flank attack under a smoke screen. Desperate fighting went on for hours. The light was fading and the Scots, uncertain of the fate of the Ulstermen, heard them shout 'Don't shoot, Jocks, we're the Paddies.' The battalions' reunion was broken up by Nebelwerfer 'moaning minnies'. A Borderer jumped into a trench and put his arms heartily round the two others in the slit. 'Well, Paddy, you old blighter. I didn't think we'd see you again!' The two old blighters were Brigadier A.D.G. Orr DSO, whose carrier had just gone up in flames, and the Paddy's CO, Lieutenant Colonel I.C. Harris!

A Sherman Tank Called 'Winchester'

Lieutenant Michael Trasenster of 'A' Squadron 4/7 Royal Dragoon Guards named his Sherman tank 'Winchester' after his school. With its two diesels it was fast, reliable, a 'motoring' tank with a good, accurate HE 75 mm gun. (The AP he said would not go through anything.) It was officially No. 27 tank and bore a charmed life, one of the few RDG tanks to go through the whole campaign from D-Day, despite wear and tear. Its pennant had been shot away – an AP shot had glanced off the side of the tank: the spare bogey had been knocked off; it had been hit by a 17-pdr HE shot from behind from a cooked-up round from Sergeant Poole's 'friendly' brewed-up Sherman; and it had bogged down on the wilder, further shores of the River Seine and had to be pulled out during Operation Neptune. Mittens or asbestos gloves were needed to load. The Browning, often red-hot with usage, needed frequent barrel changing. The fans sucked cold air in during the winter and hot air in during summer. The driver was Corporal Reg Cox MM, the wireless operator Lance Corporal 'Wilco' Willett, the gunner Trooper Stokes and the hull gunner Trooper Redford. On June 14 'A' Squadron destroyed five Panther tanks in Lingevres. Reg Cox was in the gunner's seat and himself destroyed the track and drive sprocket of the last Panther.

Essex Wood

The 2nd Battalion Essex Regiment (The Pompadours) were part of 56 Brigade (Sphinx). They landed on 6 June D-Day at midday on the *wrong* beach, 1,500 yds east of Le Hamel. The brigade (with 2 South Wales Borderers and 2 Glosters) were in support of 50th Tyne/Tees Division. During the eleven-month campaign they were successively under command of 50th Div, 7th Armoured, 50th Div, 59th Div and finally 49th Polar Bear Division. They had a number of major battles, including on 10–11 June, that of Verrières Wood, subsequently known as Essex Wood, just north-west of Tilly. In typical wooded country, the left flank of the Essex attack, 'D' Company, suffered heavy casualties from a powerful mortar attack. There was no sign of the supporting tanks or the battalion anti-tank guns and 'B' Company was overrun. Both company commanders, Major Petre and Major Watson, were casualties. The situation was critical. All the wireless sets were out of action and the only reliable communication was by the gunner FOO. All the PIAT carriers were casualties and to quote Major Elliott, the 2 i/c, 'Certain individuals had foolishly abandoned their pieces as an unnecessary burden on the battlefield.' After dark the enemy counter-attacked with flame throwers from armoured halftrucks. Lieutenant Price at Battalion HQ brought down 2 in mortar and PIAT fire and the enemy withdrew. At 0100 the 2 i/c tried to locate the Armoured Brigade HQ but they had moved, so he tracked down Brigadier Pepper at HQ 56 Infantry Brigade and explained the 2 Essex plight. But they survived despite horrendous casualties and Major Elliott was promoted to command the battalion.

Hands of Fate

On D+4 Sergeant 'Topper' Brown of 'C' Company Battalion 2nd East Yorkshires, in order to even up his sections in the line, commanded Private Lionel Roebuck, who had laboriously dug his trench, to quit it. Two ex-India regulars, 'Dixie' Dunbar and Jock Anderson, were part of some stragglers who had been 'lost' for a couple of days. They threw off their gear and joyfully took possession of Lionel's well-made dugout, delighted with what they thought was their luck. Lionel, grumbling like mad, moved some 30 yds away to join the other section and started to dig yet another 'slit'. Five minutes later a lone ranging shell landed directly on top of Dixie and Jock, instantly killing both of them. Len Brown, one of their mates, was standing by the trench side chatting to them. He caught the full blast of shrapnel from the explosion on his legs and the lower part of his body. It lacerated the flesh and ripped off his trouser-legs. CSM Pullen was immediately on the spot. Although badly wounded, Len was able to tell him that the appalling havoc of broken bodies were the earthly remains of Dixie and Jock before he was put on a stretcher and taken to the Field Dressing Station.

The Battles of Villers-Bocage

Full of their North African élan, the 7th Armoured Division was directed on Villers-Bocage and entered the little town without too much opposition on the morning of 13 June. Led by the motorized infantry of 1st Battalion Rifle Brigade and the Cromwell tanks of the 4th County of London Yeomanry, the Desert Rat column marched through the town, up the slope towards Point 213 where they were ambushed.

Although half a dozen Sharpshooter Cromwells were dispersed in two fields near the crossroads at Point 210 it was clear that the joint force 4th CLY/1st RB were taken totally by surprise by a savage (initially), single Tiger tank attack! Lieutenant Michael Wittmann, commanding No. 2 Company 501st SS Heavy Tank Battalion of 1st SS Panzer Division, was camouflaged in a little wood north-east of Villers-Bocage. No. 1 Company, under the command of Captain Mobius, was on their right. Wittmann had recorded an astonishing 117 tank knock-outs on the Russian front. Just after 0900 Wittmann knocked out the *rearmost* of the Sharpshooters' Cromwells and with his next AP shot destroyed a Sherman 17-pdr Firefly in front of it. Peter Roach, 1st RTR, wrote later: 'We believed the tale of the CLY who were ambushed in a cutting beyond Villers-Bocage. A Tiger tank had come over the top of the cutting and knocked out the first and last vehicles. The commander had then appeared from his turret, taken off his hat and bowed to the remainder, such was the feeling of immunity given by this great gun [88 mm] and armour.'

Burn your Tanks and Get Out

It was slaughter. The Sharpshooters had bunched their tanks together and the 1st RB's carriers and halftracks made easy targets. Wittmann machine-gunned the Riflemen despite vain attempts with 6-pound anti-tank guns and PIATs to tackle him. Wittmann then advanced towards the town along the Caen road and destroyed four more 4th CLY Cromwells. At 1030 Viscount Cranley spoke for the last time to Brigadier Hinde on the wireless. He then told his tank crews: 'Burn your tanks and get out.'

Instead, at 1300 Captain Mobius, with eight more Tiger tanks, appeared with infantry support and took prisoner all the survivors between Points 210 and 213. Captain Christopher Milner, 2 i/c 'A' Company 1st RB, and thirty riflemen escaped to tell the tale. The 4th CLY squadron leader, Major P.M.R. Scott MC, was killed and Viscount Cranley and many others taken prisoner. That was the end of the first stage of the battle of Villers-Bocage – a humiliating defeat for the Desert Rats.

For the rest of the day the Germans counter-attacked the 1/7th Queen's who were ensconced in the centre of Villers-Bocage. Intense close quarter fighting took place in which the German tanks were at a disadvantage.

Many acts of bravery were recorded. Lieutenant Bill Cotton MM and his troop took on three Tigers, although his tank equipped with a 95 mm howitzer gun was no use at close quarters. Sergeants Bramall and Lockwood played hide and seek and eventually set fire to a Tiger and a Mk IV. The fire brigade appeared as in a French farce to try to put out the flaming German tanks. Fierce fighting took place near the railway station and 'A' Company 1/7th Queen's, particularly CSM Baker, distinguished themselves. But with more German infantry from Panzer Lehr and 2nd Panzer Grenadier Division arriving, and amid heavy shelling, the decision was taken at about 1800 to call it a day. Under a heavy barrage of smoke and HE, coordinated by the CRA of American 155s plus 3rd and 5th RHA 25-pdrs, the two companies of Queen's and two surviving CLY squadrons were evacuated westwards back to the villages of Amaye-sur-Seulles and Tracy-Bocage.

Such a Waste

The second battle of Villers Bocage was a painful, confused, but honourable draw. About fifteen heavy German tanks had been knocked out and their supporting infantry given a bloody nose. But during the day the division lost twenty Cromwells, four Fireflies, three light tanks, fourteen halftracks and fourteen Bren carriers. The Sharpshooters had twelve officers missing, three wounded and eighty-five ORs missing, killed and wounded – a dreadful blow. Major 'Ibby' Aird now took command, and reorganized and revitalized RHQ and the two surviving squadrons. The 1st RB had three officers and eighty ORs missing or killed in action and the 1/7th Queen's had forty-four casualties. Other units also incurred losses that day, including the 5th RHA and 1/5th Queen's. Since 50th Division had not made any progress on the left (eastern) flank and there was a gap on the right between the Americans assaulting Caumont, it was clear that the Desert Rats were now exposed on both flanks. But as Sergeant Stan Lockwood of 'B' Squadron 4th CLY said: 'We felt bad about getting out. It made it seem as if it had been such a waste.'

The Diehards

There were four Medium Machine Guns Regiments in the British 2nd Army – the Cheshires, the Manchesters, the Royal Northumberland Fusiliers and the Middlesex. Eric Codling was with the 8th Battalion Middlesex Regiment, known as The Diehards, who were MMG Regiment with 43rd Wessex Wyvern Division. The Diehards also had five-men detachments to fire the 4.2 in mortars with 20 lb bombs. He soon learnt to master the complexities of laying and firing the weapon with fire control from a FOO post. He also carried a load of two packs each of two bombs, or 80 lb weight! The No. 1 commanded the mortar detachment. No. 2 laid the mortar, set the range and direction on the sights, then lined this up on an arming post set out in front. When the order to fire was given, No. 2 dropped down the barrel a bomb prepared by Nos 3 nd 4, while No. 1

continuously checked and adjusted the accuracy of the aim. Each company of 4.2 in mortars had three platoons. In addition, the MMG companies each had three platoons, and finally a company of 20 mm anti-aircraft guns. Eric was in No. 14 Platoon under Captain Pennock, 'an excellent down to earth officer, with a good sense of humour'. The 2 i/c was Lieutenant 'Nobby' Clarke. The 4.2 in mortar was in a trailer towed by a Carton-Lloyd carrier. The No. 1 was Corporal Doug Swallow, 'a young married man, a great chap.' No. 2 was Eric, No. 3 was John Perkins, 'about my age'. No. 4 was Taffy Hughes, a 'young Welshman', and the driver was 'Codger' Green, 'the eldest member, TA soldier and a greengrocer'. Eric went on: 'Our lack of experience allowed us to take unbelievable risks, like standing up to watch the nearby truck being mortared, or taking great pains to dig the mortars in and then sleeping *on top* of the ground!'

'A Coward is just an Unlucky Person'

Near Montilly after some unpleasant shelling in the evening on a crossroads, Captain Stirling 4/7 RDG found

> one chap still in a ditch by the road, pale and quivering like a frightened rabbit. It was too much for him. A few days later he walked out and was picked up in England some months later. I feel sorry for a chap like that, not angry with him, although you must take a stern line for the sake of the rest, but a coward is just an unlucky person whose natural fear is stronger than his self-control. Almost everyone is afraid in war. It was some time before I realised this. I found I was frightened myself, and I despised myself. Then I found that the others were the same. Only the completely insensitive have no fear. Others are brave in proportion to the control they exercise over that fear. A leader is a person whose men never guess that he is as much afraid as they themselves and therefore follow him into the present danger instead of following their natural inclination to safety and self-preservation.
>
> War with all its starkness and brutality brings people into a far more sensitive frame of mind. Away from the ordered calm and protection of civilised life, they feel far more urgently the need for spiritual comfort and quietness that the Church at its best has to offer. The contrast with the squalor and sordidness of the battlefields, where primitive passion rules amid chaotic din and tumult, and where death is never farther away than the next field, these things produce a frame of mind in which all that the Church has to offer is far more readily acceptable.

Life in the Bridgehead

In his book *Achtung Minen*, Lieutenant Ian Hammerton was troop leader of 1st Troop, 22nd Dragoons in charge of five Flail Sherman tanks (Crabs). On D-Day his tank's rotor jib struck a tetrahedron beach mine, was damaged and was flooded by the fast incoming tide when supporting the

Canadian de la Chaudière Regiment at Bernières-sur-Mer. For several days in wet clothes and squelchy boots his troop flashed 'here and there clearing mines or cutting through tough German barbed wire fencing at the beck and call of the Beachmaster'. From Cresserons on 11 June he supported 51st Highland Division, relieving 6th Airborne troops at Ranville. At Ste Honourine-la-Chardonnette, his gunner, Paddy, scored three direct hits on a Pz KW Mark IV tank and 'brewed' it up. But 'our Scotsmen were now retiring rather faster than decent, so we covered their withdrawal and moved back over the hill.' A 'bread and basket' anti-personnel bomb landed on the squadron harbour in Cresserons, wounding Sergeant Jock Stirling and crew, Corporal Ferguson, Johnny Munden, Dogger Butler and Dave Sawyer. Outside Douvres-la-Delivrande there was a Field Hospital with *real* nurses, a field bakery producing *white* bread and a shower unit which produced *hot* water from the nearest duckpond. Alan Walkden, a wireless-operator, introduced Ian to Sibelius on the BBC Home Service 'Promenade' Concerts. Tins of haricot oxtail were not thought much of and were used for barter, but treacle or Christmas pudding in tins was popular. Peak Frean were the makers and the tank crew wrote to thank them for their wares. Hammerton's troop helped subdue a radar station near Douvres and he went on a mine and booby trap course in Bayeux and purchased much smelly Camembert cheese. Life in the bridgehead. . . .

Lingua Franca

Hedley Bunce, a sergeant with the 3 Monmouthshires, recalls: 'Not long after landing in Normandy, a fellow sergeant, Jack Partridge, came to me and asked, "How do you say, 'Can you speak French?'" I told him, "Parlez-vous Français?" After several attempts he walked off, repeating the words fairly accurately. (He did of course mean to ask, "Do you speak English?") I heard next day that he walked up to a farm and said to the farmer, "Parlez-vous Français?" Naturally the farmer replied, "Oui M'sieur", whereupon the sergeant said "OK then, let's have some bloody eggs".'

Desert Veterans

The three famous British divisions who fought so brilliantly in the African campaigns and again in Italy, were distinctly 'sticky' when it came to action in Normandy. They thought that they had done more than their fair share already. One of the Desert Rat mottoes ran, 'An old soldier is a cautious soldier, that is why he is an old soldier.'

Friendly Fire

In the crowded Normandy bridgehead there were many cases when air forces tragically bombed their own troops causing hundreds of casualties, although this was rarely reported in newspapers. Tommy Atkins made the best of a bad situation. A popular joke current was that when the RAF bombed, the Germans ducked; when the Germans bombed, as they did every night, the British ducked, but whenever the Americans bombed, both sides ducked.

'Run Rabbit, Run Rabbit, Run, Run, Run'

This was a silly little song much loved in the early years of the war. During their first major battle in Normandy – Operation Epsom – the Ayrshire Yeomanry, 151 Field Regiment RA, were themselves being stonked by 'moaning minnies'. One Yeoman dived into a slit trench for cover from the mortar bombs and startled a jack rabbit which bolted across the field. The Yeoman was heard to exclaim, 'Get out of it you little bugger, you can run harder than I can!'

John Stirling's 'Tiger'

Near Hill 103, which overlooked Tilly-sur-Seulles, 4/7 Royal Dragoon Guards were in action around the village of Lingevres. 'All round were symbols of fresh war. The acrid mingled smell of fire and death and destruction: a German halftrack smashed and drunkenly lopsided where a tank had crushed the life out of it. Cattle in the fields where the barrage had killed them, lying on their backs, swollen and distended, with legs stuck straight in the air, for all the world like toy balloons, the hedges scorched with fire and sprinkled with bits of German uniform and equipment.' Captain John Stirling the previous day had spotted, 'My first German tank' and belted hell out of it. 'He never moved, never even took any notice.' It was a curious bronzed colour. Looks like the side of a tank turret . . . a bush? But bushes don't have numbers painted on them and what's that straight line in front of it? By God, it's a gun, a hell of a great gun. It's a Tiger! Stirling tried to bring up Michael Trasenster's Firefly, a Sherman with a 17-pdr gun.

A 75 mm is a doubtful starter against a Tiger. The crew were feverish with excitement. I got the gunner on to the target. Are you ready? Go! Technique we let fly. Bang! The tank rocked slightly. I saw a spurt of dust in front of the Tiger, but another shot was on the way and another. They were not going to waste time. As the third shot flew, I saw the tongue of flame lick round the cupola. For a moment I could not believe my eyes. Then more wildly excited than I think I have ever been, I grabbed the mike once more. 'Hullo, X-Ray 16, I've knocked out a Tiger. It's brewing up.' I babbled wildly, and back came a 'Well done!'

The Sherman clutches had gone so a tense quarter of an hour passed.

'We put the spanners away and drove triumphant to rejoin Jackie in the village.' Stirling had in fact bagged a Panther. Moreover, Sergeant Harris, 4th Troop with his Scots gunner MacKillop had knocked out an amazing *five* Panthers in the village. 'It was a sight for sore eyes and everyone was in terrific heart. The place [Lingevres] was like a fairground. For the moment the war took second place. The Colonel was there and the Brigadier. The infantry were swarming round the tanks. It was a great victory.'

Hopping back to Blighty?

Lionel Roebuck of 'C' Company 2nd Battalion East Yorkshires wrote:

We moved up into the fray only when the first assault wave on the Chateau de la Londe had overrun the German defences. A little further back in the wood, Lt Dennis Hallam and his batman, a big red-faced Irishman, were together in the same trench. Just after word came to prepare to move up forward and we were all getting ready to leave our position, a shot rang out. 'Paddy' had shot himself through his foot. After wrapping up the wound he went off on one leg, hopping back to Cazelle.

'Do Not Look Inside the Tank Turret'

Major John Leytham, 82 Assault RE Squadron, wrote:

Moving towards Hottot on 19th June, one of my AVREs was hit in the turret. The Germans put up a very fierce resistance to our attacks. They counter-attacked and it was only on the following day that we advanced and recovered the disabled AVRE. Our ARVs (armoured recovery vehicles) proved their value. Now once an armoured piercing shell enters the turret of a tank, it acts in a manner similar to a domestic incinerator. The occupants of the turret are quickly smeared around the walls of the turret. I had given orders after the recovery that none of my men should look inside. A number were foolish enough to disobey my orders. It did not improve their morale. Vehicles like this should be taken back to the rear workshops where the experts spray the inside with creosote. After a suitable interval they scrape off the remains from the walls of the turret.

First Shelling – 'Giant Footsteps'

Sergeant Bob Sheldrake, an anti-tank sergeant with the 49th Polar Bear Division, recalled:

Our attention was naturally attracted to the first ranging shot which landed 400 yards to the front and to the left of our wood. The next came down 100 yards closer and in a direct line between the first and our wood.

I could see the others wondering what to do – slit trenches had always been a nuisance inflicted on tired troops by officers. But uninitiated though we were, something in our blood, maybe handed down by our fathers from Ypres and the Somme, told us to get below the ground. Yet, fascinated, we watched them, like giant footsteps marching diagonally across the fields, marching towards us. THQ were still in animated conversation. I heard cries and the crashing of undergrowth in the trees as tank men rushed for shelter, but I shall never remember the moment I went to earth. I found myself on my hands and knees at the bottom of a tiny slit trench, ramming my head almost into the ground in an effort to get down a few more inches. What a little hole it was, yet how big seemed the opening at the top. Then as the German gunners found the range they slammed away at our poor little wood, the clang of the bursting shells and the shrapnel which rained off the trees passed over me as I lay there, gripping in one hand the identity discs which hung from my neck. When it was all over we were shaken but much wiser, made for the green fields and dug ourselves living quarters underground.

Deathtrap

Captain John Stirling of 4/7 RDG wrote:

If ever a piece of country was ideal for defence by tanks and a nightmare for them to attack in, it was Normandy in summer. The countryside is so like England. Luxuriant green grass and foliage. Tall, thick hedges bounding small pasture fields, little sunken lanes with grassy banks, clumps of grey stone buildings forming a farm or a village. A delightful spot for a picnic, but a deathtrap for an invading army. In this cover a tank or a gun could hide completely and bide its time. You only became aware of its existence when your leading tank went up in flames, and often several more went up before you had any exact idea of the position. It was difficult to see to shoot more than a few hundred yards. Instead of tanks picking a position to a flank and sitting there shooting while the infantry went forward, now they had to go forward side by side with the infantry and were duly picked off.

'Can't Manage a Rifle' or 'Rob All My Comrades'

Revd Jim Wisewell, ex-223 Field Ambulance, RAMC, recalled:

Although officially protected by the Geneva Convention which most of the Germans respected, a Field Ambulance was very much at the 'sharp end' of warfare and when evacuating casualties from the front line its personnel shared risks from shells and mortars, even if they were seldom the deliberate target of small arms fire. So some of our men were KIA and some wounded and four were taken prisoners on D+1. Major Malcolm Oxley, Privates Rogers and Scoot, with Driver Cottrell took a stretcher-carrying Jeep to Lebisey crossroads to try and bring out wounded from the 2 Warwicks who had caught a packet there. They ran straight into a German MG post and were captured. Driver Cottrell, being RASC and armed, was put into their POW cage but the other three RAMC men were taken into Caen, questioned by the Gestapo without any effect, and sent to work in hospitals treating both German and British wounded. Graham Rogers ended up in Brest and was freed by the Americans in August. Later Driver Duke and Private Moyse were awarded the Military Medal for their work in rescuing wounded on stretcher-carrying Jeeps.

There was a fierce protective pride in the 223 Field Ambulance and we took the RAMC motto 'In Arduis Fidelis' (Faithful Under Difficulty) very seriously in respect of our patients. The initials RAMC were said by the unkind to stand for Rob All My Comrades, a reference to looting valuables from the wounded, common in the Napoleonic Wars but not since. The infantry who were our special charge teased us by reversing the initials and amplifying them to Can't Manage A Rifle, a dig at our unarmed status. In fact, the wounded were always our first consideration – and they knew it. When a man has been hit and brought to the ADS for treatment he is shocked and any shells or mortars exploding nearby make him flinch. He knows that being horizontal on a stretcher makes him more vulnerable than being vertical in a trench, so, without any pseudo-heroics involved, we could cover his face with his own helmet and his chest area with ours, then lean over his stomach. It would not have been much use in a direct hit but it was good for the patient's morale! These things being so, imagine the distress of George Scott, one of our ambulance orderlies, when a shell burst near the back of his ambulance setting it on fire and jamming the doors. He had to watch helplessly as the stretcher-cases inside burned to death – and was shocked and depressed about it for days.

'These Buggers Don't Get Me Down'

'Most of our casualties in Normandy were from mortar fire on our men [Sherwood Ranger Yeomanry] standing outside their tanks. Major Seleri was caught with his entire crew save one. As I [Lieutenant Stuart Hills] was walking over to an "O" Group under mortar fire I saw "Busty" Mitchell standing beside his tank and told him he would probably be safer inside. "That's all right, sir," he said, "these buggers don't get me down." I continued my walk to the "O" Group and a mortar landed very near us during the course of it, slightly wounding Sergeant Saunders who was sitting on my right. As I walked back to my tank, I found "Busty" Mitchell dead beside his tank, his cigarette still in his mouth.'

'Advances Measured in Yards' – Operation Mitten

Captain Wheway, 22nd Dragoons: 'C' Sqn Flail tanks were under command of the Staffordshire Yeomanry whose Shermans were supporting 3rd British Division in the 8 Brigade attack on Le Landel and Chateau de la Londe. Both these objectives had originally been taken on June 22nd. Now they had to be retaken as Major W.R. Birt, 22nd Dragoons, recalls:

It was an appalling battle. The South Lancs managed to reach and hold la Londe but could not take the Chateau around which the enemy had dug in more than 30 tanks supported by elements of 192 PZ Grenadiers. The next morning the 1 Suffolk and 2 East Yorks (with 1st Troop 'C' Sqn in support) were sent in behind a barrage of terrifying weight. But they were met by heavy shell and mortar fire which pinned them and their supporting tanks to the woods around Mathieu. During that long day in which advances were measured in yards the infantry casualties were grievously heavy. Our tanks were engaged from the direction of Lebisey and accounted for eight AFVs for the loss of two of those of the Staffs Yeomanry. Though Crocodile flame-throwers were brought up to burn the enemy out of their positions, it was obviously impossible to maintain the attack. When night fell, it was called off and our Flails were drawn back into harbour north of Cazelle where they were heavily shelled.

The Padre's Story – Fog of Battle

During the battle of Fontenay (June 25th) the Sherwood Rangers Yeomanry were supporting the 49th Polar Bear Division. Padre Leslie Skinner filled half a dozen field water bottles 50-50 rum and water and took them up the line.

Ronnie Hutton on his Dingo was talking to the Infantry Officer [Royal Scots Fusiliers]. He smiled his usual kindly smile and took a sip – obviously just to please the Padre. Both he and the Infantry officer took a hefty swig. Obviously this had been a good idea! In a burst of MG fire I dived into a slit trench on top of a young soldier who was somewhat scared at my arrival. It was his first show and he was all alone. Others were dug in nearby but in the mist quite invisible. I assured him the MG fire was way up in the air. He swore at me and held up the ration box lid and held it above ground. A burst of MG fire cut it in two! It shook me. Didn't know which of us was most frightened. When firing stopped, moved out. He, poor devil, had to stay. As the mist slowly lifted, attack moving again. Casualty collecting began again, infantry and tank men alike. About 1130 hrs bringing in Royal Scots Fusilier soldier on stretcher, as approached RAP a mortar shell burst 20 yards away. Shrapnel got me across forehead and knocked me out. Came round to find Hylda (the

MO) dressing my head – lots of blood but soon conscious. Hylda told me a piece of shrapnel had penetrated my skull. My cap badge, much damaged, probably saved my life. Sent on to ADS via CCS to 84th General Military Hospital by 1600 hrs. Sisters lovely in red, white and grey. Vile headache. Increasing dizziness. [Later] Now quite deaf. Dizzy and vomiting. John Youens (Divisional Padre) and John Humphries (Hospital Padre) visited me. Afterwards said I was very angry and noisy about being sent home.

Leslie was shipped back to the UK on the *Isle of Jersey* and then to a Canadian hospital in Hazlemere. He was discharged on 5 July and rejoined the Sherwood Rangers in Normandy on the 25th.

Operation Epsom – 'Utter Desolation and Destruction'

After the débâcle of Villers-Bocage, Monty put his faith in the third attempt to take or encircle Caen. The entire VIII Corps would attack on a 4 mile front between Carpiquet, the aerodrome suburb of Caen, and Rauray to the south and push east across the little river Odon to gain the commanding heights of Hill 112. Lieutenant General Richard O'Connor, a brilliant African campaign general, but only recently a POW in Italy, was to commit

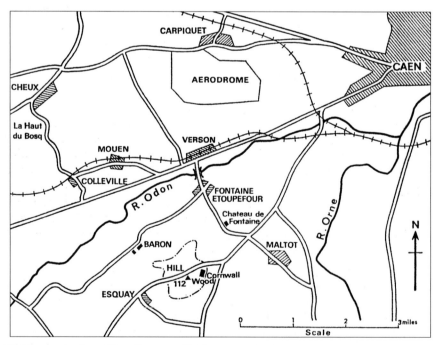

Battlegrounds of operations Epsom and Jupiter

Kent Libraries,
Registration and Archives
www.kent.gov.uk/libraries
Tel: 03000 41 31 31

Borrowed Items 05/09/2018 15:23
XXXXX9530

Title	Due Date
arching to the sound of fire	26/09/2018
e saboteur : true entures of the gentleman mando who took on the s	26/09/2018
d Lloyd George : the t outsider	18/09/2018

icates items borrowed today
nk you for using self service

15th Scottish, 11th Armoured and 43rd Wessex – all green, untried divisions – in this massive attack. To the south the equally green 49th Polar Bear Division would clear Fontenay-le-Pesnil and Rauray.

Here are some of the young 'virgin' soldiers' reports on their first actions.

At dawn on 26 June 700 guns blasted down barrages in front of the 600 tanks and 60,000 men. This was Monty's third effort to envelope Caen. The gallant 15th Scottish took a terrible beating on the right flank but despite mud and rain, tanks and motorised infantry of 11th Armoured had clawed their way by 29 June up Hill 112.

Rifleman 'Roly' Jefferson, 8 RB, recalls:

We were soon in the midst of utter desolation and destruction, corpses and shattered vehicles were everywhere and weeping, hysterical refugees were making their way back to our rear. We moved through the blasted ruins of Cheux and for the first time encountered being shelled ourselves. We had to seek out the German snipers and eliminate them. There was a vast difference between the text book soldiering when we were winning the battles on the Yorkshire Moors and the real thing which we were now experiencing. We crossed the river Odon and had to take and hold a piece of high ground beyond. One of our carriers ran over a mine and we lost the crew. Three German fighter planes came over and strafed us, so we lost another carrier. Five German tanks nosed their way out of the woods about 1,000 yards away but two were disposed of by 17-pdr Firefly Shermans of the 23rd Hussars. We dug in and there was a bloody battle between tanks. Many of our own were knocked out and burned fiercely. The tank crews who survived joined us in our slit-trenches.

'We Were Too Green to be Scared'

Major Noel Bell, 8 RB, records his feelings on his first day of action. He noticed the details of the ruined villages – gaily coloured advertisements for Byrrh and Cinzano painted on the sides of houses, enamelled signs reading 'Boulangerie' or 'Charcuterie', knocked-out German SP guns, Canadian Bren-carriers, and the surrounding cornfields littered with Canadian dead. 'All-pervading was the sweet, sickly repulsive smell of death. Dead cattle blown and stinking lay round the smouldering farms. Truly the four horsemen of the Apocalypse were riding through Normandy.' But the next morning his No. 10 Platoon supporting 3rd RTR patrolled through St Mauvieu village and then Cheux.

We rolled down the slope. Suddenly a gun spoke, once, twice and again. Some sparks seemed to fly off one of the leading tanks and the air was filled with a sound like that of a racing car passing at great speed – a rushing, whirring note. A moment's pause and the tank burst into a mass of flames. Micky said 'Eighty-eights.' We were too green to be scared for we failed to recognize the significance of it all. It had not yet registered on our minds that we were in the enemy gunner's sights and at that moment another armour-piercing shell was being loaded into the breach. It was our first taste of direct enemy action and it seemed coincidental that the shells were coming our way. We had yet to learn to be afraid. We had yet to learn to respect the German 88 mm.

'An Impregnable Monster?'

Many of the young soldiers now in action for the first time had had some experience of battle camps and firing exercises in their training in the UK. *Derrières* hugging the ground as 'boot' sergeants fired live ammo a foot above is one thing, but the first salvoes in earnest from the other side of the hill can be quite startling.

The 23rd Hussars' historian wrote: 'Those who witnessed it will always remember the shock of seeing for the first time one of the Regiment's tanks go up in flames. One moment an impregnable monster, with perhaps a crew containing some of one's best friends forging irresistibly towards the enemy, the next, a crack of terrific impact, a sheet of flame – and then, where there had been a tank, nothing but a helpless, roaring inferno.'

'We're Really In It'

Sergeant Frank Moppett, 'S' Company 1st Herefords, talked about his first action with his carrier section.

'At the start of Epsom my carrier was leading down a narrow lane on the edge of Cheux. Suddenly we were in chaos. Shots flying everywhere. Numerous dead Scotsmen were lying everywhere, one corporal lying over a branch of a tree twenty foot above the ground. A torso without arms or legs. Six 17-pounder anti-tank guns still attached to their quads all burning furiously. A group of dead Scots soldiers lying on their blankets. A Tiger tank knocked out on its side still burning.'

To his driver Moppett said: 'If this is war, mate, we're really in it.'

'Not Just a Race Course'

Troop Sergeant Jim Caswell, 'B' Squadron, 3 RTR wrote as he made his way in the dark towards the River Odon.

Small infantry battles were cracking away in the ruins of the village. The Odon was not very wide and it was the steep wooded valley which caused the most difficulty. The weather was wretched, almost continuous rain for two days, with aircraft being grounded in England. However, we received excellent artillery support [the author's 13 RHA SP 25-pdrs were in action nonstop] as we crossed the river over a small, intact bridge. We climbed the south bank of the valley with difficulty. The improving weather showed open fields ahead: more like tank country. 3 RTR was now in the lead and 'B' Sqn fought its way to the top of Hill 112. My Sherman tank had a wonderful view of Carpiquet airfield, the whole of Caen and to the east, the river Orne and the Bourgeubus ridge about ten miles to the south-east [where, during Operation Goodwood two Tigers almost annihilated 'B' Squadron]. From Hill 112 my tank had plenty of good shooting at dug-in German infantry at about 1,000 yards range. We ran out of ammo and had to go back to the Odon to replenish. Back in position I could not believe Colonel Silvertop's order to withdraw. He called the Squadron 2 i/c – no reply, nor from any troop officer. Eventually he called for *any* tank commander to answer. I, as troop sergeant, did so and proudly led 'B' Sqn off the hill to the replenishment area. We were told that two new German Panzer divisions were approaching who might have cut us off.

The Tanky's Diary – 'Swipe Hell Out of Jerry'

Sergeant Richard Greenwood was a Churchill tank commander, 'C' Squadron, 9 Royal Tank Regiment. He was in Lieutenant Peter Boden's troop with Corporal Bill Geary, wireless operator/loader, Corporal Ted Pestell as gunner, Trooper 'Tiger' Jimmy Boland as driver, and Trooper Derek Pedder as co-driver. On D+20 (26 June) 9 RTR were supporting the 9th Cameronians of 15th Scottish Division near Cheux. Fortunately Sergeant Greenwood kept a diary, 'One Day at a Time'.

We took up our start position in a large field below crest of a hill: 5 p.m. Our infantry were in position too – some hundreds of them. A sturdy looking crowd – mostly Scotties – all smiling and cheerful. They asked us to swipe hell out of Jerry. We were thoroughly conversant with plan of attack and ultimate directive. We also had a pretty good idea of where enemy's main anti-tank guns were, from previous reconnaissance. Close to our zero hour, word came through that 60 Panthers had appeared within a few hundred yards of our line of advance. Hell's Bells! Poor little 'C' Squadron. Before we started the Panthers advanced on our position and were engaged by some fairly heavy stuff – 17 pounders. After about an hour Jerry retired. He certainly didn't get through. We commenced our delayed start at 6.15 p.m. Infantry ahead, rifles at the ready. By 7 p.m. the battle was on. A/Tk guns were firing like hell and so were we. Very soon I saw one crew bale out, tank on fire. They crawled away in the long corn avoiding Jerry snipers and MG. Advance proceeded. Infantry kept 'going to ground' because of Jerry's MGs. We sprayed those woods with BESA. Tons of it and HE and AP and Smoke. Impossible to see A/Tk guns in woods. Could only fire at their 'flash'. Advance proceeded slowly. Two or three Jerry tanks appeared, all were engaged. They disappeared. More of ours were hit. Some burning, crews baling out. Found myself behaving rationally and quite calm. Was really terrified just prior to 'going in'. Eventually, we retired, waited. It seemed like hours to me. We were on the battlefield all the time.

'A Terrifying Cat and Mouse Game'

As the 5th Battalion Duke of Cornwalls filtered into ruined Cheux and started to dig in, Major A.F.C. Kitchen, OC 'C' Company, made a recce to an orchard on his right flank and found it full of Germans, so he formed a defensive flank to cover Battalion HQ from that direction. At 0900 'B' Company were making themselves at home in another orchard and heard the rumble of tanks approaching down a sunken road. Captain H. Jobson, 2 i/c 'D' Company, related what happened next.

The wireless was working to battalion headquarters and life seemed to be a little better and more like an exercise around Folkestone. During the course of the morning I was walking back to Company Headquarters having flushed a German sniper from a farm building. Cpl Ronan and I both had a fresh egg in our hands and life seemed better than ever. About 10 yards up the road we were surprised and glad to see six nice big tanks trundle up the road and turn into Company Headquarters' orchard. 'Always nice to have armour in support – pretty decent guns on them – funny camouflage they have. My God! German crosses on their turrets!' This last observation was too awful to be ignored and violent evasive action was taken by the two of us. At the same time Major [John] Fry [commanding 'D' Company] also made the same discovery and gave one of his characteristic shouts. One tank went on for 50 yards and knocked out a whole troop of 17-pounder anti-tank guns just coming up [from 333 Anti-tank Battery].

Cpl Ronan and myself soon found ourselves in Sgt Hicks' mortar pit. After a brief 'pow-wow' it was decided that he, Sgt Hicks with his PIAT and with Cpl Ronan's help, should start shooting up the tanks from the back. I went off and organised the three PIAT teams from the three platoons. On returning I had the pleasure of watching Major Fry and Ptes Jeffries and Parrish being chased all round the orchard. Each time a tank moved it was necessary for them to move also. Funny to watch, but not for them. The rest of the Company Headquarters were in their slits with the tanks actually on top and around them. Next two German despatch riders came down the road and Major Fry and I had the honour and pleasure of killing the first Germans to enter the battalion area. The German tanks then started to edge forward and knocked out the two 6-pounder guns in 'D' Company area wounding most of the crew. Battalion Headquarters was their next objective. It was a nice hull-down shoot for them at about 50 yds range. Very soon there were soft vehicles and carriers brewing up and much activity was seen by the Battalion Headquarters ditch. Our 6-pounders replied despite the fact that they were under direct fire. Lt-Col Atherton was killed in a gallant attempt to keep one gun firing. He was acting as loader as the rest of the crew was knocked out. At this time I met Capt [David] Willcocks, the Intelligence Officer.

We lay in a shallow ditch in an orchard under the barrel of an 88 mm gun with the tracks of the tank not 2 ft from us. Prayers were said amongst other things! Four PIATs were hitting the tanks up their backsides and the Germans did not like it. One fled, hit three times by the PIAT in No. 17 Platoon . . . he got away badly hit and the crew well shaken. Sgt Hicks knocked out another one at short range. Two more went round the corner and were worried by Capt Blackwell of 'C' Company who led a PIAT Party. He knocked one out and the other turned itself over in its excitement to escape. Sgt Willison's 6-pounder accounted for another when to his own surprise and everyone else's the Panther brewed up at about 100 yds range.

The hunting of the crews was the next phase and exciting sport it made. Four prisoners were captured and about nine Germans were killed.

In Action – 'That Dreadful Day'

Lieutenant Geoffrey Bishop was a young troop leader, 23rd Hussars, 11th Armoured Division.

I can see with my fieldglasses a gun being put into position. 'Gunner, traverse left, steady on 1,500 yards, by two light coloured trees. Action, yellow, one round fire' and suddenly there is the report and the blinding flash. The air is busy with the Colonel giving other orders. Then I see that Bob's tank is beginning to catch fire. His sergeant jumps out of his own tank which is just in front of mine and appears to be a sitting target and dashes over to Bob. They got the poor chap out, badly knocked about. The two drivers got away unhurt. The other two in the turret [of the Sherman] were killed instantly and could not be got out before the tank was a mass of flames. Later that dreadful day [28 June] I was to learn that poor young Peter Halyar's tank had been hit. He was mortally wounded and his operator killed. Three out of Bob's four tanks knocked out and two out of four officers killed within twenty minutes. I went on firing at the anti-tank gun but he made no reply. All that day we fought on that ground [east of Mondrainville] and in the late afternoon Tigers were reported to our north and the position looked tricky. Calmly, under perfect orders from the Colonel we withdrew to our original positions. About nine we got back into harbour, unshaven, tired out and hungry. I had been in my tank for 27 hours – it seemed like 27 days. Work to be done straight away, petrol to draw, rations, trenches to dig, guns to clean, ammo to be taken on, food to be cooked. By midnight we crept into our holes. Reveille was at 4.30 the next morning. At 0730 the Padre, haggard and unshaven, takes the burial service for Bob. All his friends are there. No other sound save the twittering of the birds greeting this sad morning. We make a simple wooden cross and Bob's beret is placed on it.

Language!

In the battle for Cheux, Lieutenant Steel Brownlie 2nd Fife and Forfarshire recalls:

The squadron came back and replenished. I reassembled what was left of my troop and was told to lead the way up to the railway by Grainville. We crossed it unopposed 300 yards from the village. This was a commanding position and I did an HE shoot on some camouflaged vehicles 3,500 yards away. Don Hall and I sat in the shelter of smoke from a burning house and watched Kenneth Matheson's Recce Troop go into the village to see if it was clear, which it wasn't. He lost a tank but no men, to a Panther sitting in or beside the church. As he was belting back past us, having done his job, Colonel Scott came on the air and asked him for his exact position. He replied, 'Position be buggered. Wait out.'

Smelling of Roses?

'Chuck' Baldwin, Platoon Sergeant No. 15 platoon 4 KSLI:

I well remember my first night in action after crossing the River Odon and getting slightly wet. We were travelling in single file when an almighty noise broke out – yes it was the 'moaning Minnies'. I have never been so scared in all my life. I dived flat against a wall into some stinging nettles and when I got up I was smothered all over with dog excrement and I mean all over, on my pouches and all down the front of me. The chaps said, 'What the hell stinks?' – it was a terrible smell, talk about coming up smelling of roses! After the first few salvoes of Minnies we soon got used to it and were prepared for the noise, but when you are travelling in the dark it is very nerve-racking.

'Chuck' became Sergeant, then CSM, and won the MM in the Hochwald battle in Germany.

The Stretcher Bearer's Story

Stretcher Bearer Corporal Ron Cookson, 4 KSLI, took part in the action to clear Baron and wrote:

My baptism of action and the Battalion's first two casualties occurred when we moved up that evening to Baron, B Company together with A. We waded across the River Odon and I remember how warm the water was at that time – up to waist level. All was peaceful until we approached the higher wooded ground, then all hell let loose with 'moaning Minnies', shelling and airbursts above us. Our first casualty was Private Askey who was killed. Then Private Jones had his leg shattered. I went to Askey first but I could see he was already dead with a great big piece of shrapnel in the middle of his back which had smashed his vertebrae.

'The Haven of Peace'

Lieutenant Steel Brownlie noted:

At dawn in a steady drizzle that soaked everyone to the skin, we motored [Shermans of 2nd Fife and Forfarshire] through the gun area, through gaps in the minefields and past German trenches, empty except for bodies. A few shells dropped close. We had gone about 300 yards when two armour-piercing shots came from the high ground on the right, sending up showers of earth and killing two infantrymen. I wheeled the troop right and saw the turrets of three German tanks nicely positioned hull-down about 1,800 yards away. AP was no use at that range so I did an HE shoot on them. They brewed up a halftrack nearby (you could see their solid shot whirling down in our general direction) but after a few minutes they withdrew. Encouraging . . . That night, after our first day in action, I don't think that anyone slept. The petrol and ammo took three hours to reach us. The enemy were only a few hundred yards away, and everybody was shattered by the day's events. Long afterwards you thought about Cheux as just about the worst and anything else seemed an improvement. You also thought about Cully, a tiny hamlet, as a sort of haven of peace.

Another Round for Luck

On the outskirts of Fontenay, the left flank of the 49th Polar Bear Division was being protected by 'B' Squadron of the Reconnaissance Regiment, under whose command was 'Y' Troop of the Anti-Tank Battery. The assault troop was sent forward to see if any enemy were present. At that moment four Panther tanks appeared on the forward edge of the wood. The first three were disposed of by one gun in four shots. Sergeant J. Bell commented: 'They were hit just where they should be hit', and his gun layer, 'The No. 1 of the gun identified the tanks as Panthers Mark V. I got sighted on the left-hand tank and the Sgt gave the fire order. The range was about 600 yards, but I got a hit first shot. Flames began to come from the

Night attack with 49th Polar Bear Division to clear Fontenay village, 25 June 1944. (Birkin Haward)

Panther. I then laid on the next tank and this was also hit with the first shot and went up in smoke. I put in another round for luck. That was three rounds fired so far. The third tank was just disappearing into the wood, but I just had time to fire my fourth round and again scored a hit. This tank also burst into flames.' The fourth tank fell to a PIAT handled by a lance corporal who later became a silk-hatted bank messenger in the City of London.

The Vile War

Sgt Bob Sheldrake, 55 A/Tk Regt 49 Division, wrote:

Hell-fire Corner [near Rauray] had been the scene of many clashes with the enemy and many of their dead strewed the road – who was fool enough to stay there long enough to move them? As tanks and carriers passed to and fro they champed over these bodies churning them to a pulp of flesh and rag. I saw a carrier make a skid turn on the corner and strip the skin backwards over a ghastly trunk until the flesh lay exposed, vividly pink and shining for the brief moment it arched as if in living torment before it slumped back into the ignominy and desecration of the mud.

So this was war – here was no glory, no proudness of scarlet uniforms and military music, but a bloody mashing, pulping of human beings. The ordinary man's war cannot be glorified, necessary it may be, but it is vile in the extreme.

A Brave Display

At Ranville, Major Martin Lindsay of the 1/5th Gordons, remembered:

> On one of these evenings we had Retreat, with the 'Road to the Isles', the 'Skye Boat Song' and all my favourite tunes. It was a brave display, the pipe band marching and counter-marching in a tiny paddock beside the main road with ammunition trucks and ambulances slowing down to see what they could see while passing. Most of the time the guns in the field beyond were firing over our heads. The officers of the Bn in their kilts, stood on the mounds of earth excavated from trenches and the men sat around in their shirt sleeves.

Operation Mitten – 'Kamerad Tommy'

The 3rd British Division were ordered to take the heavily defended farm and Chateau de la Londe from Gazelle on 28 June. The 2nd East Yorks were on the right, and the 1st Suffolk on the left under a heavy rolling barrage with tank support. Major D.W. McCaffrey, 'B' Company CO, 1st Suffolk led the dawn attack but came under very heavy artillery and mortar fire. His small staff were wounded, the wireless set was wrecked, 'and with the bad light and the noise, I lost control of the Coy. I could see nothing of the two forward platoons. At one point I found myself entirely alone.' Later. 'We entered the wood of the Chateau where visibility was reduced to about 20 yards. Eventually, with Corporal Maddern and ten men, the survivors of 'B' Company reached their objective and dug in. Stragglers came in and the small force of twenty-four was ensconced in an apple orchard with some thick trees on the forward edge.

> We were counter-attacked by six tanks who came straight at us and thirty infantry withdrawing from the Chateau came at us from the rear. We took them on [the PIAT men who went to follow up 'B' Company were by now casualties] and they went to ground fifty yards from us. Three tanks remained shooting their MGs at us from the front whilst three moved to the flanks and caught us in enfilade with both small arms and HE, firing as they advanced slowly through the gate. Things became rather bad for us in our incompleted slit trenches. When the Boche shouted, 'Kamerad Tommy', I saw the chaps nearest the tanks surrender, then others following suit. When I saw that I had lost control, I took a header into a large thorn bush, followed by Lieut Evans who was near me. The Germans searched the area but we were not located. I then had the mortification of seeing some very brave men being marched off as prisoners. They had passed through a terrific enemy concentration of fire and had seen many comrades fall. They only surrendered when their own position was quite hopeless and they could do no more.

During the day 1st Suffolk lost seven officers and 154 ORs killed, wounded or missing.

'Detonators in Place'

In the early hours of 29 June, Rex Flower and the mortar platoon of 1/4 KOYLI were dug in on the outskirts of Tessel Wood. 'The assault pioneer platoon of "S" Company had orders to lay some anti-tank mines in a hurry under cover of darkness to the west of our wood. They were allowed to carry the mines ready armed, with detonators *in place* in boxes, so many to a box. A very dangerous thing to do. All the mines exploded in one terrific explosion that blew most of them to bits. I knew most of the dead as it was my company.'

Journey's End

Gunner 'Wally' Brereton was part of an OP party, 45th Battery 81st Welsh Field Regiment RA, which supported the Highland Light Infantry Battalion of 53rd (Welsh) Division. The 'Roger Fox' carrier was driven by Frankie Silva. The FOO was 'F' Troop Commander Captain Green and Peter Bonnington was the radio operator. 'Wally' was the OP 'Ack' who carried a portable radio and field telephone, a message pad and 'panorama' drawing board. He described their semi-static OP on Hill 113 overlooking Evrecy.

A huge dugout was the Bn HQ of 1st Highland Light Infantry. At the entrance a javelin with a pennant indicated the CO, Lieutenant Colonel Torquil MacLeod, was in residence. We spent the day with binoculars glued to our eyes sweeping the scenery to the south, my rifle resting on the parapet. It was the nearest we ever got to any semblance of the Great War. Some nights I stayed on the hill and moved my telephone and message pad to the big dugout. Inside it was just like a scene from *Journey's End*. At the far end was a pile of straw held in place by a plank on which was chalked 'CO's Roost'. Several other HLI officers and our Captain Green engaged in small talk whilst I sat in the corner with my D MkV field telephone, message pad at the ready. I carried binoculars and a compass but a grey denim jacket concealed any badge of rank. In Normandy we worked in OPs in chateaux, barns, factories and church towers. Often we operated from 'Roger Fox' by the roadside.

The Tanky's Diary – 'Crack of Thunder'

After his first day of action, Sergeant Greenwood's Churchill tanks of 'C' Squadron 9 RTR had been badly mauled. Keeble had been killed by a sniper, Gotobed and Painter died of wounds and Jim Chapman was killed outright. Three days later Greenwood was back in action near Grainville.

We put up a tremendous barrage of AP and BESA. Only casualties were an NCO and OR, tank received direct hit from a mortar. We were mortared mercilessly today [D+23, 29 June] almost from the moment of our arrival. Heavy mortar is a terrifying experience. Became quite adept at diving beneath tank. Several loads of mortar from 'singing sisters' or 'moaning Minnies'. They do at least give about 3 seconds' warning by their weird wailing before exploding. The detonation is tremendous and sounds like nearby crack of thunder. These weapons have played hell with infantry [it is estimated that two-thirds of all casualties in Normandy were inflicted by enemy mortars]. And after only one day, I feel worn out. There is the constant physical effort of diving for safety, plus the awful mental strain of waiting for the explosion. At one period, we all had to take refuge inside the tank. It was too dangerous even to open hatches. Survival now seems to me more a matter of luck than anything. We are being fired at in the tanks by AP from A/Tks and tanks, and machine-gunned from the air; shelled by artillery; mortared; sniped at; machine-gunned by ground forces and then there are the countless mines and booby traps left behind by Jerry. When rummaging round his dugouts, great care has to be taken because of booby traps. They are even hanging from the trees in places. There is a great deal of artful ingenuity in Jerry's infantry. There are German corpses about too . . . just hastily buried and often partly visible.

'Killing an Obsession'

After the attack on Mouen on 29 June, Private Albert Kings, Brengunner with the 1st Worcesters, wrote: 'Good friends died at Mouen. I was both sad and angry, my hatred for the enemy had become very personal now. I felt no compassion at all, my one thought now was for retribution. I felt that as a Brengunner I had a special job to do; that was to reach one's objective as quick as possible, dig in and be in a position to defend against counter-attack and kill as many Jerries as possible. To this end killing was almost an obsession.'

Signallers Under Fire

Lieutenant John McMath of the 5th Battalion Wiltshires wrote:

J.C. Litrizza, the Signals Officer, had been severely wounded in the first engagement at Hill 112. The Signals Platoon now had to get used to a new officer with possibly different ideas. We soon learned to trust each other. After our classic victory at Maltot, I had decided to link up the rifle companies by line with advanced HQ in a ruined house at the back of the village, and give some rest to our fickle radio sets. This was my first battle experience and my first signals operation under conditions very different to training exercises. Our main concern was to protect our cable from damage by tracked vehicles. But most damage to telephone cables was by shell and mortar fire. So, there, right in front of me in the pitch dark lit by a gun flash were the skull and crossbones. I was about to lead my cable-laying party into a German minefield. The expertise of the imperturbable Sergeant King leading one cable party and some luck for me leading the other, soon established a secure communication network. It was important to give signallers out repairing damaged lines as much cover as possible and the facility to run the cable through their hands as they felt their way through the darkness looking for breaks. The real workhorse was the old No. 18 set. This R/T wireless set, for all its imperfections, its susceptibility to screening by hills, trees and buildings, the limitations of its heavy batteries and its propensity to go off set, still remained a faithful servant of the Bn Signallers. Signaller Roper won the MM for repairing telephone cable under fire and so did Corporal Angel later at Elst.

Sketches by Donald Green, 1/5th Queens Regt, 7th Armoured Division

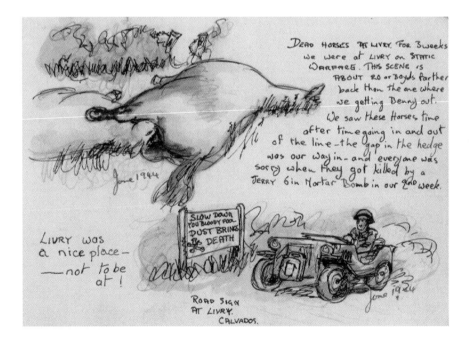

of milk – come to that – neither did I! One of our worst few minutes in FRANCE on LEFT. We had just had a shower and all were trying to dry ourselves when a FW190 dived out of the low clouds as we'd no clothes or shelter! A Bofors gun however blew its LEFT Wing of it crashed – with the pilot behind us !! CHUFF in his element milking the local cows while Tich takes his pleasures in a lighter vein he rode this cow round the field then it slung him over the hedge. The "BERGÉRE" nearly went mad.

The Truck in which Hoppy and I shared with the driver and his mate. Hoppy is here boiling the milk we have got.

SMUDGER smith   CHUFF   JOHNNY LUDOROW   TICH

Sketches by Donald Green

We were mixed in with a gun line of 4.5's, 5.5's, Long Toms and Priest and Bishop self propelled guns. the R.A. Boys assured us they were'nt half showing Jerry a thing or two. When Jerry kept slinging a counter barrage back we thought he was'nt doing so bad himself!.. It was hell had more casualties here Bocage. One of the queerest incidents I saw / Jerry TANK Commander of 9TH PANZER comes riding in with a Tiger and behind a PANTHER flying white flags from their wireless masts. They had a Sherman escort from here.

even here we than · VILLERS

July 1944

Moving round to
VILLERS BOCAGE
JUNE 12TH.

THE BOYS
"DE BUS" in a hurry at the ST. Paul Du Vernay CrossRoads. We went in
with No I Combat Team. U.S. Army, here, an Automatic Rifle has just
rattled hitted, and wounding George Read (on Back of truck) and Lt (Hood,
Hodson Standing in truck. Tanky on Right was messing about with a Yank
Automatic, Bullets hit road and ricochetted up. Everyone was in a Flat spin
for a minute or two.

Sketches by Donald Green

MORNING. June 13TH our unlucky day. We started
off by getting strafed by U.S.A.A.F
Marauders, then two blokes got shot up
by this 16 year-old sniper of a Pioneer
Bn. He came in Crying and whining
but didn't forget to ask for
a Cigarette when we didn't
shoot him. George Grace with
Bren gun very nearly did.
    only an Officer was
        looking.
From here we mosed
right on up into Villers-
15 Kilo's behind
Jerry lines.
And then the Fun
really started --------

JUST OUTSIDE TOWN OF
VILLERS BOCAGE.

CHAPTER FOUR

The War of Attrition Continues – July

Operation Epsom was a very costly near-success. Ultra/Enigma had alerted top management to the coming storm as German armour gathered and struck in a formidable attack. 11th Armoured Division were pulled down off the heights of Hill 112 to the banks of the river Odon, in case they were cut off. The main blow fell on the southern flank on the 49th Polar Bear Division who, after taking Fontenay-le-Pesnil and Tessel Wood, were in the Rauray area. The end of Operation Martlet was a terrible but successful battle fought on 1 July.

A week later Monty tried his fourth attack on Caen – a direct head-on confrontation led by the 3rd British and 3rd Canadian divisions in Operation Charnwood. Monty kept the pressure up – again at an appalling cost – as 43rd Wessex Wyvern Division tried to storm Hill 112 in Operation Jupiter in a series of classic set-piece attacks against formidable opposition. The Wyverns took 2,000 casualties in the period 10–12 July. Caen eventually fell on 10 July and thus allowed the 'grand slam' armoured battle of Operation Goodwood to take place south-east of Caen with the 11th Armoured leading the Guards Armoured and the Desert Rats in a powerful surge which started on 18 July. If all went well, Falaise might be reached. 3rd British acted as flank protection in the Troarn area.

By the end of July the war of attrition had kept the bulk of the German troops and tanks opposite the British and Canadian forces – but at huge human cost. In the first three weeks of fighting in June, the British and Canadian casualties were 25,000, of which 3,356 were KIA, 15,815 wounded and 5,527 missing (mainly prisoners of war).

These are some of the stories of four great battlefields: Rauray (the end of Martlet); Charnwood (the taking of Caen); Jupiter (the terrible struggles to reach Hill 112) and Goodwood (the charge of the armoured divisions).

The Stretcher Bearers

One of the most vital, dangerous and sometimes thankless tasks is that of the unarmed stretcher-bearers who, usually under fire, have to seek out the wounded and stretcher them back to the RAP. During the long, hot summer day after the Polar Bear Division had taken Fontenay, the enemy predictably shelled and mortared the area where the Hallamshires were holding the line. The CO Lieutenant Colonel Hart Dyke wrote:

We lost mortar platoon carriers and many of the platoon including Abbott its commander, *before* they had dug in. It was sad to see and hear their carriers, ammunition and mortars going up. Later, a mortar bomb landing at Support Company killed CSM Morton. All day our RMO Gregory-Dean worked like a Trojan under fire while so many ambulances were knocked out working between Les Haut Vents and Fontenay that evacuation of wounded was no longer possible. During the day the regimental stretcher bearers under Sergeant Goodliffe were heroic and two lost their lives. Lance Corporal Penn alone rescued 32 men, 11 of whom were saved under close small arms fire, and one even after he himself was severely wounded. Recommended for the Victoria Cross, he received the MM. Later, he had to have his leg amputated. The bravery and devotion to duty of the Hallamshires were beyond praise. Total casualties were 123 including three company commanders.

Famous Last Words

The 49th Polar Bear Division were being supported by 4/7 RDG on an attack on Fontenay-le-Pesnil where three Tigers well placed in a wood knocked out six Shermans of 'C' Squadron. The next day an attack on Rauray involved Captain John Stirling's 'A' Squadron.

We had to do a five hundred yards attack with infantry which looked fairly simple. Near the little hamlet of Brettevillette I saw an SP moving about in a farm and fired six rounds of HE at it. Sergeant Harris reported over the air that he was being fired on from the farm and I made a long-since 'Famous Last Words' remark. 'It's all right. It's only a mortar.' I saw a flash from the wood above the village. The next moment a shell hit the turret with a terrific bang. After that everything was vague and ponderous like it is in a dream. I heard Murphy shout, 'Bale out, bale out.' It seemed cowardly to leave the tank when we could still fight it. Then I saw the gun mantlet spinning slowly down the gun with a great hole in it. I realised the tank was useless and we must bale out. I struggled up and was half-way out when I saw the flash again and again that terrible crash as we were hit. Something hit me in the back and I was flung to the ground. I got up and hobbled about a bit. I was alone. The tank was on fire now and from inside the turret came the screams of a trapped animal. I got up on the front. Both the driver's hatches were open and empty. With an effort I scrambled up on to the turret. Murphy's hands were grasping upwards. I caught them in mine and gave him a hand. 'Come on, Murphy,' I almost whispered. His eyes were closed and sightless. Where his legs used to be were two little black charred stumps. The hands were limp and clammy in the last nervous convulsions of the Death that was spreading a yellow stain across his face. The operator was peacefully dead on the floor.

John Stirling was evacuated to RAP, FDS, to Bayeux base hospital, to the RAF hospital at Wroughton and EMS Hospital in Worcester. Seven weeks later Stirling was back with his regiment.

Three Casualties

Private John Longfield 1/4 KOYLI took part in the battles for Fontenay-le-Pesnil and Tessel Wood and describes three of the casualties.

With enormous artillery fire support we attacked up the hillside at the other side of the village. Some of the shells were falling short. One fell very close – a small splinter from it hit the man next to me. It went in through his foot [he had thrown himself on the ground] and came out at his knee. He was screaming in agony. There was nothing I could do except call for the stretcher bearers and carry on up the hill. [Later.] In Tessel Wood itself I came across an enormous bomb crater. Sat on the edge was a German, his arms resting on his knees. I was about to shoot him when he heard me, looked up and raised his arms. There were no hands on the ends of his arms. I was so horrified at his predicament that I considered killing him to put him out of his misery. [Stretcher bearers carried him away, and he survived.] After we had taken the Fontenay Tessel Wood area, I found the youngest lad in the company lying on his back in front of a hedge, his tin hat over his face. I lifted his tin hat up. The front of his head was missing and there was a grey mash of brains mixed with blood. The poor lad was only 17 years old. He had got into the army by falsifying his age. What a dreadful waste!

One afternoon, I guess my nerves must have been pretty shattered at the time, I thought to hell with this, opened my tin of cigarettes and lit up. I didn't smoke one cigarette, I smoked most of the tin lighting one from the previous one.

Mobile Anderson Shelter

Generally speaking, the infantry/tank cooperation within the three fine armoured divisions – 7th (Desert Rats), 11th (Black Bull) and the Guards – was brilliant. Tightly knit 'battle groups' such as 3 RTR had with 4 KSLI and welded together by 8 RB motorized infantry and 13 RHA SP 25-pdrs were perhaps the epitome of all-arm cooperation. Godfrey Harland MC was a Company CO of 1/4 KOYLI in the 49th Polar Bear Division and wrote:

Our pre-D-Day training had included some (mighty little) infantry/tank cooperation but during that limited training there was not time to develop that vital rapport between infantry and armour which can help both to perform well on the battlefield. We had never before met the 24th Lancers or anyone else in 8 Armoured Bde until just before our first battalion attack against Cristot in Normandy. It was our marvellous good fortune to find ourselves supported by the 24th Lancers Sherman tanks during the big early battles in the 'bocage' area of Normandy. Their support was bold and skilful. After we had taken Tessel Wood a whole Squadron remained with 1/4 KOYLI for the whole night to add to our fire power on our exposed right flank where Panzer Lehr were threatening a formidable counter-attack. I was talking to a Lancer tank commander when a hefty German 'mortar' stick started dropping all around us. He said, 'If you don't mind I'll just drop down inside my mobile Anderson shelter!' He closed the lid down leaving 1/4 KOYLI feeling rather naked outside! At Rauray on 30 June they supported our 70 Brigade in that ferocious battle and their CO, Lieutenant Colonel W.A.C. Anderson, received many congratulations. Alas, our later support from armoured regiments equipped with Churchills was less effective. They were reluctant to do what we wanted them to do and rarely cooperated wholeheartedly.

The First Battle – Point of the Arrow – Suffolk A/Tk Gunners

'As daylight dawned [over a cornfield near Rauray] we watched our first 25-pdr shells come down on a line of trees across the field to our front. The "Guv" pointed to a hedge on a bank some 25 yards to our front behind which crouched dark shapes and small groups of men. "That's the front line, 'Shelley' [wrote Sergeant Bob Sheldrake], we're the point of the arrow at last. Tell everyone to dig like hell because at first light we'll get a hell of a pasting here." We did. Across that 100 yards of grass lay the enemy and the grim battle was on. The artillery threw over everything they had. All sizes of shells whizzed overhead to come crashing down on the enemy: our mortars were pumping bombs over from all directions and the Brens were puttering away mingled with rapid rifle fire. The rasping, quick action rattle of German Spandaus cut into the corn around us and then they backed them up with a heavy stonk on our position. They threw mortars at us, with now and then "moaning Minnies", multiple-action mortars which at the moment of release gave off a weird wailing sound calculated to strike terror into those waiting to receive them. They shelled us with 88s which reached us almost as soon as we heard the guns fired and the corn wavered and shuddered, clinging desperately to its little roots, among the smoke that enveloped all. The whole area quickly became a ragged shell-torn corner, dotted here and there with slit trenches in which we cowered and waited for what was to come. Now and again a Sherman tank would come along, fire a few rounds and withdraw. It was always our fear that we would be run over. The smiling eyes of the driver, as we desperately waved him aside, were very reassuring. It was no picnic for them for two or three were brewing up in the vicinity, adding billowing smoke to the cloudy scene.'

'Toasted White Bread and the Beveridge Plan'

Eric Codling, of 8th Battalion Middlesex Regiment, supported the Wessex Wyverns with his 4.2 in mortars. Diary extracts read:

> The first week in July we were near Tourville on the Caen–Villers-Bocage road and had 3 casualties from mortar bombs. Our Brigadier, a veteran of WWI, said the conditions are now similar to the very heavy artillery fire and trench warfare of 1914–18. We constructed some very deep and strong dug-outs. Our 4.2 in mortars really came into their own as Arty ammo is in short supply due to the bad weather and storms in June. We have plenty of mortar bombs to break up incessant counter-attacks. Saw the RAF heavy bombardment raid on Caen [450 heavy bombers on the night of 7 July to prepare the way for Operation Charnwood the next day. The old city was flattened. The Germans had withdrawn key troops from the town before the air raid.] We did not know that the devastation caused by the bombing was to prove a bigger hindrance to the Allies than to the Germans in the coming battles to take the city. [And] 9 July – recce party to orchard in wooded area south of the River Odon. The bodies of enemy soldiers lay where they had fallen, some in the river, a few inches deep, which was where our water supply was drawn from. 1,200 mortar bombs carried and stored for next barrage. After 4 weeks of hard biscuits, *white* bread, first for four *years*, appeared. Firing all day. Mortar barrels became hot enough to toast the delicious white bread on. After a while the battering on our ear-drums caused us to reel about like drunks, such was the deafening noise. Mortar barrels had to be taken down and rolled in the lush grass to cool them because licks of flame coming from the barrel mouths, after a bomb had been fired, threatened the next bomb about to be dropped in. One of a group of German POW sheltering from a bout of shelling picked up a copy of the *Daily Mirror* lying by a trench. Headline report about Beveridge health care scheme for postwar Britain. One German who could read English said Hitler had introduced a similar service *ten years before!*

Tactics

Lieutenant Colonel T. Hart Dyke was a notably effective battalion commander. 'We suffered our first casualties from enemy mortars. I walked round to see how the men were taking it and ordered them to dig *shallow* trenches which kept their minds off the shelling.' The Hallamshires were being shelled in their Forming-Up Point (FUP) before an attack near Les

Haut Vents. A couple of hours later, 'We dug in properly with good fields of fire. When the Battalion HQ Signal and two Medical 15 cwt trucks were knocked out by shells, this taught us *never* to leave our unarmoured vehicles in the forward area but to dump and dig in our stores.' When their neighbours, the 4th Lincolns, lost the whole of their carrier platoon from shellfire 'due to their moving in error across a forward slope, this taught us the necessity of traffic signing, drummed into us at home but now rather neglected.'

During the attack on Fontenay the 10th Battalion Royal Scots Fusiliers (147 Brigade) were on the left of the Hallamshires. 'I could get no news of them. For ever after I always attached a liaison officer on *my* wireless link, *privately* to any battalion with whom I was working.' The RSF suffered heavy casualties when forming up for the attack because – a cardinal sin – 'they had *not* secured their FUP and start line before the main attack.'

Cheer Up, Mate – Here's a Fag

Sergeant Wally Caines, i/c the Signal Platoon of the 4th Dorsets, wrote about his first action (2 July):

A few shells fell in the area: the unit suffered several casualties, some badly wounded. The medical services were excellent. One could see the wounded being brought in by the stretcher bearers, who would sweat in streams after their strenuous slogging to and from the RAP, a hundred yards away from Tactical HQ. One could hear the wounded moaning, sometimes crying with pain as they passed by. The boys would walk alongside saying 'Cheer up, mate', and stuff a lighted cigarette in their mouth. A cig always helped soothe the pain, this was well known to all.

The Empty Battlefield

Private John Longfield of 1/4 KOYLI was the Brengunner in his platoon.

Of course I did not see any Germans – just spotted the area where their fire was coming from. And I don't suppose that they saw many of us. The general rule was that anyone who *was* seen – unless he was moving fast – was killed or wounded. A battlefield, large or small, generally looks pretty empty of men, except perhaps in a set-piece attack – and then one does not see much of the defenders until one is right on top of them. As the days passed, casualties mounted from small arms fire, mortars and artillery.

Reinforcements came in to replace those who had left. In some of these I noticed the importance of the psychological factor. Naturally everyone was scared but quite a few expressed the view, 'I could not kill anyone.' When it came to the crunch, I hope they changed their view. Even a fraction of a second's hesitation in deciding to pull the trigger can be fatal. In fact the reaction should really be automatic. I am sure that not enough emphasis was laid on this in our training and that it had unfortunate results in some cases. . . . I remember one of my colleagues was most concerned about a particular German he had killed. This German had burst through a hedge in front of my pal who had immediately shot him in an automatic reaction. Later on he told me he was worried because he thought the man wanted to surrender. It really preyed on his mind. Presumably, all front-line infantrymen had nightmares for years after the war ended.

The Team

Sergeant Bob Sheldrake, 'A' Troop 55th Anti-tank Regiment (the original Suffolk Yeomanry), described his team. George Savage drove the portee,

A grand old lady of many winters and many exercises, now the ammo truck, named 'Flo' after George's wife. Lieutenant O. Martin, 'A' troop commander, tall, lean and with a respectable sandy moustache which belied his twenty years, was a Cornishman affectionately called 'The Guvnor'. 'Wilco' Adams with his long, white face was the wireless operator in the Bren gun carrier. Jimmy Todd, short, tough and reliable, was the carrier driver (who cooked as well) and Bert Ennis was the Guvnor's batman. Dave the jeep driver was a natterer who begrudged every minute of the day that kept him away from his beloved Hereford. The four 17-pounder A/Tk gun No. 1s were ginger-haired Sergeant 'Math' Bowers, Sergeant 'Jas' King and Les Bullman and Norman Asher. Later on, Andy Anderson became the Guv's new batman. He was worth his weight in gold, for he could really cook. Each gun crew was self-supporting, cooking all their own food. We always managed – when either Jimmy or Dave was cook. We didn't do so well when I took a turn but when Wilco had a go it was unbearable, his cooking was too bad to be true.

Houses

There were two schools of thought about the use of houses as defensive points in the Normandy battles. It was well known that isolated houses and farms were always made registered fire targets by the Germans – thus most British units in or near the front line would avoid them like the plague. On the other hand, Rommel had fortified over a hundred farmsteads south-east of Caen, which defied and halted the great tank onslaught of Goodwood. Lieutenant Colonel Hart Dyke recalled: 'If accommodation was available I got as many men as possible into houses whenever I could for this was with the primary objective of getting all-round field of fire. The Norman houses were very solidly built and gave real security from *any* form of shell. This was contrary to the teaching then in vogue. The Germans adopted these tactics so well at Vendes so we copied them and never regretted it. Slit trenches were of course dug out and manned at Stand To.'

The Dead Jerry

'A German machine gunner who had been positioned to cause the maximum havoc to our advancing columns [1st Worcesters in Normandy] had been dealt with effectively and lay dead in the roadway. Without thought or hesitation each vehicle in the convoy ran over the body. As my own 15 cwt [Corporal William Gould's] signal truck approached it was evident that my driver intended to do the same. It was too much for me to contemplate and I rasped out "Stop". The driver obeyed but said in some bewilderment: "Why? It's only a dead Jerry; he is past feeling." I stepped down in the roadway and dragged the mangled body into the ditch. I thought of his mother or his wife . . . I felt easier in my conscience for this small mark of respect for a fallen enemy. We became so brutalized in the heat of battle.'

Counter Mortar Fire

The dreaded German Minenwerfers, known as 'moaning minnies' because of their ghastly sobbing noise after they had been fired, were the most lethal hazard. It was difficult to pinpoint them as they could be moved quite quickly to another firing site. Lieutenant Colonel Hart Dyke, CO of the Hallamshires of 49th Division, noted:

> The 49th Division produced a wonderful counter-mortar and counter-battery organization which swiftly dealt with any enemy fire. Compass bearings, called shell-reps and mortar-reps, were sent in by each company *as soon as* an enemy gun or mortar fired on us, or on the Bn on our left [at Tessel Wood]. Our artillery officers, Harold Sykes or Mickie Carter, whichever was in the line with me, then did the necessary wherever we could get a trisection. By the time we left that area we had definitely obtained fire superiority over the enemy.

Morale

'Many men and some officers began [July/August] to suffer from battle neurosis as time went on and the toll of casualties mounted. To differentiate between those really ill and those feigning illness through cowardice was a difficult task, the solution of which seriously affected the morale of the Bn [Lieutenant Colonel Hart Dyke's Hallamshires]. Padre Thomas was loved by all for his quiet Christian courage and his bravery under fire which later earned him the Military Cross. Doc Gregory-Dean had distinguished himself at Fontenay and when he was wounded, Doc Griffiths his replacement (who earned an MC with the 6th Dukes at Bois de Boislande) – in their capable hands those able to carry on were returned to their companies, while those who were mentally unable to do so were evacuated through medical channels.'

The Real Battlefield

Lieutenant Geoffrey Picot's excellent book, *Accidental Warrior*, depicts his battle experience as a Platoon Commander in the 1st Hampshire Regiment. These are his views on the 'Fog of War', morale and reinforcements.

You may have difficulty in imagining a *real* battlefield. You and a couple of pals can be hundreds of yards away from anybody else. You may not have much idea where friend or foe are. You fire from a concealed position to a hidden target. And how on earth do you find out what is going on? . . . The battle is now beginning to die away, as battles do. There is no referee to blow a whistle when time is up. The firing just gets less and less until all is quiet. It is easy to make yourself scarce in battle. All you do is find somewhere to hide, stay there till the shooting has stopped, then look for your unit and say you had lost your way. Such soldiers should be court martialled for desertion.

I recall the advice a senior officer had given me. 'If at nightfall the situation is chaotic and desperate, just sit tight and wait for daybreak and you will find everything will be all right.' Here was one lesson of war. The enemy is not always in good shape. When you are unhappy and fearing an attack, so perhaps is he.

If a Bn suffers light casualties, it is easy to absorb their replacements. Morale, cohesion and team spirit can be maintained. But when there are heavy casualties [at the second battle of Hottot, the Hampshires suffered forty-three killed in action] particularly among the senior officers, it is much more difficult to maintain these qualities. The private soldiers naturally do not respond so well to the command by strangers. By now, of ten key men in our fighting outfit, battalion and rifle company commanders and their seconds in command, I think only one was still with us. It is surprising that the Bn continued to fight so well, although I doubt whether it ever again performed so superbly as it had on D-Day.

Home from Home

Major Bob Moberley, 2nd Battalion Middlesex Regiment, 3rd British Division describes the creation of one of his Normandy 'homes'!

Life in the bridgehead soon developed its own pattern. The old slogan says that a soldier's best friend is his rifle. A far better friend is his shovel. The soldier soon learns in action to dig *at once wherever he is* and to dig deep. Then if he stays in one place for a long time, he improves his hole. It probably becomes L-shaped. The short arm of the 'L' is the proper slit-trench and weapon pit [Middlesex MMG and 4.2 in mortars], sited tactically. The long arm of the 'L' is the 'abri' or dug-out where a man can sleep lying full length. He roofs it over with planks or an old door, thickly covered with earth or with earth-filled shell-boxes. This may save a man's life in an orchard or wood because shells are liable to burst in the trees above, and send shrapnel down into an open hole. This added protection is safe except against a direct hit. The hole is furnished with straw on the floor, and cupboards made of ammo boxes in the walls. Also a system of drainage, so rain cannot come in at the 'door'. Once a man has dug his hole, the next thing he learns is how to get into it *very* quickly indeed whenever necessary, and how to judge when a shell or mortar bomb is coming *his* way! There is a distant 'burrum' of guns or the long groan of a 'moaning Minnie' bringing forth her young. Every ear is cocked. Every man is in his hole in a split second, in a record-breaking jump, spring or dive.

Caen – 'The Stricken City'

Harry Jones was a Platoon Commander with 2 KSLI, 3rd British Division and in his 'Personal Account' recalls:

From 26 June to 6 July we held the front at Bieville, and when out of the line, at Beuville. During the RAF bombing of Caen, Colonel Maurice, the CO was killed. As we were preparing to move to Square Wood there was the sound of heavy bombers approaching from the Channel. Looking up in the sky I was amazed to see wave after wave of bombers flying fairly low heading in the direction of Caen. Later there was the thunderous roar of tons of bombs falling on the city. The noise was indescribable. Suddenly the sky was overcast and a vast white cloud was blown from the city toward our position. This dense cloud, made up of rubble, debris and other unmentionable objects from the stricken city suddenly enveloped us. We were unable to see more than about five yards. [Later in Square Wood.] The remainder of the night was spent in probing the enemy positions with the occasional crossfire breaking the silence, and from the enemy a barrage of hand grenades. At one point I took the Bren MG and fired bursts into their positions, shouting words of abuse *in German*, challenging them to 'come out and fight'. Thankfully the challenge was not accepted! At dawn a German soldier, hands raised in the air in surrender, walked to our scrapes in the ground and threw a hand grenade at my sergeant. Fortunately it missed and exploded harmlessly. I told one

King's Own Scottish Borderers in Caen. (Imperial War Museum, London)

of my toughest soldiers to fix his bayonet and force the German to advance with us to Lebisey Wood. [The following day Harry's platoon went through Lebisey.] The scene was one of utter devastation. The ground was cratered with innumerable shell holes and the trees looked like the scarred and shattered woods of WWI. There were mangled bodies lying around. On our right the dreaded water tower still intact, but battle-scarred. [The KSLI advanced to Point 64. Caen was just a mile away.] I was urging 10 Platoon forward. I felt a dull thud in my left arm just below the elbow. I looked down and saw blood oozing through my battledress tunic.

Harry crawled under a knocked-out tank, made his way back to the RAP, then to Field Hospital, then DUKW to a hospital ship. 'My battle for Normandy was over.'

Second Army Bombardment of Caen

Major Raymond Birt, Signals Officer 22nd Dragoons:

It was an astonishing ten minutes. From the edges of the sky to the hedges nearby, the world was rocking and shaking with noise and the flash of guns. Our RHQ armoured cars were shaken by the hot blast of roadside batteries. Soon a thick fog of smoke settled down across the fields in the still morning air, and the crack of the guns merged into a steady beat of exhausting power and authority. What was it like to be on the receiving end of such a weight of fire? The German soldier dug into the slit trenches in the art of whose preparation he was necessarily most skilled, could only await the end of the murderous rain of steel that beat against him, knowing that when it was over he would not only have to face a seemingly inexhaustible supply of tanks, and attack by determined infantry, but that the sky too, would be filled by aircraft screaming down upon him with salvoes of rockets and a deadly sweep of machine-gun fire. But he still fought with skill, with courage and with obedience.

The Charnel House of Charnwood

Diary entry for 8 July 1944, Operation Charnwood, when Caen north of the Orne was taken, by Jim Wisewell of 223 Field Ambulance.

At 4 a.m. the barrage began . . . it seemed that every gun in the neighbourhood was hurling shells at Lebisey. . . . Then the infantry went in.

At 5 a.m. the first wounded came back, cheerful, optimistic. We splinted fractures, covered wounds with sterile dressings and relieved each other for breakfast at 6.30 a.m.

As the day wore on, sunny and scorching hot, the tide of casualties rose. Dozens and dozens were carried in. Our treatment centre always had 3 upon the trestles being attended to and soon the approaches were lined with a queue. Hour after hour we worked and evacuated, and still the flow continued. Ghastly wounds there were, of every type and state of severity. Heads with skulls so badly smashed the bone and brain and pillow were almost indivisible; faces with horrible lacerations; jaws blown completely away leaving only two sad eyes to plead for relief from pain. Chests pierced through with shrapnel and lungs that spouted blood from gushing holes. Arms were mangled into shapeless masses left hanging by muscle alone and waiting the amputation knife. There were abdomens perforated by shell splinters and displaying coils of intestine, deadly wounds. Buttocks were torn and in some cases spinal injury had followed bringing paralysis.

But the leg wounds! Thigh-bones splintered; knees without kneecaps; legs without feet; red, mangled flesh and blood flooding the stretcher.

And others trembling uncontrollably, sobbing like children, strapped to the stretcher and struggling to be free; screaming and, when a shell landed near the ADS, shouting, 'They're coming again! O God, they're coming again.' Not heroes, but sufferers nonetheless.

We ate our lunch of biscuit and corned beef with bloody fingers and when relieved by 9th Field Ambulance at 6 p.m. we had treated 466 British soldiers and 40 Germans.

The Signaller's Role in Battle

'It is vital in an Infantry Battalion, that the CO shall at all times be kept in contact with his four rifle and HQ Companies. A platoon of about 40 men are trusted to provide that information: an officer (Lieutenant or Captain), two Sergeants, two Corporals [of which William Gould, 1st Worcesters, was one], three Lance Corporals with about 30 trained signallers. All are fully trained in reading Morse code, wireless communication, line-laying and line communication. If well trained, they can read maps. Two men are allotted to each formation in the Bn. The four companies of riflemen, the Carrier platoon, the Motor platoon and any attached such as heavy machine-gunners. A Corporal is in charge of line-laying with a squad of men to operate with him. The two signallers with the Coy COs had a No. 18 wireless set netted by Bn HQ with a range up to four miles. The line-laying squad carried with them two field telephones and up to two miles of cable on drums which held 600 yards each. One or other means of communication was usually put out of action, necessitating the use of the other. Wireless sets drifted off net, and cable laid on the ground was often cut by enemy missiles (or friendly tanks). When both methods failed, a man had to take his message verbally. The signaller was often at a disadvantage, always on the move backwards or forwards, thus constantly exposed, often escaping shellfire by flinging himself into ditches.'

Operation Jupiter – the Plan of Attack

The enemy still held the high ground immediately east of the river Orne. From the slopes of Hill 112 and the ridge of Maltot his FOOs, mortar and artillery retained perfect observation to the west and south. Major General 'Butch' Thomas, GOC of 43rd Wessex Wyverns, was given a small army to secure, during Operation Jupiter, the high ground between the rivers Odon and Orne, and between Hill 112 and Maltot, and exploit eastwards to Feugerolles. Under his command were 31st Tank Brigade and 4th Armoured Brigade, plus 46th Brigade of the 15th Scottish Division. In addition, two AGRAs (Army Group Royal Artillery) and the divisional artillery of the 11th Armoured and 15th Scottish divisions were to support the attack. Initially, 130th Brigade on the left and 129th Brigade on the right were to capture Hill 112 and the road leading to Chateau de Fontaine. The village at Eterville, then Maltot and the high ground to the south-west would be captured and 4th Armoured Brigade with 214th Brigade would pass through as far as the river Orne. To 46th (Scottish) Brigade was given the task of left flank protection by occupying Verson and then Eterville when captured. The artillery plan involved a 3,500 yds barrage – a gun to every 35 yds plus 4.2 in and 3 in mortar support and Typhoons to take out AFVs on the roads.

4th Dorsets at Eterville – 'Shells like Hailstones'

The 5th Dorsets were to open their brigade attack to capture the village of Fontaine Etoupfour, the 4th Dorsets to attack and capture Eterville, and in the third phase the 7th Hampshires would take Maltot. Sergeant Wally Caines described the attack on Eterville:

> One could hardly hear oneself speak for the continuous and thunderous roar of the barrage. Typhoon and fighter bombers strafed with rockets and bombs on a small wood in front, raking and killing the enemy. Little opposition was encountered, but several casualties by enemy artillery and 'moaning Minnies' as they were called. German POWs rolled in within a few minutes of the attack opening. They looked exhausted and terrified. One German crawled out of his fox-hole seen walking to his captors with his hands up was shot dead through the back by one of his own comrades. Just before HQ 4 Dorsets reached the village, a hell of a barrage came down upon us: several were wounded. We were split up having to take cover. We then became somewhat disordered. After some terrible minutes dodging shells and mortars, the odd few of us decided to remain until the barrage eased up and then move on. Shells were still raining down like hailstones. The battalion's casualties were pouring into the village church beside many scores of Germans lying around wounded. Everyone was

82nd Assault Squadron RE support Devons and Hampshires at Hottot, 10 July 1944. (Birkin Haward)

told to dig in for their dear lives' sakes. The Bn had by now received a large number of casualties and the MO and his stretcher bearers were working like niggers to dress the wounded and get them evacuated to the Advanced Dressing Station. Our very brave and gallant padre volunteered to find a German MO to attend to their wounded. An hour later to our astonishment he returned with an enemy MO. Both worked alongside dressing the wounded. I dug for two hours or more nonstop, smoking endless cigarettes, taking swigs of my water bottle.

'A Cat and Mouse Game'

On 10 July the 7th Battalion Hampshires were ordered to take the village of Maltot. Nineteen-year-old Private D. Davies, 'B' Company, was wounded during the attack and captured. His report afterwards read:

We were told the village was only lightly defended [not true], there was no artillery barrage and we only had two tanks on the start line. It was a bright, sunny morning. The Bn advanced with two companies up and two behind across large, open country, rolling plain covered with wheat about hip-high. 'B' Coy was deployed with two platoons up in line, with the other platoon behind. Coy HQ was behind us [No. 15 Platoon]. The two Churchill tanks running at either side of the two forward companies were beating flocks of small birds into the air. Caen, visible in a thick pall of smoke, was a few miles to the left [north-east] of us. One tank was hit by an 88 mm shell almost immediately. The other tank took out the '88' with two well-placed shots. Then we walked into a very heavy barrage of 'moaning Minnies'. 'B' Coy were badly hit. No. 15 Platoon was down to seven men. Lieutenant Friend was wounded but Major J.J. Tomkins, our CO, came up to steady us. As we continued the advance we came under MG and rifle fire from well placed and camouflaged slit trenches. The Germans would keep hammering at us until we got close then would scamper back on hands and knees through the wheat. We caught a number of them and disposed of a few by lobbing grenades down the trenches. We were maddened by the slaughter caused by the 'moaning Minnies' and were for a brief moment out of control. We were now over the ridge to the north of the village. We could see the grey stone houses on either side of the road, about a mile away with a church prominent to our right. We came under more heavy machine gun and rifle fire as we moved down the slope and suffered more casualties. Our tank was peppering the defensive positions and took out another '88' dug in among the bushes. We chased the remaining enemy troops out of the gardens, killing a few on the way. The village looked deserted and the houses deserted. A German Mk IV tank then blasted us with MG fire and explosive shells. [Later that day.] We played a cat and mouse game with the Germans, each side taking pot shots at anything that moved. Some time in the afternoon I was hit by shrapnel from two hand grenades, knocked out for a while. In the evening the Germans rushed us and took 5 prisoners, three of us wounded.

Davies was wounded again, taken to Fallingbostel Camp and survived.

'Hell's Bells! My Tank was Being Fired At'

Sergeant Greenwood's 9th RTR Churchill tanks were in support. From Verson they helped the 4th Dorsets launch an attack on Eterville on 10 July:

Very soon we opened up with HE on the village. There were as yet no signs of any 88s. The infantry kept steadily on walking warily through the deep corn, but always going forward . . . forward. Our BESA fire passed over them, but it must have been uncomfortably close. Grand fellows those infantry lads, so brave and calm. I felt terribly grateful towards them when I saw them amongst the trees. They would report any hidden A/Tk guns and tanks. My vehicle was behaving well and putting down smoke fire. Crew worked splendidly. Damned hard work too. And how we smoked cigarettes! Mortars were still troublesome, as good as any air force to Jerry! [Later that day, Eterville having been taken, 'A' Squadron passed through 'C' and 'B' to carry out an attack south of Maltot.] Things weren't going so well. 'A' had been hammered pretty badly. Once again that terrible fear. Well, we went in via scenes of recent action . . . dreadful scenes. We plastered the woods around Maltot with MG and plenty of HE. [Sergeant Greenwood's gunner knocked down a church steeple.] Got two lovely hits with HE: the steeple toppled. It *might* have harboured an enemy observer. And then I noticed one of *our* tanks on fire. What on earth was happening? It seemed like a counter-attack in force judging by Major Holden's appeal. Suddenly I heard heavy gunfire and the swish of shells. Hell's Bells! *My* tank was being fired at. Two misses! Darned if I could see any gun flashes or tanks. I peered frantically through the periscope. The major's voice . . . he wanted help . . . smoke. He got smoke . . . all of us poured it out as fast as we could. In a matter of seconds, our former peaceful hill crest was pretty well littered with burning vehicles. Very soon infantry appeared running towards us and away from Maltot. Were we withdrawing?

'C' Squadron lost two Churchills, and three or four damaged. Casualties included Lieutenant Drew, Lieutenant Chapman and Corporal Crewe. Sergeant Purdy's vehicle was burned out: he and his crew were missing. 'A' Squadron had only three tanks left, several casualties and seventeen missing.

Disaster at Maltot – 'It was Hell'

The 7th Battalion Hampshires tried to capture the small village of Maltot near Hill 112.

The CO informed us [Sergeant Wally Caines, HQ Signaller, 4th Dorsets] that 7 Hampshires had met overwhelming opposition in Maltot and were in fact almost surrounded, 1½ miles to our front. The majority of our Bn formed up in an open green field with two Coys up and two in reserve. We entered the village supported by tanks protecting the flanks and met with terrific opposition from a Panzer Division. Our tanks were knocked out from all directions. German Tiger tanks were cleverly concealed in orchards and German MGs fired from all angles. Neither us nor the Hampshires stood an earthly chance of securing the village. It was I'm afraid a great disaster. Most of our tracked vehicles were knocked out by enemy 88 SP guns. Our A/tank gunners did not even have the time to place their guns in position. We were up against terrific odds. Comrades were laying around everywhere, many killed, many badly wounded. TAC HQ were crossing a cornfield on the outskirts of Maltot. Jerry allowed us to come up close, thus cutting us off. Suddenly the whole party were cut down by a burst of fire from a Spandau. It was hell. No one dared put his head above the corn. Self-propelled guns fired practically unceasingly. At 1900 hrs orders came to withdraw. Some men were without rifles or ammo, many lost their complete equipment. But by dark almost everyone was dug in, in possession of some sort of fighting irons. The main signals equipment had been destroyed by shellfire, all stores blown up, no communication facilities in the Bn. Most wireless sets had been knocked out or left behind in Maltot. All of us were cold as stones, extremely worn out, dog tired. It had been a terrible 24 hours. Something I will never forget as long as I live, seeing men fall, hearing the wounded cry and moan with pain as they were wounded. I could never express in my own words the horror experienced on this day.

Forty-eight Dorsets were killed that day, and several hundred wounded or captured on 10 July.

Edgar Allan Poe's Hell

Chateau Fontaine. 'We dug in around Battalion HQ who were in a building called Chateau Fontaine. . . . What we faced from the Germans on Hill 112 was the heavy shelling by every calibre of gun reminiscent of the 1914–18 War and barrages,' wrote Private D. O'Connell, carrier section with the 7th Battalion Somerset Light Infantry. 'Every blade of grass seemed to be targeted by German shells and bullets, attacks by their infantry came by day and night. The noise was ear-splitting and those that did not seek a slit trench were either dead or wounded . . . our lot was fraught with fear, danger and death every time we moved from our slit trench. Edgar Allan Poe could not have described the hell on those slopes . . . our officers were dwindling through death and wounding. We only had one or two officers left in the company. Our own Officer had been killed and it was left to our

Sergeant to look after us. The toll of dead from the German shelling and attack had risen considerably . . . our graveyard increased.'

'Smelling and Fighting Mad'

Sergeant Reg Romain was with the 6-pdr Anti-Tank Platoon of the 5th Battalion Wiltshires. These are excerpts from his Normandy journal.

From Brecy we travelled through St Manvieu Norrey then left the road to sweep across country to La Gaule. My first sickening sight of death in the fighting was to see two of the Royal Scots infantrymen straddling the barbed wire as we entered the village. We were digging in on our objective when a flurry of mortar bombs came down amongst us. I dived into what I thought was a disused German slit trench – it was a latrine hole. I came out quicker than I went in – smelling and fighting mad. [The Wiltshires attacked across the main road near Tourville, heading for Hill 112.] I lost two close friends here, Harry Tranter and Harry Weaver.

After crossing the dried-up river Odon, Reg's platoon hauled their anti-tank guns up the slope under 'moaning Minnie' bombs and into Baron along the road near Calvary. Soon other best pals were killed – Ronnie Law and Reg's driver Reg Carter. 'We had now been going for over a week without any sleep or proper meals.' Supporting an attack by 5 DCLI to secure Hill 112, Reg wrote, 'Again under shell and mortar on our start line, I spotted a hole in the ground and dived for cover, only to find a dead Jerry lying in the bottom again. The smell was awful. Zero hour came at the scheduled time and our rifle companies moved off. I shall never forget the moment I watched our men go forward into the hell of tank fire, mortar, machine gun, shells, you name it, Jerry was slinging it.'

Horror on Hill 112

Corporal Doug Proctor, in Lieutenant Sydney Jary's 18 Platoon, 4th Battalion SLI, witnessed an appalling event after Jupiter.

During a company night attack on Hill 112, one of our soldiers had been hit in the lower chest by a rifle or MG bullet. Passing through his body, it had not killed him outright. The bullet's devilish course lay through the soldier's webbing equipment pouch which contained a 77 phosphorous smoke grenade. Caught on barbed wire, the poor soldier lay disembowelled, for all around to see, his writhing body a smoking mass of burning phosphorous. Responding to his agonized screams to put him out of his misery, his platoon commander shot him through the heart and finally through the head, after the poor man's final frenzied plea, 'Not there, sir, through the head.'

The Diehards During Operation Jupiter – 'Foxes in a Trap'

The 4.2 in mortars of the 8th Battalion Middlesex Regiment were in constant action in the terrible battle to try to recapture Hill 112, as Eric Codling's diary notes.

> For most of the six days of battle it was impossible to get out of the mortar pits, such was the punishment received. One of the most bitter slogging matches of WWII. We ate, slept and even natural functions had to be carried out in that confined space below ground. The small waterproof bags that covered the mortar bombs' tail units were in plentiful supply! Risk of Tannoy breaking down, relaying orders to mortar-crews. On the night 15/16th July to our surprise a member of another crew leapt into our pit during the heavy pounding on us, very distressed, babbling incoherently. His pit had received a direct hit, wrecking it, and throwing the crew out of the hole. Amazingly no one was injured. In panic he had rushed to the nearest slit trench occupied by Sergeant McLeod. Having recovered his wits, he asked the sergeant to move up – no reply. By the light of shell flashes, he saw the sergeant's head was missing. The bottoms of his trousers and web anklets were soaked in the blood of the dead sergeant.
>
> A German propaganda leaflet was seen. These told us we were caught like foxes in a trap, better to give ourselves up! Wounded horses and cows had to be shot to put them out of their misery. The putrifying carcasses inflated like enormous balloons, breeding ground for flies. The stench was indescribable. Large horseflies took their toll in the heat as we dug trenches without shirts on. A severe bout of shelling faced us with the choice of tin of cold pork and veg – or nothing. I went hungry!

Life in the Open

Major B.E.L. Burton of the Queen's described the period 1–18 July with the Desert Rats:

> We always lived in the open. Houses and barns were used as recreation rooms but all troops slept out. For the most part we leaguered in fields and orchards, tucking ourselves away in any available cover. Slit trenches were dug. When the weather was fine and warm it was lovely and very healthy. In wet weather bivouacs had to be improvised out of ground sheets and gas capes but it was not really possible to keep the bedding dry. Food in the early stages consisted of compo packs containing rations for 14 men for a day. Everything was tinned and ready cooked, only requiring heating – contents varied but one got very tired of 'compo' after a time.

When the 'build up' allowed, field service rations including fresh meat, bread and tea were issued instead. There is no doubt that the rations were very good. The cigarette issue averaged fifteen a day. Mail from home came regularly and quickly. The homeward mail at first was slow. Companies went regularly by turns to Bayeux for baths and cinemas. But also we had training infantry with tanks – a careful slow system of cooperation in bocage country.

The Battlefield Teddy

'The slit trench was surrounded by churned-up earth in what remained of the garden of a small French cottage near Eterville not far from Hill 112. The trench was unoccupied, but traces of its previous occupants lay all around. A gas cape, wet with the morning dew. Clips of .303 cartridges were on the parapet and an entrenching tool lay embedded in the ridge of spoil that made the paradox. In the bottom of the trench lay a cluster of "36" grenades, a large pool of blood and an unravelled field dressing. None of these surprised me. [Lieutenant Sydney Jary, 4th Battalion Somerset Light Infantry.] My eyes rose, my throat tightened and tears came. Sitting on a tiny ledge cut into the side of the trench was a small light brown teddy bear. He wore a red and white ribbon collar with a bell attached. I was just twenty years old and this was my introduction to battle. My reaction to Teddy's dilemma did not augur well for the future.'

Night Work – 'A Travelling Bomb'

Many infantry units were worried when their friendly Tanky friends disappeared at dusk and left them to their fate. Trooper 'Jack' Thorpe was the co-driver/hull gunner in a Sherman tank, 2nd Fife and Forfar Yeomanry in 11th Armoured Division. He had one tank destroyed during Operation Epsom and another during Operation Goodwood, when he was badly wounded.

Each day commenced with a night guard (stag), if we were not driving through the night on an approach march to a new Start-line in time for H-Hour. Night guard was shared by all the crew [Sergeant Clifford Jones, Lance Corporal Pat O'Brien, Trooper Bert Long, driver Trooper Dennis Robinson and Thorpe], each man being sentry to his own tank when in night leaguer for an hour or more at a time, whilst the rest of the crew relaxed either in a blanket, on the ground in a slit trench, or underneath the tank, or curled up inside on the turret floor, or sitting in his seat drooped over the gun or draped over the driving sticks, but there was no relaxing until the tank had been serviced. Each Squadron formed lines, one tank behind the other and each Squadron alongside each other, with space between every vehicle to allow them to manoeuvre. The outside

Squadron's tanks were placed so that their guns could swing outwards in case of a surprise attack. All round the perimeter of the square, our infantry were dug in to help defend the armour, very vulnerable at night. 'A' Echelon would drive up to the line of tanks and deliver petrol in four gallon jerry-cans and ammo needed. 75 mm rounds of HE, AP and Smoke. Each round was packed in individual cardboard cases which had to be unpacked and *carefully* passed up by hand into the turret where the gunner placed them into the turret racks.

Belts of .300 MG ammo were delivered in tin boxes containing 250 rounds of mixed shots in sequence, such as AP, tracer and ball. The Quartermaster (SQMS Blackie) came along every three days to give each tank a box of American Compo Pack rations. This provided 14 men's rations for one day, or five men for three days (just). The real luxury was the cigarette rations of full-size Woodbines in two round tins each containing 49, also tuppenny bars of Duncan's chocolate and a daily ration of three boiled sweets each. We would nibble all day the packets of hardtack biscuits to allay our hunger. The SQMS brought up our mail which was handed to each tank commander. The petrol tanks were down both sides of the tank alongside the engines and together held 80 gallons and with 60 rounds of howitzer ammo, plus boxes of MG belts, we were riding on a travelling bomb. The driver and co-driver checked and maintained the engines and batteries (used for engine electrics and wireless equipment), the greasing of wheel bearings and suspension, the cleaning and condition of the tracks which picked up all sorts of debris/fencing or barbed wire wrapped round the sprockets and suspension. The gunner cleaned and oiled his 75 mm gun and MG, checking and setting up his gun sights, maintaining all the hydraulic traversing gears and turret ring, removing all spent cartridges, servicing all weapons, including our Bren used for the defence, Thompson sub-machine guns, Sten gun, signal flare pistol, smoke mortar and Mills grenades. The wireless operator who was also the gunloader, looked after the wireless set, maintained the aerial, headsets, microphones, sockets and intercom in good order. Sleep was precious. We needed it more than food. Our tasks continued all through the day, even when we were in action.

Operation Goodwood – 'A Real Showdown'

'The Second Army is now very strong. It has in fact reached its peak and can get no stronger. It will in fact get weaker as the manpower situation begins to hit us. Also the casualties have affected the fighting efficiency of divisions. The original men were very well trained. Reinforcements are not so well trained. So I have decided to have a real "showdown" on the eastern flank and to loose a corps of three armoured divisions into the open country about the Caen–Falaise road,' Montgomery wrote to Alan Brooke on 14 July. Rommel had foreseen this attack after the fall of Caen on 8 July.

General Eberbach of Panzer Group West had fortified over forty strongpoints of villages and farms in five defensive lines crammed with tanks, anti-tank guns and infantry. Moreover, from the heights of Bourguébus, the German FOOs could scan the whole battlefield. On the morning of 18 July the greatest air bombardment of ground forces took place as the RAF and USAAF pounded some, but certainly not all, of the fortified strongpoints. Major General 'Pip' Roberts, GOC 11th Armoured Division, had been forbidden to use the combined infantry/armour tactics for which his troops had trained for years. In Africa fashion, the infantry brigade attacked on the right, armoured brigade on the left. It was very nearly a disaster. A few miles of Norman soil gained at a terrible cost.

Goodwood – Gigantic Support

The Adjutant of 33rd Field Regiment RA, Captain J.A. Brymer, described the immense support for Goodwood:

The main fire support was to come from the RAF plus the divisional Artilleries of 2 and 3 Canadian Divisions, 3 British and 51 Highland Divisions, 7, 11 and Guards Armoured Divisions, 4, 8 and part of 9 and 2 Canadian AGRAs with 107 and 165 HAA regiments totalling three regiments RHA [3rd, 5th and the author's 13th], sixteen Field, fourteen Mediums, three Heavy and two HAA Regiments. In addition HM Navy supported with 21 guns. Goodwood opened with concentrated RAF bombing [8,000 bombs] on a gigantic scale during which the regiment fired on 'Applepie' followed by Counter Battery and concentrations in support of 8 Brigade. Throughout the morning [18 July] the fire was almost continuous and was by far the most extensive programme that the regiment had been called upon to perform. During the whole day the regiment [twenty-four Sexton 25-pdrs] fired 9,600 rounds, 400 rounds per gun. Mention must be made of the superb ammunition supply by the RASC.

Unfortunately the Germans were now expert at reading the Allied intentions. Their forward positions were thinly held and often regarded as expendable. When the immense bombardment slackened or ceased, Tiger and Panther tanks and Panzer Grenadiers would be rushed forward to occupy the various strongpoints. It was a pleasant, sunny morning and the division, to a man, saw, heard and wondered at the air armada saturating the German front ahead. It seemed as though nobody could survive that terrible onslaught. But they did.

The Sherman Tank Crew

'Dent, the operator, was a good looking, dark kid with a nice smile. Litchfield, a funny looking cove with a receding chin was the driver, a tireless worker, and a good driver. Gordon was the co-driver and finally Charlie Sanson, the gunner, a big country fellow with nice brown eyes, untidy hair and an enormous pair of shoulders and hands. That was my [Lieutenant Geoffrey Bishop, 23rd Hussars] crew. I went round the other tanks, commanded by two sergeants, Dixon and Smith, a ruddy-faced Yorkshireman. Then a conference with Bill Shebbeare, 'C' Sqn leader to meet the other officers, Peter, Bunny, Jock, Mike, Pratt and Peter Robson.'

Operation Goodwood – 'Crestfallen Bunch of Yeomen'

W.R. Moseley was Gunner/Wireless Operator of Sergeant Doug Bellamy's Cromwell tank, 3 Troop 'B' Squadron, 2nd Northants Yeomanry, 11th Armoured Division Armoured Recce Regiment. Lance Corporal 'Dick' Dixon, a Cornishman from Helston, was Wireless Operator/Loader, Lance Corporal Albert Cunningham was the driver, and Trooper Ken Wrathall was the co-driver.

> We harboured north of Ranville amongst the 'D' Day gliders and then crossed the river Orne over Pegasus bridge during darkness and headed south, but east of Caen, towards Bras and Hubert Folie. It was a beautiful summer day. We advanced through cornfields as far as the eye could see with little resistance. Things became tougher. We came on a field thick with blazing and brewed up tanks, the remains of the Polish Armoured Brigade. Towards late afternoon we encountered strong

Tanks of the 11th Armoured Division advancing across the Caen plain during Operation Goodwood, July 1944. (Imperial War Museum, London)

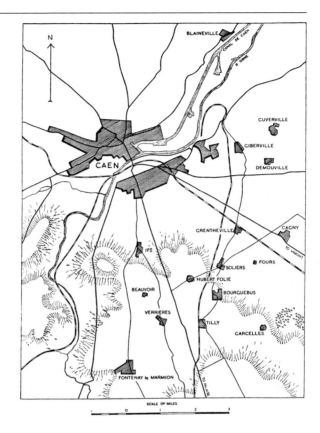

Operation Goodwood

resistance from hull down German tanks and 88s in a wood. [Moseley's tank was hit in the rear by an 88.] The tank shuddered violently and stopped amid a shower of sparks. Dougie shouted 'Bail out'. [Moseley got caught up in his Sten gun which had jammed as the turret traversed.] We made a dash for another 'B' Squadron tank where Corporal Trevor Cox, the driver was lying alongside badly wounded in the leg. We then made a second dash to another tank [Sergeant Tite's] and climbed aboard the outside. [Moseley scrounged another Sten gun from Jack Austin.] I felt less naked perched on the front glacis plate. The turret was traversed to the rear and both guns were blazing away to good effect. We moved off towards a railway embankment some distance to our rear. Then an AP shell ploughed through the armourplate and shattered the idler wheels, but missed the co-driver's and my feet by inches. Another thud quickly followed. The tank slewed to a stop. A cry of 'bail out' sent us all running for the embankment. Major Stancombe ordered us all back to a crossroads to wait for 'B' Echelon to pick us up. There we sat, a sorry, weary and crestfallen bunch of Yeomen amid the lurid flames from burning tanks and that revolting smell of burning bodies – under mortar 'stonks'.

Goodwood – So Ended a Disastrous Day

'We started to move slowly forward in the direction of Fours. Within a few seconds Peter Robson's tank was hit by an .88 and went up in smoke. All the crew baled out safely. Jock Addison reported a Panther in the village, which he was trying to engage. This was the last coherent message from the rest of the Squadron [to Lieutenant Geoffrey Bishop, 23rd Hussars]. They were all brought under heavy and accurate fire. Within a matter of minutes about five tanks were on fire and another three out of action. The MO had a temporary Dressing Station in a little white signal box on the railway line. Casualties started streaming back from the burnt-out tanks. The chaps were all blackened, their clothes burnt and most had lost their berets. A tank which had survived came roaring back with a lot of wounded lying on the back of it. [Geoffrey was the only surviving officer. His CO told him that the line of the railway would be held to the last man and the last round.] All very dramatic. Everything was now in a state of chaos. The Squadron on the right was also being heavily engaged by the enemy and losing tanks rapidly. It seemed only a matter of time before the rest of the regiment were written off. Things remained tense and uncertain for the next couple of hours. As the light began to fail, two German tanks were seen advancing on our right flank. [The tanks were hit by the Hussars.] This seemed to deter the Hun. The sky was lit by the flames from our own blazing tanks and the whole battlefield seemed to be littered with burnt-out Shermans. It was a sorry sight. So ended a disastrous day, heralded as the greatest tank battle of the war. Nothing could have been a greater failure. Everyone had seen the last of some of his best friends.'

'A Jab of Morphia, Swig of Scotch'

During Goodwood the Desert Rats were the reserve armoured division, following behind 11th Armoured Division. Major Bill Apsey MC, 1st RB, was:

> Shocked to see so many brewed up tanks of the Fife and Forfar Yeo and Northants Yeo. . . . Our casualties were mounting from shell and mortar fire but we couldn't get them back so carried them with us. 'I' Company took over Grentheville from 8 RB (11th Armoured Div) and were shelled incessantly. We moved forward in the morning to clear the line Soliers to Bourguébus with supporting tanks and artillery. Two platoons moved into Soliers and started to clear it. All went well so I left the gunner and tank OPs who were with me to catch up with the leading platoons. I remember walking towards the crossroads and suddenly found myself sitting in the road. My leg

looked a mess but no pain. Almost immediately I was on my back with my left arm useless. Damned mortars – you could never hear them coming. Somehow I crawled to the side of the road and was then conscious of a blow in the back. Third time lucky? Fourth time? Suddenly silence and my batman, Rifleman Jackson and others rushed over and put me in the back of a tank. A jab of morphia, swig of Scotch and I was on my way to the RAP.

Bill Apsey was badly wounded and invalided out of the army. 'In the ambulance were two tank boys horrendously burnt, both died on the way back. My fighting war was over after three years and three times wounded, I had against all the odds survived. I still ask myself, "Why me?"'

The Queen's during Goodwood

Private Robert Boulton wrote during Goodwood:

Our carrier section pulled off the road just opposite the dressing station of the 1/5th Queen's [who had twenty-five casualties during Goodwood], who were doing an attack. A long and continuous stream of casualties were coming in. I remember saying there would be nothing left of the Bn if this went on much longer. Worse still, there was a poor lad who had most of the bottom of his back blown away. There was nothing to be done for him so he was just put outside on the stretcher. The poor devil screamed for about two hours. Morphine seemed to have no effect. He was pleading for someone to finish him off. Our sergeant had been in the war from the start and even he was white and shaken.

Slow Obvious Steps

1/7th Queen's, who sustained twenty casualties, including two officers, reached Bourguébus by the evening and 1/6th Queen's stayed in Grentheville, Soliers and Fours. Peter Roach described the Queen's during Goodwood:

Marching solidly through the village went our infantry company – slow obvious steps, no hurry, no eagerness, no fear. A bevy of shells fell and with them one man, now with one leg. His comrade behind stopped and bent over him and then straightening up, undid his gas cape from off his pack and spread it over the peaceful figure. Quietly and with barely any disturbance to their movement, they had passed through the village.

'Troarn – Symbol of our Deepest Tribulation'

The 3rd British Division were left flank guard during Goodwood. 1 KOSB was on the right and 2 RUR on the left with the tanks of the East Riding

Yeomanry in support, as 9th Brigade advanced eastwards at midday from Escoville towards Troarn. Major H.S. Gillies, OC of 'C' Company, wrote:

Cambes had been a grim and desperate experience. Troarn will ever be the symbol of our deepest tribulation. We passed through the ruins of Escoville. In open fields west of Sannerville we were ordered to halt. From our left flank we were observed from the Bois de Bavant and suffered numerous casualties. Thirst and heat were beginning to trouble us. Several men collapsed. On our advance towards Troarn the going was difficult with huge bomb craters. Utter fatigue set in, tortured by thirst, soaking with sweat, borne down by the weight of our equipment, we clambered over great piles of rubble that had once been streets. Although the enemy was considerably disorganized, 'C' Coy leading was held up by MG fire on a sunken road on the outskirts of Troarn.

The CO, Lieutenant Colonel G.D. Renny, was twice wounded but refused to go back. By 1900 hrs 1 KOSB were dug in at La Croix de Pierre.

Our casualties by now extensive. We were cut off from our transport [and tanks] by the craters, running very short of water and food. We dug in as we were to resume the advance in the morning. The night was most unpleasant. Most men too exhausted to dig trenches just lay down in the orchards and tried to forget their hunger and thirst in a few hours of disturbed sleep. Our wounded in a desperate situation, short of medical supplies: no ambulances could get through. Walking wounded had to stay: no hope of negotiating the miles of craters in the darkness. During the night, the enemy shelled and mortared our positions. They brought up fresh reinforcements, sent out patrols which inflicted more casualties on 'A' Coy. 'D' Company HQ was hit several times by shellfire, 'B' Company had several casualties in a booby-trapped farmhouse and 'C' Company came under fire from a railway signal box.

The Underrated Enemy

Jack Harrod, briefly 9th Brigade Intelligence Officer, could see and hear how Goodwood was faring.

We had again made the most popular of mistakes: in a flush of immediate success, we had underrated the enemy, forgotten his discipline and staying power, his fighting qualities and proneness to hit back. Across the plain [south-east of Caen to Bourguébus] the enemy fell back . . . to a strongly prepared line and our armour seeking battle with the German Mark IVs after a Libyan pattern found the way barred by an impenetrable screen of powerful anti-tank guns. . . . He had no intention of giving ground in the wooded country round Troarn where he had been untouched by the bombing and could not be reached by the tanks. Troarn was to be held to the last possible moment.

Tinkers' Carts – 'Char Up Now'

Rifleman Roland Jefferson was a 19 Set Signaller with the 8th Battalion Rifle Brigade. He describes the battle-hardened battalion after Goodwood.

Our carriers and other vehicles took on the appearance of tinkers' carts. We had pots and pans and biscuit tins hanging on or fastened to the vehicles. The best way of making a cup of tea was to put some sandy soil in one biscuit tin and pour in liberal quantities of petrol. Then fill another tin with water, place the one on top of the other and put a lighted match to the petrol. These field stoves didn't take long to boil up sufficient water for a mashing. We would pierce holes in tins of stewed steak, or soya links, or whatever goodies we received in our compo rations and put them into the water to get a hot meal. The more adventurous would *fry* eggs, but boiled eggs and boiled potatoes to go with the nutritious but monotonous rations were almost the order of the day. Any water left over after these cooking operations came in handy for a warm, luxurious shave. I never remember being short of water or petrol [thanks to the efforts of the RASC] as these with packs of rations were brought up to us every night by the Echelon. We carried several jerri-cans of petrol. These were replaced nightly by simply trading empty cases for full ones.

Barbée Farm Burial Party, 21 July

On the 15th the Hallams plus 'D' Company 1/4 KOYLI made a local attack on Vendes and Barbée Farm. It was a failure and the Hallams lost twenty KIA and the KOYLI six. Rex Flower, with the KOYLI Mortar Platoon, described the situation:

The bodies had been in the hot sun for six days. The stench was awful. Indescribable. It was a terrible thing to see them, that had been young men in the prime of their life. There was the inevitable dead cattle and horses, also a number of dead Germans grotesque in their tight fitting helmets. Their heads were swollen larger than their helmets, so that there was a large overlap. It was a charnel house. We started on the right. The first was a Sgt from the Hallams. The enemy had a nasty habit of putting grenades under corpses (even their own). When someone came to bury the body, instead of burying him, they joined him. They were lousy swine. The Padre and the Warrant Officer i/c had brought a rope. The corpses were pulled out gently and buried in shallow graves as the earth was baked solid.

Moulded into Warriors

'Individual reactions to battle varied widely [Lieutenant Geoffrey Picot]. I should make my own clear. At the prospect of fighting I was horrified.

Machine-gun bullets, shells and casualties are terrible companions. I saw that very few had been in battle longer than I had. Most of those who landed on D-Day were soon wounded or killed. How much longer could I defy the law of averages?

'It was then that a subtle military factor rescued my morale. I could see that most men were absorbing the strain reasonably well, so I decided I had better try to look as if I was. Only later did I learn that all were frightened and most took pains to conceal their fear. Nearly all of us played this concealment game. Thus, a man pretending to be brave gave bravery to his comrades; as they, with their pretence, likewise gave bravery to him. But first we all had to be moulded into warriors.'

Operation Express

Operation Express was a highly detailed plan to take Maltot, not from the west as in Epsom and Jupiter but from the north. Now that Caen had fallen and with the territorial gains of Goodwood, the third onslaught on this wretched village stood a better chance. On 22 July, supported by two AGRAs and 7 RTR tanks, two battalions of the 43rd Wyvern Division – 4th and 5th Wiltshires – with 4th Somerset Light Infantry in reserve, set off in dreadful weather. Anthony Jeans describes how the 4th Wiltshires met bitter resistance in the woods by the river Orne and the amazing gallantry of Lieutenant Donald Pope of 'C' Company.

> Donald decided to go in with the bayonet under cover of his Brens and 2 in mortar and shouting to his chaps to follow, he ran forward firing his Sten gun from the hip. He had not gone far across this 50 yards of hell before he was hit again. He fell, but scrambled up and ran on, only to be hit again, this time in the other leg. He decided it was too big a job for him as only two men had followed him, so he started to come back, but was hit a fourth time. This time he went down for the count right in the middle of No Man's Land.

> Donald was hit four times, survived and was awarded the MC. Eventually, at dreadful cost to both infantry and 7 RTR Churchill tanks, the village was taken. The Wiltshires took 400 prisoners and recaptured 600 British rifles lost with their owners in the first battle of Maltot on 10 July.

Tribute – 'Continuously in the Lead'

When Major Mickey Gold returned to take over command of 'B' Squadron of the Sherwood Rangers Yeomanry he found that many of his old friends had become casualties.

> I miss them all and in particular I would like to pay tribute to the memory

of four sergeants, three of whom were killed in action in June, and one who died of wounds received on the beaches. They are Sergeant G. Green, Sergeant L. Biddell, Sergeant W. Crookes, Sergeant W. Digby. They were great friends these four and were largely instrumental in creating within the Squadron an exceptional spirit of friendship and loyalty. They were as proud of their squadron as we are of them. To say they did their duty is an understatement. They were leaders and magnificent examples to us all. As I say, we were all close friends, a friendship proven of daily companionships, danger shared, difficulties overcome. As friends we mourn them. As leaders, their equal does not exist. But their tradition they have left with us. We cannot measure what they did for England. Sufficient to say that throughout the Desert campaign until the fall of Tunis, and from D-Day in Europe until their deaths, they were continuously in the lead.

CROMWELL TANK OF 5.R.T.R. "AJAX" (ABLE 2) LAYING SMOKE IN REPLY TO WIRELESS MESSAGE FROM ME. THIS INCIDENT I DIDN'T SEE BUT IT IS DRAWN FROM MEMORY. WE WERE IN A FIELD WITH HEDGES EVERY 50 YDS. INF. WENT FORWARD CLEAR "BOUND" CALL UP TANKS AND REPEAT TO NEXT BOUND. TANK IS AT "MAPLE" BOUND WE WERE 50ˣ FORWARD AT "PINE" ENEMY WERE IN NEXT BOUND "ELM" THIS TANK DROPPED ONE SMOKE BOMB BESIDE HOPPY WHO WAS ALSO LAYING 2" MORTAR SMOKE. ANOTHER TANK HIT THE TREE WITH ONE ABOVE LT. GREENALL AND ME. WE WERE IN A FLAT SPIN, SWEERING COUGHING AND CHOKING WHEN THE SMOKE CLEARED — SO HAD JERRY TALK ABOUT A PANIC.

TANK OFFICER GUIDES TANKS FORWARD

3 DAYS leave started while we were here, to BAYEUX. We were put on trucks and wheeled back to Bareux on July 14TH FRANCES National Day We went to the "MODERNE Cinema" and sat with rifles and Bren guns across our knees watching ABBOTT AND COSTELLO in "HIT THE ICE." We were then taken back to our particular little corner of hell !!

Sketches by Donald Green, 1/5th Queens Regt, 7th Armoured Division

The German in the Orchard. This village had got in the way of our ARTILLERY creeping barrage. During a bombardment Jerry will pull his troops out then rush them in again on trucks, tanks etc. They did that here — Too bad the 51ST HIGHLAND DIV. (HD) had moved in first, we took over and contd. our advance from here George RICHARDSON and JOHNNY LUDFORD ARE here passing a Jerry who was one who didn't get out.

COVERVILLE JULY. 19ᵗ

N

Air attack on the Bailey
Bridges - Churchill and London-
and concentration of
our armies just south of
the River ORNE.
Many fires were started
among the vehicles
Flack from LIGHT,
Medium and Heavy. A.A.
guns as playing **hell**
with the blackout.

night of
July 18th 1944

We were without any cover at all here, out on the
open plain SOUTH of the ORNE we seemed naked to
everything, shrapnel coming down was our worst enemy
and every shell seemed to burst just above you
Blackpool illumintions compared to this was a mid winter blackout.

Sketches by Donald Green

CHURCH TOWER
USED AS R.A.
OBSERVATION
POST

HOUSE BREWING UP
FROM JERRY SHELL.
MADE GOOD AIMING
MARK.

TANK OF
8TH HUSSARS

BORGUEBUS

We made
this place
at midnight.
He stonked
us and I
got cut off
in the
confusion.
I made it
back to our
lines in time
to get 4hrs
sleep in a
Jerry air-raid
shelter before
he started
to come
back at us.

July 20th
21st

10 lb shell
hole.

He scooped 2 Direct hits on our
trench with these shells, it never even
dented the roof.

This sketch was at height of battle. RAIN pouring down and MORTARS, HURDY GURDIES, SPANDAUS, BRENS, OERLIKONS, 210's, 88's, 4.5s, and everything going off all round. HERE HOPPY is on look-out while I try to contact H.Q. on 38 set. It was "dead" with a lump of shell in it! Borguebus smelt something wicked. A few dead things about probably accounted for that. In the middle of all this we were told the Canadians were taking over at night. But we were to move out while it was light, that was bad as Jerry had us under close observation.

July 21st

Sketches by Donald Green

ran to side of wall where 3 Canadians, were, Another shell dropped close they were peppering down now, CANADIAN ON LEFT OF THE 3rd WINNIPEG RIFLES cried out, he was hit, I started to bandage him, his pal looked at Hoppy he said "Your MATES DEAD chum!" soon after that there was a terriffic flash, NEARLY A FORTNIGHT LATER I CAME ROUND PROPERLY — IN HOSPITAL — IN BLIGHTY.

July 21st.

Canadian hit in leg.

2 in Mortar

Hoppy.

MYSELF.

HOPPY'S GAS-CAPE BLEW OFF, HIT ME IN FACE

CHAPTER FIVE

August Break-out

The tide was turning, but slowly and painfully, so Monty launched another massive attack: Operation Bluecoat on 30 July south-east of Caumont. This violent bruising operation was more successful. The 11th Armoured Division seized Beny Bocage and the 3rd British Division reached Flers and found Vire empty. Despite the failure of 30th Corps to make expected progress, 7th Armoured to the north and 43rd Division to the west seized the heights of Mont Pinçon in a fine action on 6/7 August. Although Bluecoat was called off in mid-August by intense German counter-attacks, it was clear now that a German collapse was not far off. Two Canadian offensives on the eastern flank – Operations Totalize on 7 August and Tractable on 14 August – were not conclusive but reached the outskirts of Falaise. On the 16th General Von Kluge, the German Commander in Chief, ordered a full-scale retreat. 2nd SS Panzer fought the Canadians and Poles to keep the 'Argenton–Falaise' pocket open. Monty issued a directive on 20 August: 'I call on all commanders for a great effort. Let us finish the business in record time.' The RAF Typhoons had a field day tearing remnants of the SS Panzer divisions apart. The gap was closed on the 21st and the German losses in Normandy totalled 450,000 men, 1,500 tanks, 3,500 guns and 20,000 vehicles. It was a great victory. Better still was the exhilaration – so good for morale – of the final break-out and chase up to the Seine. 43rd Wessex Division, involved in a five-day battle in Operation Neptune, then seized a vital bridgehead at Vernon.

The Mate you saw Go Down

Private Rex Wingfield of 1/6th Queen's wrote about his comrades in action.

Waiting for action is frightening but once the battle or the patrol starts, fear vanishes. In battle so much is happening at once, you're so busy that you haven't time to be scared, you haven't even time to think. You do things instinctively. But at night or in some pause in the battle you have got time to think. The mate you saw go down. The tank which 'brewed up'. The shell which stuck in the ground two feet away and failed to go off. When Ted fell, did he try to break his fall? If he did, it probably meant that he was only wounded, but if he seemed to sag at the neck, knee or ankle you knew what that meant. You look into the dusk. A solitary man is digging a trench. You watch him carefully. If he digs slowly and apathetically you know his mate is dead.

Leg-pullers

Lieutenant Geoffrey Picot, of the 1st Hampshires Mortar Platoon, recalls how, 'Sergeants Johnson and Wetherick were great pals and leg-pullers. Johnson had missed part of the early campaign because of malaria, probably contracted in Sicily. He could have stayed in England because of his malaria. Wetherick told me, "But he came out here because he wanted to be with *me*. He is lost without me!" But Johnson's version was that he came out to Normandy to look after Wetherick. "He'd be lost without *me*," said Johnson.'

'My Bleedin' Holidays'

Kenneth West, with 11 RSF on the outskirts of Frénouville, met an irate French farmer protesting at the damage done to his cornfield where an RAF Typhoon had just crash-landed. Beside himself with rage, he was told in French by Ken's mate George, 'C'est la guerre, Monsieur.'

The blue overalled farmer bemoaned his losses. In four years of war the Germans had never burned his fields. The British had dug holes, defiled his ground, driven tanks and lorries through his crops. In three weeks we had ruined him *and* killed his cows. George suddenly lost his cool. 'You ungrateful little bugger, we've come to liberate you lot. If you're not satisfied we'll all go home and let the soddin' Jerries reoccupy your land. I'll never come here again for my bleedin' holidays.'

Censorship

In Normandy security-conscious staff bureaucrats decreed that personal diaries could NOT be kept and that all letters home should be censored. As the vast majority of BLA did not know *precisely* where they were, or care, nor did they have any information of *any value* to the enemy, the censorship procedure was a chore that went automatically either to the regimental padre or to the most junior officer in each unit. To a twenty-year-old subaltern (Patrick Delaforce, 13 RHA) it was an eye-opener to see how other families corresponded and on what subjects. There were frequent mentions of undying love, sex, food, booze, some reactions to the immediate war, often comments about the troop or platoon leaders, which were intended to be read. There was, however, one form of secret coding by which the majority of letters ended, often scrawled on the back of the envelope. S W A L K was the most popular – Sealed With A Loving Kiss. Others were perhaps more demanding: B U R M A – Be Undressed Ready

My Angel, and NORWICH – Nickers Off Ready When I Come Home. But some devoted lovers had cryptograms which needed a cypher expert to decode.

An Armoured Division's Role in Battle

When Rex Wingfield joined 1/6th Queen's of the Desert Rats he was given a very good brief by his new 'muckers'.

The job of an armoured division is a highly specialized one. It is a spearhead. The point is three regiments of tanks and in close support of each of them is a company of the 1st Rifle Brigade in halftracks (and carriers). The blade is you, riding in Troop Carrying Vehicles (TCVs) – three battalions of infantry. You now belong to the 1/6th Queen's Royal Regiment. You also belong to 131st Lorried Infantry Brigade of the 7th Armoured Division. An armoured division probes and pushes its way through or around opposition. It does not bash blindly ahead. It does not stop to 'mop up'. It moves on and hopes to God that its supplies last out, or catch up. The limit of the advance is the limit of those supplies. An armoured division is basically restricted to main roads but it can use good firm tank-country. Tanks make their way ahead. If they meet machine guns they deal with them. If they bump anti-tank guns or anti-tank

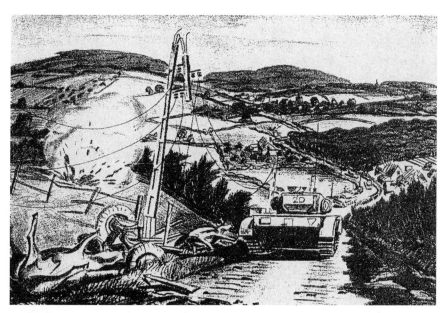

Moving south from Caumont with the 43rd Wessex Wyvern Division, 31 July 1944. (Birkin Haward)

ditches – it's the infantry's job to deal with those. Anti-tank guns are cleared by infantry flank attacks. Infantry also clear and hold anti-tank ditches until AVREs bring up tank bridges or 'fascine' tanks to fill up the ditch. At night the tanks laager on some prominent feature or natural obstacle such as a hill or river. Round them in all-round defence are the infantry. During the night supply columns battle their way to you – we hope! By next day your TCVs have brought up an *ordinary* infantry division to relieve you and on you go again! From dawn to dusk you have rocket-firing 'Tiffies' constantly circling round – and all the division's artillery to play with. We don't have to worry much about wood or street clearing. That's not our job. That's for ordinary infantry divisions – very costly in men. If *our* tanks go and play with someone else we're taken out of the line because we're not strong enough to hold anything.

Tank Support for Infantry

Major John Stirling, 4/7th Royal Dragoon Guards, wrote: 'The theory which had been preached for combined tank and infantry attacks, was that the attack should go in waves, with tanks followed by infantry, followed by more tanks. Experience soon showed that to have the tanks leading at all – was a mistake. In close country, tanks *must* go side by side with the infantry, and in more open country they could best give support from a position slightly in the rear, and to a flank.'

Jary on Weaponry

Lieutenant Sydney Jary, 4th Somerset Light Infantry, wrote:

In a fire fight between a German and a British platoon their MG 34 and MG 42 won hands down against our Bren and Sten. We were amazed at the crushing fire of those very rapid firing guns. Their infantry seldom used rifles, but carried boxes of light MG ammo – an endless supply.

The Sten was a wretched weapon. It had no locking device at the moment of firing. The quality of steel used for the magazine springs was poor. It should hold 32 9 mm rounds. Our experience was to restrict it to 25 rounds in a new magazine and 20 rounds in an old magazine. The German Schmeisser was a far superior weapon. The best sub MG was the Italian 9 mm Beretta with two triggers, one for single shots, other for automatic. One could load its magazine without the aid of a magazine loader. A lot were captured late in the German campaign after Italy had surrendered.

[At the foot of Mont Pinçon] powerless and crouching in a hedgerow, I tried to identify the Spandau positions. This proved impossible as they still kept up their crushing display of firepower. In my ignorance I expected that the enemy machine-gunners would soon expend their ammunition. They did not. Nor did they in dozens of subsequent battles. There must have been about 12 Spandaus firing at one time. This devastating display of firepower stopped the Bn dead in its tracks.

To the Races?

'Just before Bluecoat H battery 13 RHA were in laager just off the centre line waiting to integrate with 3 RTR. It was a lovely summer's day. The sun shone. Birds twittered. Three Shermans, half a dozen half-tracks and eight Sexton Rams waited patiently in the tree-lined bocage field with its thick green grass and clover. It was like a summer garden party or fête. The BC prowled. Troop commanders by their OP tanks listened for the "off". The two troop leaders checked their maps and looked out possible gun positions a few miles up the centre line. Gun crews gossiped. The night had been noisy as usual, but breakfast – bully beef and marmalade pudding – had been undisturbed and on time. There were no slit trenches in the great field; no steel helmets in sight. RHA bars and sparkling brass pips adorned the shoulders of the eight officers (a sniper's delight). Suddenly, literally out of the blue, there was a burst of thunder followed by thick, violent, noisy hail. We were lucky that it was only one 88 mm, targeting airburst right on top of us. It went on for half an hour. Metal fragments sprayed the sides of many of the vehicles, hissed noisily on top of the Shermans and cascaded round the field. Nobody took the slightest notice. "A bit noisy, don't you think?" "Really rather good shooting," or "Wish *we* had some 88 mm." The garden party went on. Officers strolled idly across the meadow under the hail waiting for starter's orders. It was no coincidence that the names of the flat race meetings, Epsom and Goodwood, were chosen for the great Normandy battles. There were a few casualties. Nothing serious. The 13th went to war again.' Lieutenant Patrick Delaforce was then a raw young Troop Leader.

Ferdinands at St Pierre

Private Len Stokes was a Rifleman with 'B' Company 7th Somerset Light Infantry. On 1 August the Wessex Wyverns at the start of Bluecoat had reached St Pierre du Fresne.

In the dark on the road, two enemy halftracks drove right into our midst, firing their machine guns like mad. One was knocked out with a PIAT gun, the other got away. By 2 a.m. 'B' Coy was in the village of St Pierre. Company HQ was in a large stone farmhouse with a vast courtyard. The three rifle platoons had to dig trenches. At dawn I was on sentry duty and reported the sound of a tank approaching. A little later I crossed the road to visit a platoon. I looked left and looked down the barrel of the biggest gun I had ever seen, on the biggest tank I had ever seen. [Ferdinands were a rare breed of SP guns, on a big tank body, with a fixed turret that did not rotate.] It fired a solid shot into our FOO in his Bren gun carrier, killing him. The mist in front of our position now suddenly cleared. Several hundred enemy soldiers were seen to be coming down the hill towards us, and overran our forward post. Major Whitehead, a really first class officer, the Coy CO, managed to call down very heavy artillery fire on the enemy who were caught in the open. The barrage was also called down onto our own positions to clear the enemy infiltrating. The German attack was smashed to smithereens. The tank [Ferdinand] was knocked out with a PIAT. We took 40 POW. The ground was littered with enemy dead. The Major received the Military Cross but was seriously wounded six days later.

The Chaplain's Diary – 'Consumed by Fire'

An entry from the diary of Revd Leslie Skinner, Sherwood Rangers Yeomanry:

Friday 4 August. Rejoined Doc. Went up with CO in jeep to 'A' Sqn [at St Pierre du Fresne]. Heavy shelling. Hear Birkett and crew [Sherwood Rangers Yeomanry] buried by Infantry. On foot located brewed up tanks – Watson and Heslewood died of wounds at Dorset's RAP – marked grave and buried two Infantry left behind by RAP. Only ash and burnt metal in Birkett's tank. Dorset's MO says other members of crew consumed by fire having been KIA. Searched ash and found remains pelvic bones. At other tank three bodies still inside – partly burned and firmly welded together. Managed with difficulty to identify Lieutenant Campbell. Unable to remove bodies after long struggle – nasty business – sick. 'C' Sqn still wanting me for 2 burials, but after three unsuccessful attempts to reach them had to give up. Ground between us and their position too exposed. Heavy fire each time I tried. They buried Troopers Howie and Mitchell themselves and left me to mark graves, etc. Shelled again during evening. Caught in one heavy burst while talking to new men just arrived from 24 Lancers. [Their regiment had just been broken up.] They will remember our introduction.

The Advance on Mont Pinçon

It is 1,200 ft high and its sides are very steep. The weather on 4, 5 and 6 August was hot and close, threatening thunder. Dust stirred up by moving vehicles, bursting shells, marching feet, hung chokingly heavy upon the fetid air. From its crest the Germans controlled a wide area south of Villers-Bocage and several vital roads. On the west side the ground was close and wooded with a river cutting irregular gullies across the approach roads. The 43rd Wessex Division plan was for 5th Wiltshires to secure the lower slopes of the hill and for 4th Wiltshires to capture St Jean le Blanc to the south-west. No fewer than eight infantry battalions of Panzer Group West's new defence line were concentrated there on a 4 mile front. Ondefontaine had been captured by the Wyverns in 36 hours of furious fighting and 130th Brigade were involved in battling their way to the northern slopes of Mont Pinçon.

Fighting under a Burning Sun

Major A.D. Parsons described the 4th Wiltshires' advance:

4 August. An uncomfortable feeling as we rode along closely packed on top of the Sherman tanks of B Sqn, 13/18th Hussars and our already overloaded wheeled and tracked vehicles. On the way to Mont Pinçon the countryside resembled Devon, steep and wooded hills, lanes with high banks, large undulating cornfields. Weather was very hot and sunny, the roads lay thick with white dust and dead horses. There was a new threat of roadside mines. 5 August. At Ecures a large chateau was burning, the bridge was blown and both banks were mined. On the way to St Jean le Blanc up the steep slopes it was slow, costly bitter work by 'C' Company, eight hours of desperate fighting under a burning sun. Our FOO, Captain J. Fletcher was tireless, invaluable. Lance Corporal Jenkins ('A' Coy) commanded a platoon reduced to seven men, and for his daring later received the MM. All three NCOs had been hit. That night 'C' Coy dug in, hungry and exhausted with the sad task of burying their dead. As night fell the tanks withdrew. Our only friends the Gunners. Captain Fletcher fed every man in the Company with biscuits, bully beef and water from his carrier. Enemy tanks or SPs were defending St Jean le Blanc. A bitter and largely fruitless day's fighting in difficult country under the hot sun, little or no food. We lost twenty-two killed and thirty-nine wounded. A bitter day for the battalion.

An Audacious and Brave Adventure

To the north, half a mile away, the Somersets were similarly mown down. But at La Varinière two Shermans of 13/18th Hussars raced across the bridge to be followed by six more tanks and sixty surviving Wiltshires. They secured the vital crossroads of La Varinière and, leaving the near-exhausted infantry, seven Hussar tanks from 'A' Squadron led by Captain N.N.M. Denny, Lieutenant Elliott and Lieutenant Jennison's troops set off up a very narrow steep track. One overturned, another had its track blown off, but by 1900 under cover of a smoke screen the Hussars had seven tanks in an all-round defensive position on the summit. At 2000 Lieutenant Colonel Dunkerley arrived with the rest of the Hussar squadron – an audacious and brave adventure. The wretched, exhausted 4th Wiltshires were back in the fray with Major A.D. Parsons leading 'B' Company up at

2100. Their CO, Lieutenant Colonel Ted Luce, was the first of the battalion to reach the top but went back down again to encourage his men. During the day the Wiltshires lost thirteen KIA and forty-nine wounded. Soon 130th Brigade fought their way up on the north face. From the top Lieutenant General Brian Horrocks, with his CCRA Stewart Rawlins beside him, could deploy the fury of 300 British guns onto the enemy who now planned to defend the river Noireau with equal tenacity. Eric Codling's 8th Middlesex noted 'rushing forward throwing caution to the winds to support the small band of 4 Wilts and 13/18th Hussars who had slipped through the enemy defences under cover of darkness to establish a tenuous hold on the summit. A bitter and confused struggle took place. At the end of the day our OPs were on the heights to cause havoc on the retreating German troops and transport.' The storming of Mont Pinçon was a crucial victory.

'Stretcher Bearers were Busy Again'

The 3rd Monmouthshires, a lorried unit in the 11th Armoured Division, had lost 240 men in their first four weeks of battle in Normandy. Only one hundred had arrived to replace them. Major J.J. How was a Battalion Company CO. He describes their start to Bluecoat.

The Monmouths, reorganized after their losses on the start line, had pushed on to reach the main road just west of Caumont.

We wondered where the enemy were. There was that eerie silence one feels when one is being watched from some hidden place of observation. We entered a park-like area with tall trees. Suddenly the flood gates of hell opened and we were drowned in the scream of shells, the wail of mortars and the detonation of missiles exploding all round us. We flung ourselves down and pressed our bodies into the long damp grass with hearts racing and stomachs turned upside down.

It stopped as abruptly as it had started. There was silence. We rose up hesitatingly, looking around. There were shouts: 'Keep moving!' – 'Don't close up!' – 'Stretcher bearers!' We passed some dead of the 15th Scottish, who were attacking on our left. The shells were falling again. We were still under observation. They followed us everywhere. We ran down a grassy slope and halted at the stream in the valley below. The clouds had disappeared and the sun was clawing its way through. The shelling and mortaring grew heavier. We moved into the bed of the stream to get some protection from the banks. The stretcher bearers were busy again.

There was the sound of machine-gun fire not far ahead. Word went round that we were waiting for the 15th Scottish. They were held up in the village of Sept Vents. It must have been almost midday when two Sherman tanks came down the slope and joined us. One was hit on the engine casing by a falling shell. The crew threw themselves out of the hatches as flames billowed up. A great mushroom of smoke rose in the air. Ammunition was exploding in a series of flat bangs and cracker-like bursts. Sparks and bits of smoking metal were thrown out to lie smouldering on the damp grass. The man next to me put his hand to his eye. Blood came streaming down through the fingers.

Operation Bluecoat – 'Prisoner in Paradise'

The 11th Armoured Division had advanced through bocage country, had taken Beny-Bocage and 23rd Hussar Shermans were holding the line between Presles and Chênedollé. Geoffrey Bishop describes the scene on Friday 4 August:

All is quiet for a while – brilliant sunshine – but the awful tension persists. 'Prisoner in Paradise' suggests itself as the title for a story. This beautiful Normandy scene, the soft wooded hills, the good rich earth, a balmy summer's day, and yet fear is there – fear of the unknown – a tearing, screaming shell blasting through your little iron fortress, taking with it your legs and your friends – fear of the unknown – a sniper in an adjacent hedgerow quietly preparing to kill you unawares. August the fourth – it is my sister's birthday. I think of a tennis party in England. The time ticks by. We have a meal – a very good stew, cooked under the stern of the tank. [For four days the Hussars stay locked in mortal combat.] Sunday 6 August. How long can this go on? Eleven lonely tanks and a few dug-in infantry on this shell-torn hilltop. It must be a highly sought-after spot by the Jerry. The senior NCOs are distressed with fatigue and anxiety. There is a feeling that we have been left here to die. At last the black night settles over our grim little battlefield – I found our little Scots MO in a sunken lane bright and cheerful as ever, dealing with a lot of pretty bad cases.

The battle on the Divisional front raged for over a week but the Black Bull Division held on to their gains and fended off daily counter-attacks.

Corporal 'Basher' Bates' Victoria Cross

185th Brigade was soon to be in desperate trouble. 'Around midnight [5 August] I made contact with Brigadier Jack Churcher [of 159th Infantry Brigade, 11th AD] who pointed out a burning ridge in the distance and said [to Major Humphrey Wilson, Royal Norfolks], "There are the Monmouths or what is left of them, be careful how you go as we are only in wireless touch with them. Be prepared to take over from them at first light."' Heavy mist on the morning of the 6th initially hid the Norfolks take-over moving south-east through Burcy towards Sourdevalle. When the hot sun broke through, 'B' Company under Major Cooper-Key were spotted and became an easy target for intense mortar fire from 10th SS Panzer Division. 'A'

Company under Major MacGillivray made a detour to avoid Burcy, but suffered seventeen casualties. 'C' Company under Captain H.J. Jones were also badly hit as they followed up. By 1700, however, the relief of three of the Monmouth's rifle companies had been achieved. Half an hour later a very heavy artillery stonk fell on the rear of relieving Norfolks, setting most of 'F' Echelon's vehicles ablaze. The two battalion COs pooled forces (called Nor-Mons) totalling only 550 men but supported by the Shermans of the 2nd Fife and Forfar Yeomanry. At 1815 'B' Company was attacked and partly overrun and by 2030 'C' Company was down to thirty-five, all ranks. The desperate situation was not helped by friendly US Thunderbolts firing their cannon on the hapless 'Nor-Mons'.

'The scene was indescribable,' wrote Humphrey Wilson, 'blazing vehicles, dead men and cattle. The Thunderbolts gave us a good strafing. 'B' Coy "got on the air", told Bn HQ by wireless that it was being heavily counter-attacked. In this attack Corporal Bates won the Victoria Cross.' Known as 'Basher', Bates was commanding the right forward section of the left forward 'B' Company and, seeing the situation was desperate, seized a light machine gun and charged the enemy through a hail of bullets, firing the gun from his hip. Although hit three times, he went on charging and firing until the enemy started to withdraw. It was a truly brilliant, heroic effort. He died of his wounds, two days later.

A Tiger tank moved through 'C' Company, the 3rd Monmouths killing many men in their slit trenches. 'The enemy came on and on out of the sun. Our artillery worked wonders and everyone had a shot at the Boche,' recalls Humphrey Wilson. 'At about 1930 some twenty Shermans of the Fife and Forfars arrived and everybody took on a new lease of life. By 2130 hours the last of the enemy had disappeared, a great number had been killed, a large number wounded and the rest just went back.' But 10th SS Panzer Division had fought like demons.

Sourdevalle had cost the Norfolks 176 casualties, including thirty-two KIA. For five more days the Norfolks stayed there licking their wounds often under heavy Nebelwerfer fire. 'After a time the whole area reeked of death.' In the battle of Sourdevalle, Sergeant C. Hopkins won the DCM. Though wounded in the leg, he engaged and hit a Tiger tank with a PIAT. CSM T. Catlin, Sergeant G.A. Smith, Corporal C. Thirtle and Major W.E.G. Bagwell, among others, won awards for gallantry.

Close Shave

Lieutenant Patrick Delaforce, 13th RHA, wrote:

At dusk I laid out 200 m of trip wire and flares in front of Fox troop gun position. 8 RB were in the green meadows and copses of the Normandy bocage just in front of us. Nevertheless we did not want stray Panzer Grenadiers slipping into our patch during the night. We had three

Defensive Fire targets registered about 2,000 m ahead to protect the Mons and KSLI. During the night we brought down battery shoots on the DFs as well as half a dozen regimental targets. It was a long, hard, noisy night. But we certainly stopped 10 SS Panzer dead in their tracks. At dawn Fox troop stood to as usual and I walked round the four Sexton Ram 24-pounders, making sure the crews were awake and more or less on the *qui vive*.

To my surprise, out of the early morning mist appeared Norman Young, my troop commander. I saluted and greeted him. 'Morning Norman, come slumming with the workers?' He looked me up and down. He knew about the night's noisy entertainment. He knew that Fox troop had had no sleep at all, as he had called down the DFs himself. We were all tired, dirty and rather irritable. 'Have you shaved yet, Patrick?' he said in a clear, carrying voice. I took a deep breath and counted slowly to ten. I thought rapidly of several mutinous answers such as 'Sod off', 'What the hell do you think we've been doing all night?' or a feeble, 'It's not yet daylight.'

'Imminently, Norman,' I said, 'Imminently,' and left it at that. I was 20. My early morning crop of whiskers was undistinguished. A few days later my CO, Lieutenant Colonel Bob Daniell DSO, awarded me my Royal Horse Artillery jacket – a coveted award – which would allow me, if I survived, to wear splendid chain mail blue patrols and round silver ball buttons with service dress. It was a crazy war!

'Dust Means Death'

During that long, mainly hot summer of 1944 the non-metalled roads and lanes were baked by the sun. Any traffic movement raised clouds of dust indicating a target which German mortars and 88 mm guns found irresistible. The culprits on the road ranged from RASC trucks to (very important) red-tabbed senior officers. So the signs went up. Rifleman 'Roly' Jefferson and his 8 RB Company of 11th Armoured Division had a difficult time in early August towards the end of Operation Bluecoat.

For four long days and nights we were in the village of Presles and supplies were becoming a problem. Each night a carrier had to go through to the other end of the village to collect the necessities of food, fuel and water. 'Dust means death' was a familiar cry. Wherever possible, signs were erected stating just that. It was difficult to move a carrier with its caterpillar tracks without raising dust. It was not easy to get volunteers to drive out for the supplies. The fairest way was to take turns. I was mighty glad when I got back safely from my run. We were under almost constant mortar and shell fire but we kept our heads down most of the time and casualties were light. We were sadly depleted. Quick transfers were made to even out section strengths.

Potato Picking

Rex Wingfield, 1/6th Queen's, describes a dangerous task which all front-line troops had to undertake from time to time. It was known as Potato Picking.

We spread out lying on our stomachs, and took out our bayonets. They were nasty looking things like a meat skewer, and they had an end like a screwdriver. They looked horrible. Worst of all they were damned short. Inch by terrifying inch we moved forward going through the drill. Bayonet upright held above the ground, swing forward, swing back, swing left, swing right. That tells you whether there are any trip-wires around. No? Grip the bayonet lightly but firmly at an angle of 45 degrees to the ground and prod gently. If you prod straight down, you won't know what hit you. If you find a mine dig all around it and watch for any connecting wires. Render safe by shoving nails into the plunger. The Army Drill book always assumes that an infantryman had half a ton of nails in his ordinary essentials. But those bayonets were damned short. A shout from the right and a nasty flat cheese of a Teller mine was found – and another and another. We found a belt about two hundred yards long and twenty deep, a mixture of Teller anti-tank and S-mines. An S-mine was a pleasant little toy, which shot 4 feet into the air and then exploded about 300 ballbearings as well as its own casing into a nasty scythe cutting down anything in its way. Slowly, carefully, with death three inches from our pale faces, we prodded, located and rendered them harmless, every minute cringing for the huge flash which would be the end of Eight Platoon. We cleared the minefield. It took six hours. The tanks ground slowly through the white tapes and into the fields.

'A Little Gentleman's War'

There was no doubt that Major 'Algy' Grubb, a Company CO with the 1st Worcesters was a 'card': tall, blond-haired, intelligent and idiosyncratic.

It may now seem rather an incomprehensible thing to say, but it [fighting] could be great fun. What was really tiresome was when the shells came, then you had no chance. Tanks and things make it a hell of a bloody game, but a little gentleman's war was a great deal of fun. At that time, after the experience we had been through, one was attuned to it, inoculated against it. You really were, you became a little elated, unbalanced even. On reflection it appears odd that you could enjoy such a thing, but it is an example of an extraordinary reaction of the body that I think is largely due to the generation of adrenalin. In moments of intense danger, one became elated to such an extent that it bordered on insanity. When it was over, there was total collapse. When it was all over, I collapsed into a very small slit trench and went completely out. A tremendous thunderstorm during the night filled my trench with water to just below my nose. On one occasion I was out for 24 hours. Nobody could wake me. At Mont Pinçon my 'B' Company started with 88 men and ended with 5. I was mad with elation upon something that I felt was impossible.

'Algy', the Mad Major, went on to win a MC, but took so many outrageous risks that in the Reichwald fighting, to help him stay alive, his CO and Brigadier sent him back to the UK to run a battle school.

Tank Driving

'A good tank driver is, first and foremost, one who maintains the vehicle so that it is as reliable as it can be made to be. The crew's lives depend on the tank engine starting instantly when required and not "conking out", at any time, for any reason, except enemy action. A stationary tank in action can often be a sitting duck waiting for an AP. But a *very* good tank driver also knows how to give his crew a reasonably balanced "ride", so that they can get on with *their* jobs of gunnery and wireless and, in the case of the commander, observation. This demands a little more from the tank driver than the skills traditionally required of a chauffeur: looking ahead, not accelerating and braking suddenly. Going across country through hedges, over ditches, into ruined buildings the tank driver needs considerable judgement in order to avoid throwing his crew about like dice in a shaker. It is quite easy to get hurt inside a tank without anyone shooting at you; safety belts were not provided and if they had been they would not have been worn as you need quick movement, especially the loader/wireless operator. If the tank brewed, the split second releasing a safety belt would have had you fried. A good driver knows what demands he can make of the tank's suspension, mixing his braking and accelerating in rapid alternation sometimes.

Imagine driving an ordinary motor car with all the windows painted black except for a ten inch diameter of clear vision in front. The car is travelling at a fair speed on a flat road, slowing down as the road becomes rutted and then driving it over a series of small boulders; then quickly tilting the car over at speed round a corner.' [Norman Smith, Cromwell tank driver, 5th RTR.]

Tactics – Battle of the Somme?

Sydney Jary, aged twenty, commanded 18 Platoon, 4th Battalion Somerset Light Infantry. The thirty-six men consisted of three rifle sections each of ten men, including a Brengunner plus Platoon HQ with 2 in mortar detachment, a PIAT, the Platoon Sergeant and the CO's batman/runner. He reckoned that British infantry platoons and companies were overtrained in, and bored stiff with, basic infantry tactics, which as far as they went were very good.

Many of the Battle School instructors lacked battle experience and imagination. Thus the battlefield became our teacher, and inevitably it exacted a grim price in blood and time. Infantry had to fit into the big picture, rarely operating without artillery and armoured support. The most successful actions by 18 Platoon were fought *without* the support of either. We had learned in a hard school how to skirmish, infiltrate and edge our way forward. The right or left flanking platoon attack so beloved of the Battle School staff would rarely succeed in the Normandy 'bocage'. I remember being 'locked' into the timetables of meticulously planned large battles. These inevitably left the junior infantry commander no scope for exploitation. If you found a gap in the enemy defence, adherence to the artillery programme, which could rarely be altered, effectively stopped any personal initiative. The irony was that this support was planned and given to the infantry with the best of intentions. The battle of the Somme had also cast its shadows on our artillery and armoured commanders. The Germans were expert at holding off opposition with a screen of Spandaus supplemented by odd snipers. Inexperienced troops can be held up for hours by these delaying tactics, as we ourselves were in Normandy. By pushing on fast, bypassing MG posts, the enemy's screen inevitably collapsed.

Operation Totalize

We made our way to the factory area of Cormelles, the assembly area. We [22nd Dragoons] were to take part in a daring plan that night [7 August] – an attack in darkness, aided by movable moonlight [searchlights reflecting downwards from clouds], south-eastwards, astride the Caen–Falaise road to smash through the enemy's strong defence. It was daring because it was to consist of four parallel columns and the entire first wave was to be on tracked vehicles. Even the 51st Highland Division would be carried in Kangaroos, tanks minus their turrets. Tanks are almost blind at night and the enemy line was held by the Hitler Youth Division – all fanatical young fighters – in prepared positions. The RAF would give close support bombing and every gun in the beachhead would follow up with a rolling barrage. A brave navigating officer in a Honey light tank led, followed by a troop of Churchills; a Flail troop behind them, then a long string of Churchills with the Kangaroo infantry bringing up the rear.

Many of the tanks in front of Lieutenant Ian Hammerton were bazookered and Corporal Adler's Flail was brewed up in Tilly-la-Campagne.

Hammerton's Flail tank plunged into a huge crater, a track broke, and could not move. The next week [14 August] the RAF bombed in four waves the 22nd Dragoons and destroyed most of the Echelon of the Polish Armoured Division.

The Fife and Forfarshire Troop Leader's Journal

'8 August. Before first light we crept cautiously to the same positions [near Chênedollé]. All quiet. I crawled round the burnt-out tanks. I had a list of the wounded who had been evacuated, so knew what bodies to look for: crumpled heaps on this seat or that. The enemy had really gone. In the afternoon we were relieved by the Scots Greys. Our squadron comprised only Pinkie and my 4 Troop, five tanks in all out of nineteen. At La Quelle we found a grinning Jimmy Samson. Lance Corporal Martin with the mess truck, mail, etc. and I [Lieutenant Steel Brownlie] immediately had three large whiskies and soda. We were there for four balmy days refitting, absorbing reinforcements, taking shower-baths, marking maps, lying in the sun, eating a roast goose. . . . A grenade went off in the pocket of a C Sqn officer, killing him.'

The Breaking Strain

'The mortaring and shelling increased in violence, especially on the two forward [17-pdr anti-tank] guns. In the morning I [Sergeant Sheldrake] had to go and bring one of the men out. We finally got him out of the slit in which he was huddled, wracked with sobs. Much has been written by many writers about cowardice, but only men who have known what these men had been through have the right to judge. This man was no coward. The strain had been too much for him. Weeping unashamedly in front of his mates, cringing at every small noise. I had to hold him down by physical force whenever it mortared while we were on our way back together. At THQ, Dave and I got him on the jeep and set out for Battery HQ [Suffolk Yeomanry]. We were unfortunate to be passing through a village when it was shelled. It was too much for him. He yelled and struggled, nearly spilling us all out of the jeep. We were glad to hand him over.'

Snipers

Everyone hated snipers. They picked off the young leaders with relative impunity. Major Godfrey Harland MC was a Company Commander with 1/4th KOYLI in Normandy. 'In a static position if a sniper's position was identified, I would either ask the nearest tank, if one was handy, to give the sniper a "squirt" with its BESA or Browning, having pointed out the tree or trees where he was hiding – or – if no tank was available send a section on a sniper's "stalk" using cover to get near enough to use rifle or Bren or both to "dislodge" him. During an attack the "drill" was to ignore them and rely on our supporting tanks to spray the trees and likely hiding places with machine-gun fire.' Very few snipers – particularly the fifteen- or sixteen-year-old Hitler Youths tied to their trees – survived to tell the tale.

'Me Ruskie' – The Signaller's Story

Graham Roe was a Corporal Signaller in 'C' Company of the Hallamshires and frequently had to go out into No Man's Land to repair telephone cables which had been cut by the enemy or chopped up by mortar and shell fire. Or of course by friendly tanks and carriers!

It was my custom to lie down on my back to repair the cable across my chest. I did not present a target for an enemy sniper and I had a better view of anyone approaching me. It was a sunny day but the sun was in my eyes. Suddenly I found myself looking into the muzzle of a rifle. I could make out the silhouette of two burly soldiers in field grey. My heart sank. This was either the end or I would be taken prisoner. I sat up with a jerk. The words of Psalm 46 came into my thoughts, where God is my refuge and strength and a very present help in trouble. I waited. One of them with an apology for a smile, handed me a leaflet promising a safe passage, if they brought the leaflet in, and *surrendered*. One of them banged his chest and said, 'Me Ruskie'. Plucking up my courage I said in German, 'Bleiben sie da' and finished joining the cables.

A Picture of War

Major Creagh Gibson, commanding 'A' Squadron 5th Inniskilling Dragoon Guards, wrote home to his father:

August 14th 1944. We came out of the line last week after some weeks in battle. I will endeavour to give you an account of our daily life but it is difficult to be descriptive because of security. I cannot say which formation I am in [7th Armoured Division], although it is probably quite clear to the Boche!

The battle divides itself into two different types; one when we are working with a similar formation to ourselves and the other when supporting infantry. Armoured battling has been on a very small scale on our sector because of the very enclosed country. There is no doubt that the Boche has made good use of the terrain. He has proven himself to be clever, subtle and crafty. A few determined men, well sited and camouflaged and manning an anti-tank gun, can give an armoured regiment a very bloody nose in a very short time. They lie up in the ditches and hedgerows and cannot be seen. The first indication of their presence is when a leading tank is knocked out. Even when this happens, you cannot tell from whence the shot came. They seem to use some smokeless powder and there is no flash. They also employ many snipers who have very accurate rifles with telescopic sights. They play havoc with the crew commanders who frequently have to have their heads out of the turret to observe. These snipers are very brave and continue shooting for a long period after the forward troops have passed. Many are caught but it is certain that some get back through our lines to fight again. The general method of advance in this sort of country is to attach a squadron of tanks to a battalion of infantry. The infantry try to ensure that there are no nasty people manning anti-tank guns or carrying bazookas. The tanks deal with machine-gun posts to protect the infantry. The cooperation between the two arms is difficult but we are getting better at it.

On a typical day we get out of our protective trenches at about 0430 hours and 'stand to' till just after first-light, which is between 0530 and 0600 hours. We are usually only a field away from the infantry who hold the line at night. As soon as it is light enough each vehicle crew cooks breakfast which may consist of anything from tinned soya sausage to tinned bacon and beans with bread or biscuits and tea. It makes a very good meal and everyone is quite ready for it. It is often the only cooked meal of the day. There may already be one or two troops of tanks in support of the infantry and these have to be relieved. The advance begins through the thick countryside until a strongpoint is met.

During the past week, prisoners have been coming in readily but not before they have been soundly shelled. Each pocket of resistance has to be dealt with. Artillery fire is called down and tanks deploy to get in a shot from a flank. We have excellent artillery support which can be called down on to targets only a hundred yards ahead. The enemy dig very narrow slit trenches which give them excellent protection, but their casualties are very high. They also dig in their tanks and these are a devil to deal with. They can only be dealt with by an armour-piercing shot and when a tank is brought into position where it can observe, so can *it* be observed. Rocket-firing Typhoon aircraft are often called for to deal with them. Provided the target can be identified, they can usually destroy a tank. The aircraft comes down in a steep dive. The combined roar of the engine and the rocket has a devastating effect upon the morale of the defenders.

I have spoken about 'being in the line'; in fact there is no line. Pockets of resistance are left behind which have to be cleared. This pushing, probing and clearing up goes on throughout the day and until dusk when we form what we call a 'loose laager', i.e. groups of tanks dotted about. Our casualties have really been very light. Those we have suffered have nearly all been caused by mines, shelling or mortar fire. We are perfectly protected inside our vehicles but you have to get out sometimes and it is then the chaps get caught.

'Little Hope of Survival'

When Private Rex Wingfield joined 1/6th Queen's his Section Corporal lectured the newcomers.

Now consider our case. We're in trouble 24 hours a day. We get used to the idea of danger until even Death is the normal thing, so we build up a way of life, a state of mind, at first a resistance to Death, a fight for life, but that finally becomes a submission and resignation to constant danger. You've heard the old gag, 'Any change in Infantry is bound to be for the worse.' If you accept that, you've conquered Fear. Death doesn't worry you any more. We have little hope of survival. We accept that and spin it out as best we can. We don't have any distractions like comfort. Our life goes along smoothly at a permanent level of tension. *We're as good as dead.* A slit trench, after all, is the nearest thing to a grave we'll be in while we're alive. It *is* a grave!

On the Way to Argentan – 'The Stench was Overpowering'

'On the 15th we spent the night north of Vassy and befriended a small black cat. German resistance was being broken down and we passed into the Falaise pocket all the time driving the enemy eastwards where they were trying to escape to the Seine,' wrote Rifleman Roland Jefferson in his journal *Soldiering at the Sharp End.*

The 3rd Mons forded the river and our column crossed on a platform of brushwood. We moved forward slowly. The whole scene became increasingly more indescribable. The whole area was strewn with dead Germans and horses and wrecked transport, guns and knocked-out tanks of every description. We had to pick our way through the wreckage. Sometimes there was no other way through the devastation but to drive over the corpses. The stench was overpowering. Prisoners were giving themselves up in their hundreds. 'G' Coy 8 RB rejoiced in capturing their first German General. Some wore the unmistakable [Runic] sign of the crack SS troops, still their arrogant selves. The prisoners were a nuisance to us. We simply bypassed them and sent them back in long columns. Bulldozer tanks tried to clear the roads. There was simply nowhere to push some of the German debris, it was piled so high. Literally thousands of German dead lay around. We eventually got through and the sun shone brilliantly as we passed through the ruins of Argentan.

'The Sheer Ferocity . . .'

By the middle of August, Lieutenant Sydney Jary had led his platoon for nearly two months and was now a veteran of the 'bocage'.

For the infantry and armour of the British 2nd Army the sheer ferocity of the fighting in Normandy came as a salutary shock for which they were, in some ways, unprepared.

At our level we were unaware that the best German divisions were deployed against us, although at the time it certainly seemed to be so.

During exercises in southern England, my previous Battalion had practised infantry attacks supported by tanks. Nothing in these exercises prepared me for what was to come. It was in Normandy that we first tried the real thing with the Armoured Regiment that usually supported us, the Nottinghamshire Yeomanry (Sherwood Rangers). After our first attempt, I was left with a profound pity for them. Hopelessly out-gunned by the German Mk IV, Mk V (Panther) and Mk VI (Tiger) tanks, they suffered grievous casualties. The German 75 mm and 88 mm anti-tank guns also wreaked a terrible havoc. To add to these perils the German infantry had by far the most effective short-range and anti-tank weapons. Their bazooka was larger and had a longer range than that used by the American infantry and was in all respects superior to our PIAT. Their smaller Panzerfaust was probably the best conceived weapon of its type in any army. Lurking in woods and hedgerows, German infantry, armed with either of these weapons, exacted a heavy toll of any of our tanks that strayed from the immediate protection of our rifle sections.

Denied scope for manoeuvre, our tanks were reduced to the role of blind, slow and highly vulnerable infantry support guns. Their primary task was to knock out enemy machine-gun positions with 75 mm high-explosive shells and these they could seldom see. Consequently, and it was very difficult, we had to devise a means of identifying these cunningly concealed targets for the tank commander. We soon learned not to climb onto the tank and shout. Due to engine noise he could seldom hear and, for us, it proved a lethal pastime. We tried firing Very lights towards the target and also Bren bursts of all-tracer rounds, but neither was satisfactory. The most successful arrangement was for the tank commander to throw out a head and breast microphone set, but even then engine noise made it difficult.

The Padre's Bloodbath

'Thurs Aug 17th. "C" Squadron SRY on other axis had a rough time. Wounded evacuated along Infantry stream. 8 men killed, 5 still in tanks. Went back to start line then forward along "C" Sqn axis. Buried the three dead and tried to reach the remaining dead in tanks – still too hot and burning. Place absolute shambles. Infantry dead and some Germans lying around. Horrible mess. Fearful job picking up bits and pieces and re-assembling for identification and putting in blankets for burial. No infantry to help. Squadron Leader offered to lend me some men to help. Refused. Less men who live and fight in tanks have to do with this side of things the better. They know it happens, but to force it on their attention is not good. My job. This was more than normally sick-making. Really ill – vomiting. Buried all five in a 43 Div cemetery set up at cross-roads in Berjou.' [Revd Leslie Skinner.]

No Sorrow . . .

'At a burial in an area just to our rear the Padre [1st Battalion Hampshires] said, "If the Christian religion means anything at all, it means that this is not the end of this soldier. We believe in the Christian religion; if we did not, we could not be giving him a burial such as this. And the Christian religion means that his soul and spirit live on: only his body stays in the earth. We cannot feel sorry for him because he has gone to a better place than this. We can feel sorry for his family and the friends he has left behind but not for him, no."'

The Argentan–Falaise Corridor – 'A Ghastly Sight'

Towards the beginning of August the German 7th Army and its reinforcements found itself in a rectangle bounded by Vire, Falaise, Mortain and Argentan. The vital Mont Pinçon was seized on 7 August and General Patton's Shermans were marauding in Brittany. To the south of Falaise the Americans, British, Canadians, Poles and some French were putting immense pressure on the retreating *Wehrmacht*, although Hitler had forbidden its withdrawal until 10 August. The surviving Panzers and SS troops fought their way through the corridor hell-bent for the river Seine, leaving the foreign troops [Russians, Poles, etc.], the second-rate troops and the wounded to fend for themselves. Sergeant Wally Caines, 4th Dorsets, wrote in his diary:

22nd August, near Falaise massed slaughter had taken place by Typhoon fighter bombers. The recce party passed through this area. We travelled one road and actually our vehicles passed over the top of many hundreds of crushed German dead bodies. Vehicles of all types of German transport littered the whole area. . . . How that lot looked and stunk, dead bodies were running over with maggots and flies. It was indeed a ghastly sight seeing these dead Nazis bursting in the blistering heat of the day. The road was about 1$\frac{1}{2}$ miles long and never before had I smelt anything like it. The Typhoons had done a great job of work. Day after day we saw them charging down from the heavens above spitting their deadly fire at the retreating German Army.

'Sheer Bestiality'

'I think it was the most exciting and sensational time I shall ever have in my life. We drove south first through Condé-sur-Noireau and Vire. Then we swung east towards Argentan and the Seine. At first we [John Stirling back again after his wounds with 4/7th RDG] moved gingerly. At every corner and every wood one waited to hear the familiar boom and snarl of a piece of "hard". But the noise never came. It seemed incredible after all these weeks, that we could motor ten miles down a main road without being fired on. But the ten miles mounted to twenty and still there was silence and still the speedometers ticked on. We could not understand that the rout of the German Seventh Army was now almost complete, that the Falaise pocket, round whose outskirts we were driving, was the scene of the biggest disaster the victorious Wehrmacht had ever experienced. This was the real thing. This was the Breakthrough. We saw the remains of a retreating army. Burnt-out vehicles that the RAF had caught, abandoned vehicles that had broken down, derelict vehicles that had run out of petrol, dead horses, broken wagons, scattered kit and equipment. We saw the brutal sadism of the SS. Everything had been thrown out of the French houses, breakables broken, materials ripped, pistol shots through the cider barrels, an axe for the windows and farmhouse and all the livestock killed and removed – to establish the supremacy of the Herrenvolk over the lesser people – and sheer bestiality.'

'Not Coming Back'

In the last two weeks of August the Recce Regiments who had not been fighting in their true role in the bocage country were let off the lead. The Inns of Court were the spearhead for 11th Armoured Division, the Cherry Pickers 11th Hussars for the Desert Rats, and the 2nd Household Cavalry for the Guards Armoured Division. Lieutenant Brett-Smith, with the Cherry Pickers, wrote in his diary:

Jory, St Pierre-sur-Dives and the Poles gabbling unintelligibly on our frequencies but fighting like lions, then Livarot (later Lisieux, Fervacques and up to the River Risle near the Forêt de Montfort). For the first time we were cracking on *and not coming back* and it was exhilarating. The guns were firing nineteen to the dozen, found it hard to keep up, let alone the Echelons. Livarot had a timely Calvados brewery and with a quiet pull of the bottle we rushed off to chase the enemy back across the Seine. He did not need much chasing. Now and again the Luftwaffe showed itself but was swamped by our excellent air support. In fact one was, as like as not, strafed by Thunderbolts and not Focke-Wulfs.

The Armoured Car Crews

Major Bindon Blood, of 43rd Recce Regiment with the Wessex Wyverns, wrote:

I can see the men who fought them now – I can see them in the cold dawn light, tired, unshaven, patient; car crews moving up into action, too tense to smile back at my hesitant one. Each crew a team: the commander, his resolution a rock on which any uncertain mate could build; the gunner, often more sensitive than the average, with his dual watch on 19 set and BESA; the driver, glimpsed with a quick flash of clear eye through his hatch, sturdy and humorous. Men from the carrier sections, an earthier breed, back from patrol, clutching Bren or Sten or Schmeisser. The assault troop corporal; his task to hold together men who sometimes felt they 'had the dirty jobs'. The lad who shivered when he heard our own shells going over, but was going on; B Echelon driver, beret on the side of his over-long hair. . . . 'Hello, all stations Jig Able George – report my signals – all stations . . . '

Armoured Car Cover

'The Inns of Court moved on recce in front of the Division (11th Armoured from Briouze, through Argentan, La Ferne Fresnel, L'Aigle and Rugles to Conches). Those who led this advance will remember all these towns with a mixture of joy and sorrow. Lieutenant Richards and Trooper Climie were killed near Courmeil, Troopers Brown and Price were killed near Tilly and Sergeant Clarke and Lance Corporal Roberts wounded in the same action. Corps HQ tribute was that no formation had ever had armoured car cover such as had been provided by the Inns of Court during those days.' [Lieutenant Peter Reeve]

'Merci, Merci' – The Platoon Commander's Story

Lieutenant Geoffrey Picot, 1st Battalion the Hampshire Regiment, wrote in his book *Accidental Warrior*:

Operationally we were very lucky and had very little fighting to do. We combed woods, sent out protective patrols, caught a few stragglers, and that was about all. But, of course, when one went out on patrol there was tension in the air, for one did not know the area would be clear until one had been there and investigated. One might have to fight and, with the war racing to its finish, this was not the time to become a casualty. Ken Edwards, who continued to lead our column, was very wary. Approaching any village he looked anxiously to see whether their flags were flying. If so, he knew they had been liberated and he led the column in with an easy mind; if not, he went very cautiously, observing all the while.

I shall never forget those tumultuous days at the end of August when France warmed to its liberation. Apples and pears were thrown at us as we passed through the villages, bottles of local 'fire-water' were placed in our hands, little delicacies of food that we knew people could ill spare were showered upon us whenever we stopped for a moment, and it was all given with moving eagerness.

The young and middle-aged waved flags, shook our hands, danced in the streets, kissed and behaved with enthusiasm and excitement.

A woman walking on her own along a country road clapped her hands continuously and said, 'Merci, merci' all the time our column of 130 vehicles rumbled past her.

Old men wept for joy; old men who had fought their war and won it a quarter of a century previously and had lived through the shame and horror that had come to them when the next generation did not win over again what was really the same war. Outside one house a bearded man in shabby clothes stood rigidly to attention and at the salute while we passed. At a street corner nearby an elderly gentleman stood and solemnly beat a drum as we rolled by. He beat a deadly monotonous tune, but so firmly were his feet set apart, so decided his beat and so fixed his expression that one could see he regarded this as a military duty and he was as conscientious about it as if the whole success of the campaign depended on whether he beat his drum in a dignified manner or not.

In some villages the population brought chairs out of doors and sat on these all day long as different troops drove through. It was indeed for them the occasion of a lifetime. On all faces were such expressions of thankfulness and joy as I had not seen anywhere before. I was confident that they would remember Britain with gratitude for the rest of their lives.

For us also it was unforgettable. All the troops were deeply moved.

Absolute Fury

'D' Company 1/4th KOYLI were ordered to take Ferme d'Elbeuf on the approach to the Forêt de Bretonne. John Longfield wrote of the attack.

First of all three inch mortars put down a short barrage, then we moved into the attack. We had to move out of cover, climb a hedge and cross a field to reach the farm. [John got caught on barbed wire but threw himself across it.] We charged rapidly over the field to arrive at the low wall of the farmyard. Here most of us stopped and started firing from behind the wall but I had jumped over the wall, put my Bren gun down on the brickwork of a Jack and Jill type circular well with a tiled roof and opened fire. The sound echoed back from the depths of the well like a 6 pounder gun. From haystacks in barns in the farmyard, Germans dropped down all over the place. Bullets were flying round in such quantities that I am surprised that anyone survived. As the yard cleared, I fired at Germans crossing the gate to get out at the other end of the farmyard. I was in an absolute fury because they weren't all dropping down. The other fellows had come over the wall and we swept through the farm and out at the other side. Officers were calling us to come back but all the men wanted to do was kill Germans and they only came back when all in sight had been disposed of. We took 8 prisoners and D Coy lost 10 casualties. Heaven knows how many we killed.

Out of the Line – 'Sing our Hearts Away'

'For a change instead of being automatons of destruction we could be human beings again. Normally we would spend a night in delicious sleep after a hard fought battle and arise the following morning when the sun was high in the sky. [The Sherwood Rangers Yeomanry, after their battles during Operation Blackwater, were out of the line near L'Aigle.] We remained there for quite a few days and had a very pleasant time [23 August] playing cricket, football and enjoying the beautiful surroundings in typical summer weather. We would cook our breakfast in the most palatial fashion with long preserved rations, talk a little over our cigarettes, replenish our tanks and do the odd maintenance jobs. Then we would strip naked and wash luxuriously in pails, dixies or petrol tins until we shone like marble. When all was done we would lie in the sun, read, sleep or attack our correspondence. Mail, apart from leave, is the most beneficial tonic a soldier can ever have. I have seen men overwhelmed with joy or nearly in tears when the mail, productive or otherwise, has arrived. We had church services too which always went down well. As the Padre once said, "Every man in a slit trench is a Christian." We felt that life was good. We would barter our tinned rations with the locals for eggs, butter, wine or chickens and cooking our meals was the main item of the day. We had ENSA shows and organized baths. But I felt, and I am sure the men felt too, given good weather and peaceful surroundings, the more they were left to themselves during the day the better. About eight o'clock at night we had a sing-song. Bennett in my troop [Lieutenant Stuart Hills] was an excellent performer on his piano accordian. While the sun fell, we would sit round a fire, drinking our NAAFI ration of beer and whisky, local cider and calvados and sing our hearts away – music is a fine thing for morale.'

'Chocolat? Bon-bons? Cigarettes pour Papa?'

The Flail tanks of the 22nd Dragoons were rarely needed for minefield clearance on the break-out. The German rearguards scattered some mines, which could be cleared by the sappers or Infantry Pioneers. Major W.R. Birt enjoyed his 'Great Sweep' northwards.

Except for the customary troubles of a long march across country with machines as awkward to handle as Flails, it had been a rewarding journey.

Liberation?

There were along the way some terrible areas of devastation – at Lisieux, for example, and Rouen. There was also grim but in some ways gratifying evidence of the rout of the German armies, whose motley processions of tracked vehicles, lorries, and horse-drawn carts had here and there been caught by the cannons and rockets of Allied aircraft and lay tossed in ruin among hedges scorched by fire. But for the most part it was a journey at last through undamaged country, through villages unbelievably free of destruction, past fields and orchards rich with their unspoiled harvests, by lovely half-timbered houses whose roofs were marked by no worse scars than those of their ripe old age. It was, too, a triumphant progress among people whose whole being was seized with happiness and welcome. The flags were out, and the bunting. We were waved through with greetings of flowers, salutes, and kisses. At every stop the cars and tanks were swallowed up by a mass of people eager to shake us by the hand, to embrace us without qualification, to say over and over again: 'It was long coming; it was long coming.' *Welcome!* The word greeted us in the shop windows, in banners strung across the roads, and in the songs of carefree crowds who came out to see us pass. Gratitude showered about us in the shape of apples, pears, tomatoes, cucumbers and chickens. Biscuits and tins of bully were passed back in exchange – and before long the children had got to know in what manner the British armies were supplied; among the voices we heard the soon familiar chant of 'Chocolat? Bon-bons? Cigarettes pour Papa?'

CHAPTER SIX

Operation Neptune and the Great Swan

The RAF had done a magnificent job in the bombing and destruction of all the bridges over the river Seine. Fortunately it meant that very few German tanks, AFVs or trucks had escaped north. It also hindered the Allied armies thrusting north. The Canadians, the 49th Polar Bear Division and 51st Highland Division (the latter with old scores to settle) were responsible for the clearance of the Channel ports, in particular Le Havre. The first priority was to force a bridgehead at Vernon and allow the sappers to build pontoon bridges across. Major General 'Butch' Thomas and the 43rd Wessex Wyverns were responsible for Operation Neptune, a four-day battle at the end of August to cross at Vernon. The Polar Bears had a damaged bridge at Rouen to cross before they could go west to capture Le Havre in Operation Asconia, with 51st Highland investing the port from the north-west coastal sector.

The month of September was a glorious one for the Allies. Paris had fallen to the Americans and the Free French Division. Once across the river Seine the Guards Armoured (lucky devils) thrust for Brussels, the 11th Armoured Division for a five-day battle for Antwerp and the Desert Rats for Ghent. The ambitious, daring, doomed battles of Market Garden were still to come in the middle of the month. Much has been written about the gallant Airborne, little about the determined attempts to relieve them. The end of September saw the Germans cobbling together desperate ramshackle battle groups who fought for parts of Belgium and most of Holland with skilful rearguard actions.

'Not a Bad Day's Work'

'On the last three days of August, we [Lieutenant Stuart Hills and the Sherwood Rangers Yeomanry] travelled 20, 54 and 27 miles respectively, passing through Acos (where we took 35 prisoners), St Remy (which we took after a short battle), Vesty, Les Thaillés Cahagnes, north to Armentières and Savignies. At one stage over open country we were able to adopt the old desert formation and it was a grand sight to see all the tanks going flat out – it almost developed into a steeplechase. Apart from the not very intense opposition we met, it might have been a pre-war motoring tour. Everyone was in high spirits, the weather was fine, in fact life was good. In every village we passed through we received terrific welcomes. Sometimes we were able to halt to receive the fruits of little victories. At others we went through in a cloud of dust, hardly being able to see or hear the cheering bands. On Sept 1st we crossed the Somme at Longpré-les-Argoeuves. We led the whole way, travelled 50 miles and cleared the town of Doullens which was strongly held by the A/Tk guns and pockets of infantry. We had five tanks hit (Sergeant Cribben was killed). "C" Sqn did a left flanking move and shot up a German column at about 5,000 yards range. In Doullens "A" Sqdn knocked out five guns and took over 100 prisoners and overran a flying bomb site. Not a bad day's work.'

'Hang on to Them'

61 Recce Regiment were leading 50th Tyne/Tees Division out of Normandy towards and beyond the Seine. Major Philip Brownrigg relates a macabre story.

They were the most exhilarating days of the campaign. Our task was to protect the left flank of 30 Corps in their armoured dash to the Somme. We were on our own on a virgin route, anything up to 70 miles ahead of Divisional HQ. One beautiful morning we drove 40 miles before breakfast. There were several engagements, some of them quite sharp and we collected an enormous number of prisoners. 'C' Sqn went over a small bridge on the Somme. Here Lieutenant Laing's troop of armoured cars was caught on a long open road by a Panther tank. He ordered his vehicles to put out a smoke screen and *both* the car patrol and the Panther withdrew. Later, Laing moved forward to the next village where his troop took 40 prisoners. It was evening and he had to return to his squadron, so he handed over his prisoners to the French FFI. Laing, a Scot with a strong accent, told the French 'Hang on to them for me. I'll collect them in the morning.'

The French did just that. They hanged the 40 German prisoners and told Laing the next day. 'That's what you told us, wasn't it.'

Operation Neptune

The river Seine at Vernon is over 650 ft wide. It has a high steep escarpment of 300 ft on the north bank and was defended by the battle group Meyer, part of 49th Infantry Division. They were armed with machine guns and plenty of 20 mm dual-purpose Flak guns, but negligible tank support, no Nebelwerfers and no 88 mms. The railway bridge was demolished and the only road bridge had two spans lying in the river. It could be crossed by infantry in single file under fire. Initially everything went wrong. The 5th Wiltshires tried to cross in storm-boats. 'A' Company were almost wiped out as boats were wrecked or stranded but a few DUKWs ferried the rest of the battalion over. The 4th Somersets landed on submerged islands and had two companies marooned. The 1st Worcesters tried to cross the battered road bridge and failed. Eventually the Wyverns built up the northern bridgehead, although 'A' Company 7th Somersets were captured and a company of the 5th Duke of Cornwalls overrun in a dawn counter-attack. It took 500 sappers 28 hours to construct the 40 ton Bailey bridge called 'Goliath'. It spanned 684 ft and was opened to the Armoured Divisions 48 hours after the first assault. Other bridges called, of course, 'Saul' and 'David' were built by 582nd and 583rd RE field companies. In the four-day battle the Wyverns lost 550 casualties but they took 500 German prisoners and killed several hundred. It was a famous Wyvern battle honour.

Stretcher Bearers Killed

'During Operation Neptune "B" Company 1 Worcesters came under very heavy fire from machine guns hidden in the undergrowth on the Vernonnet–la Chapelle St Ouen road. I was in the leading section as we moved up the hill towards our objective. Suddenly a Spandau opened up, I heard a cry behind me, someone had been hit. We went to ground either side of the road. I was hidden from the enemy by a hump in the grass verge. I looked behind me to see Bert Smith lying there wounded and calling for stretcher bearers. Two bearers came ambling up the road in no time, armed only with a stretcher and their Red Cross flag. One couldn't help admiring the way they worked in full view of the enemy, protected only by their Red Cross flag. They lifted Bert onto the stretcher and picked him up. Something happened then which I shall never forget. The German machine gun fired on them killing all three. My best friend Joe Cartwright and another chap were both shot dead right across the road from me. Sergeant Kerrigan was also killed by a MG burst which hit him across the chest and throat.' [Albert Kings]

Operation Astonia

Le Havre, a great ocean port surrounded by water on three sides, was defended by a garrison of 15,000 troops under Colonel Eberhard Wildermuth. They had a whole series of deep inland bunkers harbouring seventy-six field, medium and AA guns. Harfleur, 2 miles from Le Havre, had to be cleared first. The land investiture took time as both the Polar Bears and the Highland Division had to get across the Seine at Rouen. A terrible softening-up period by the Royal Navy and the RAF – for the Fuehrer had, of course, from his Berlin bunker forbidden surrender – now took place. It was a brutal business that killed 5,000 French civilians and did little damage to the garrison sheltering in their bunkers. When Operation Astonia finally took place, on 10–12 September, it was a superbly planned operation with excellent cooperation by infantry with their supporting tanks, 'Funnies' and Flail tanks to clear the minefields, backed by huge artillery barrages. It was a

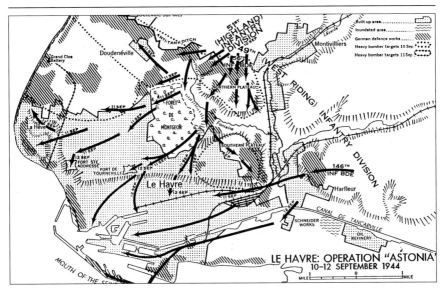

Operation Astonia

text-book attack, *but* the German garrison had few tanks, few 88 mm guns and relatively few Nebelwerfers. The Polar Bears lost 550 casualties but took nearly 8,000 prisoners. The 51st Highland Division, attacking from the north-west, had a similarly successful battle. The huge dock areas had been so badly damaged that shipping could not use Le Havre until 1 November.

'Help Yourselves'

At the battle for Le Havre, 1/5th Gordons attacked through three gaps in the Boche minefield, called Ale, Rum and Gin. 'Meanwhile a lot of prisoners were coming back and it was most encouraging to see that they were being led by their officers. They lined up in front of me [Martin Lindsay]. "There you are," I said to the men who were near me, "the Master Race. Help yourselves." They soon had a fine collection of watches, fountain pens, pocket knives and not a few French francs. Then I put the prisoners on to improving the track. Some of them had our pink leaflets on them. They seemed very good propaganda to me. On one side was printed, "Why die in the last week of the War? You are between two Allied armies and the sea, and your holding out will help no one."'

The Great Swan – 'Heroes of a Different Age'

Rifleman 'Roly' Jefferson's 8th Battalion Rifle Brigade supported 3rd RTR, 23rd Hussars and 2nd Fife and Forfarshire Yeomanry Sherman tanks on the great armoured drive northwards from the River Seine.

At dawn we moved off to cross the Seine at Vernon on a pontoon bridge, courtesy of 43rd Wessex Wyvern Division. The accelerating advance took us through Guiviers, Guitry, Mouflaines and Valmesnil but we were checked by opposition at Etrepagny. After a skirmish we took a lot more prisoners and pressed on to Longchamps. There the village priest, brandishing a pistol, beckoned us towards the church. We found 30 Germans who had given up the fight and made them sit around in the graveyard. But we had to do some house-to-house fighting there. On the 30th we sped through Neufmarché and through the night made a tremendous drive of fifty miles to Conty just short of Amiens. Although early in the morning, the French population came to life and offered us any drinks we wanted. It was a party atmosphere. The French called us all 'Tommy'. We realized we were now in the battlefields of the First War which our fathers had known so well. A common joke was 'Come away from her, she's probably your sister.' At first light we found ourselves sitting astride the approaches to Amiens. [Later on.] The bridges over the River Somme were intact. There was some fighting but nothing like that in Normandy. At times we could hardly move for the frantic cheering crowds who swarmed onto our vehicles and showered us with fruit, flowers, champagne and wine. We were embraced by women, children and old, bearded men with tears of joy streaming unashamedly down their faces. We pushed on again. It was farcical. The celebrating population were holding us up during the day. Another night drive took us through famous First War battlefields of Arras, Loos and Lens. We told ourselves we would soon be re-occupying the trenches which our fathers had so bravely defended in their war. We passed too, numerous huge War Cemeteries. They all looked so neat and tidy, even though under German occupation for four years. We choked back emotion as we contemplated with pride those heroes of a different age. We travelled by day and by night. We passed signposts marked Ypres. As we neared Armentières, we joked about whether we would meet the Mademoiselle made so famous in the First War song. There were signs to Dunkirk too. At least we were avenging the humiliating defeat inflicted by the Germans there.

The Padre's Adventures

Padre Leslie Skinner, with the Sherwood Rangers Yeomanry, had some unusual adventures. On 2 September at Douellens he heard that Sergeant Cribben of Recce Troop had been killed on flank axis $1\frac{1}{2}$ miles away in the village of Flesselles, still held by the Germans. He left his driver and truck, entered the village via ditch and farmyard and made his way to the village parsonage. Sergeant Cribben's tank was still there, 200 yds away near the village churchyard. The wounded had gone. The bodies of Sergeant Cribben and Trooper Sharp were beautifully laid out in the parsonage in white shrouds, having been washed, etc. Graves had been dug in the churchyard under the nose of the Germans. 'I made out name details – saw to correct marking of crosses and gave them to the village curé to place in position after the Germans had gone. Curé worried no coffins ready. Farmer produced some hessian and I stitched the bodies up. Curé in robes led funeral cortege down street to churchyard as I watched from window. The Germans had watched the funeral procession and seen the service 30 yards from their tank, without interference.' Ten days later the padre buried ten SRY across the canal in Stelen parish church and decided to bury another eight in Geel churchyard. 'During these burials as I read service, shells flew over very close. Nobody believed my assurance "Anglais" – not even me! When a shell actually hit the church, the Belgian crowd fled, leaving my driver and me to finish the service. Next shell hit church wall above our heads. We both instinctively dived for cover. Only time in my life I have actually been *in* the grave during service. At time did not seem at all odd – merely sensible. Few moments later service resumed and finished.' Church steeples were inevitably shelled to deter gunner observations officers and/or snipers occupying them. The battle for Geel was the bitterest for SRY since D-Day. Eleven tanks were destroyed and twenty-three SRY KIA.

Moving up by Bounds

'We did not dream that our victory in the Normandy battle was going to pay such a rich dividend that not only towns, or even provinces, but whole countries were about to fall into our hands, and that in a few weeks we would be rejoicing in Brussels. The nature of the advance astonished us. Our wonder grew with every kilometre we travelled, every town we entered, every frontier we crossed.

While we were still at St Pierre, Colonel Turner explained to us [Lieutenant Geoffrey Picot and the 1st Hampshires] the form future operations were likely to take. He said generally the battalion would travel behind an armoured force, and whereas the armour might have to keep going continuously, we would move by bounds, waiting till the tanks had a lead of ten or twenty miles and then travelling that distance in one spell. We would then harbour up and wait possibly a few hours or a few days till the armour had gone twenty miles ahead again, then bound forward to catch them up. The tactical role of the armour was to get moving and keep moving; our tactical duty was to mop up everything they left behind and form a firm base behind them wherever they went.

Our battalion column contained something like 130 vehicles; thus if lorries were forty yards apart we would take up three miles of road. We had to watch the spacing, because if vehicles bunched too closely together they would present a tempting target for the German air force. On the other hand, if they were spread out too much we would occupy a lot of road space and that would make progress slow, as we were just a small part of a great column.

On a typical move an armoured division, with 200 tanks, three battalions of lorry-borne infantry and a vast assortment of other vehicles, would lead, followed by an infantry division of which we were but a ninth part. With ambulances, supply vehicles, repair trucks and lorried equipment for supporting weapons added in, the two divisions would contain thousands of vehicles, so if the infantry were to be anywhere near the armour, and supplies anywhere near either of them, each vehicle would have to keep reasonably close to the one in front of it.

We were frequently warned to expect opposition from the German air force, for as we drove eastwards we would be approaching their bases, but not once did they trouble us. On these long moves from Normandy to Brussels no infantryman footslogged. Speed was essential in pursuing this defeated enemy, so riflemen were bundled into lorries, Bren gun carriers, jeeps, vehicles of all descriptions – but mainly 3-ton TCVs (troop-carrying vehicles) – and driven forward. When fighting was likely to develop they jumped out of their vehicles and ran into battle formation. The scare over, or the battle over, whichever it proved to be, back in again, and press on.'

'Amiens Tonight'

The 11th Armoured Division poured across the river Seine, heading north from Vernon. By 30 August the Inns of Court, followed by 3 RTR/8 RB and 23rd Hussars/4 KSLI, had converged their centre lines at Marseille-en-Beauvais, some 40 miles due south of Amiens. The memoirs of the GOC, Major General 'Pip' Roberts, record the next dramatic move: 'Ike [General Eisenhower] said to Monty, "Amiens tonight." Monty said to 'Bimbo' [Lieutenant General Dempsey] "Amiens tonight." Bimbo said to 'Jorrocks' [Horrocks, 30th Corps Commander], "Amiens tonight" and then the planning started.' It was a bold plan to drive the superb tank force through the night to seize the Somme bridges in Amiens before daylight. 29th Armoured Brigade centre line was from Crevecoeur by the main road to Amiens, and 159th Infantry Brigade (with tank support from the 2nd Fife and Forfarshires and 15/19th Hussars) would take winding country roads through Conty and Taisnil to Amiens. When the General had finished giving his orders it had been a lovely fine warm evening with the moon fullish at 2300. The phrase 'Moonlight tonight' sounded good. In the event the march began in pouring rain in pitch darkness and stayed that way most of the night!

A Night March

Roden Orde, 2nd Household Cavalry Regiment, wrote:

A night march through enemy territory is at the best of times a tense affair. The drivers peer out of visors intent on avoiding falling asleep or landing in the ditch. The armoured car commanders also stare ahead trying to penetrate the gloom for signs of the enemy and checkups on the right route. The operators live in a strange world of their own at the bottom of the turret tormented by crackles and demonic wireless noise while map boards and chinagraph pencils drop on their heads. Gunners grip the trigger mechanism as much for support as anything else for they are almost blind at night. Over everyone the desire for sleep descends in recurrent and overpowering waves.

Normally armoured cars bear a role out of all proportion to their size, as they are the eyes and ears of the Corps Commanders. Advancing usually on a wide front, they constantly report back by wireless to their LO at TAC Corps HQ.

Much credit is due to the Resistance movement. They provided advice about German troops ahead, although it was a sensible rule of thumb to divide their figures by three! They also provided guides, guarded prisoners and bridges and, above all, offered a marvellous reception which was very good for morale. '*Vive les liberateurs. Vive les Anglais.*' Anyone who took part in the liberation from Normandy to Antwerp on the Great Swan will always remember the startling, intoxicating welcome.

Sudlow's Shooting Gallery

Major Noel Bell, 8 RB, tells the story:

Reports came in from civilians that there were approximately 5,000 Germans still in Amiens, and at that early hour and having had no sleep this information shook us a bit. It was now getting light and we could see enemy columns and single vehicles streaming into the city along the roads parallel to our own. After some discussion, negotiation and argument as to who should go first, the leading section [of RB] carriers and the leading troop of tanks [3 RTR] advanced *abreast!*

A series of individual platoon battles then took place with Lieutenant Donald Sudlow and Co destroying lorries, staff cars and sections of infantry with three Bren guns. The action was known as 'Sudlow's Shooting Gallery', with fifty POW and the same number killed or wounded. A bridge was blown in front of 11 Platoon's eyes but the main bridge was saved. Breakfast tasted wonderful that morning and despite our weariness we felt on top of the world.'

Noel Bell's 'G' Company totalled seventy riflemen, but Bill Close's 3 RTR squadron was at half strength with ten Shermans. Resistance men showed the way through the sleeping city. Fortunately, the 2nd Fife and Forfarshire later seized two bridges across the Somme. Noel Bell noticed signs of hardship and privations suffered by the townspeople, and much looting of food stores and dumps followed liberation.

Lucky

Steel Brownlie, Fife and Forfars, recounts: 'Civilians were out in force and one hit me in the face with a bunch of flowers when I was doing 35 mph. *Merci bien!* I found the bridge at last undefended though a few small shells came down. [Later] we harboured in green fields near Coisy [4 miles north]. I was orderly officer which meant sitting all night beside the wireless tank with earphones round the neck. But there was a large rum ration which I supplemented. I was happy, still alive, doing my job, and winning. Lucky.'

It was a Riot

7th Armoured Division swept north from the Seine on the left flank heading for Ghent/Gand. The historian of the Queen's noted the 'flat country where 131 Queen's Brigade had fought 4½ years before, long poplar lined roads, rich farms, orchards, ugly little villages but bright with flags and excited civilians. In May 1940 1/5 and 1/6 Queen's had been part of the BEF rearguard in fighting near Oudenarde.' The Recce Troop of the Skins (5RDG) went through Lens, a scene reported by John Pilborough.

A victory parade where the people thronged the streets, cheering every vehicle that went by. Sweeping south of Lille and Roubaix we drew clear of the drab scenery of slag heaps and crowded dwellings, factories and cheering people and at nightfall [on the 4th] crossed the Belgian frontier at Toufflers [suburbs of Roubaix]. If our reception in Northern France had been enthusiastic, here it became ecstatic. The red, white and blue French flags gave place to the red, yellow and black colours of Belgium. There was hardly a house without one and most cafés and houses had several. There was dancing and music in every café, 'Tipperary' was sung, the black-out was forgotten. It was a riot.

It was a relief to get out of the drab industrial north of France, despite the warmth of the welcome, into the more interesting Belgian Flanders. The advance was north-east parallel to the Schelde/Escaut Canal. General Verney noted, 'Except for one blown bridge at Warcoing we had a clear run through. Our reception in Belgium exceeded even the tremendous scenes we had already experienced in France. It was quite unforgettable and most inspiring.'

Girls, Flowers and Wine

Major Arthur Crickmay, 5 RTR, recalled:

I had arranged a stonk [by 5 RHA] on the road block into Ghent. I remember hearing the shells exploding and also seeing the smoke, just as

Ronnie Morgan came up on the air and said he was in a very difficult position. I couldn't get anything very concrete out of him (he was obviously worried about security) and so I followed him round, rather expecting him to be pinned down with Boche swarming all over his tanks. To my amazement I found him in a built-up area in the middle of a crowd of some hundreds of euphoric Belgians with girls, flowers and wine in about equal proportions.

The Desert Rats eventually rounded up 10,000 Germans in and around Ghent, Oudenarde, Deinze and St Niklaas, all for a total loss of 100 casualties in the period 4–8 September.

The Laws of War – 'A Party of Trippers'

After taking Ghent, the Desert Rats were faced by a wide canal. Private Rex Wingfield, 1/6th Queen's, was sent out on patrol to search the barges. 'The day was still but the green woods twenty yards away on the other side of the canal seemed full of the menace of the unknown.' After several adventures,

We put our tails between our legs and slunk back to Bn HQ. We moved to a truck for tea laced with rum, then reaction set in. We realised what we had just done. We had forgotten most of the caution patiently taught us in training. There wasn't a rule for survival we hadn't broken. First, we had sauntered across 400 yards of open country like a party of trippers. Next I had risked the patrol by sticking my neck out in a mad dash on a towpath. Finally, we had missed two sitting ducks [enemy] at twenty to thirty yards. Our retreat through the woods had been slightly more professional and certainly more noisy than a herd of eccentric elephants.

By all the laws of war we should be dead ducks. But we had got away with it. We thought of what might and should have been. We shivered. We shook. We shuddered. Our teeth chattered. We were bathed in sweat. A large dose of neat rum brought back the warmth to our chilled bodies.

Liberation – 'Hot Pancakes'

'As we rumbled on our way through town after town, the people cheered until [on the way to Lille] they hadn't the strength to even ask for cigarettes. I [Sergeant Bob Sheldrake] have noticed it so many times. The tanks nose their way through a town while the civilians hide in their cellars. The infantry bearing the brunt as always, pass through to nothing more than a sniper's bullet, but by the time the guns go through, the civilians have left their holes to cheer them on their way.' Of course there is a rule of thumb – 'B' Echelon always seem to have plenty of cigarettes and chocolate and tins of food to hand out than the hard-pushed Tankies and PBI. But across the border in Belgium, the Suffolk Yeomanry on their way to Liege noticed the change in the colour of the liberation flags. 'The crowds cheered and laughed just the same. They sang and rode with us and fell off and they didn't care. In one town when I was riding in the carrier, they showered us with boxes of matches, in another we had ice-cream; yet another provided hot chips, all handed to us as we slowed down in the towns. We never made a halt except in the open country. One good lady, as the gun-quads changed down and finally stood panting on the road outside her house, rushed out with a plate piled high with hot pancakes and fed the dusty but happy troops [of 49th Polar Bear Division].'

The Taking of Brussels

Lieutenant General Brian Horrocks ordered the Guards Armoured Division to take Brussels. 11th Armoured and 7th Armoured Divisions muttered oaths to themselves. 'Lucky so-and-sos, trust the Guards to get to the delights and fleshpots of the capital whilst we have to slog away to Antwerp and Ghent,' or words to that effect. The Welsh Guards group of Shermans and infantry advanced on the right flank, starting from Douai on 3 September to try to beat the Grenadier battle group on the left flank. The Household Cavalry armoured cars led the Welsh Guards into the Grand Place on the evening of the 3rd, having covered 70 miles that day. At Point à Marcq the Grenadiers had a stiff fight and the King's Company suffered fifty-three casualties. Brigadier G. Watkins' 5th Guards Brigade guarded the Royal Palace of Laeken, still inhabited by the Queen Mother. The Guards had a magnificent welcome which went on for days – wine, women and song, and all that. General Horrocks quite rightly ensured that Brigadier Piron's Belgian Brigade, composed of Belgians who had fled to Britain and had been trained and equipped by the British Army, escorted him in the triumphal entry into *their* capital. On 7 September the Guards Armoured Division was in action again as the spearhead of the 'Garden' part of 'Market Garden' to seize the Meuse–Escaut Canal en route for Nijmegen and Arnhem.

'Only Two Black Eyes and One Broken Nose'

Sea-girt British islanders, unconquered for nine centuries, may find it difficult to comprehend the sheer ecstatic, passionate welcome that their 2nd Army received in those exhilarating four weeks during the break-out from Normandy in August 1944. Three countries had suffered – for four years – a wicked, savage, repressive regime of Nazi rule. And suddenly, sometimes in a matter of minutes, hours, occasionally days, young khaki-clad soldiers brandishing ferocious weapons would carefully and methodically clear out – like professional rat-catchers – the enemy within.

We left St Romain after the capture of Le Havre, on the 19th for the

Dutch–Belgian frontier. The whole route was lined as far as the population would permit with wildly cheering people. Fruit, tomatoes and flowers were hurled into car vehicles as we passed. We were fortunate in reaching Nijlen after three long days travelling under these ideal circumstances with only two black eyes and one broken nose in the [Hallamshire] battalion. The reception in Belgium was even more enthusiastic than that in France. We moved from Nijlen via Lierre to Oostmalle in MT. The whole city turned out to wish us God speed, and our vehicles were liberally covered in fruit and flowers. The whole route beyond was thronged with cheering waving people, many with tears of thankfulness running down their cheeks. It was a very moving experience and seemed more suitable for a Victory March than a prelude to battle. [Lieutenant Colonel Hart Dyke]

The Belgians sang 'Tipperary'

The British Army was back in Belgium again, as Lieutenant Geoffrey Picot, 1st Hampshires, recalls:

In 1940 children politely threw flowers of welcome at the soldiers. In 1944 the country was absolutely delirious with joy. Four years had made a difference. One could quickly detect a dissimilarity between the French reaction and the Belgian reaction. The French sang the 'Marseillaise', the Belgians 'Tipperary'. The French shouted: 'We are free', the Belgians, 'Welcome to our liberators'. When we were in France we did not consider the French attitude to be lacking in gratitude or profuseness. We thought the people were as warm-hearted as they could be. We could not imagine a better reception. It was only when we reached Belgium and were actually accorded an even more rapturous welcome that we thought of the difference between the two countries.

I looked closely at the people who lined the route here, as I had in France, because I always wanted to see what men and women looked like after four years of German occupation. At this time my parents and my sister were in German-occupied Jersey, and I was relieved to find that the man in the street did not look disastrously ill or under-fed. A little thin, yes, and very eager for a square meal, but their hardships did not seem to have been so severe as to cause permanent harm.

The citizen army was greatly in evidence. One saw small groups of them everywhere, with British Sten guns over their shoulders. I suppose this was the first time they had been able to show themselves in public and they seemed very eager to be in the forefront. They obtained many prisoners. Some they ferreted out themselves, others were given to them by British troops. And as every truckload of prisoners was driven through the villages the inhabitants turned out to hiss and boo those who had caused them so much grief. The Germans showed great reluctance to surrender to the patriot army because they knew what to expect from those they had ill-treated. They more easily gave themselves up to us, probably hoping for kinder treatment.

The Taking of Antwerp – 4–7 September

The defence of the vital city and inland port of Antwerp was entrusted to 15,000 troops, modestly equipped and of poor quality under Major General Graf Stolberg-zu-Stolberg. General Horrocks ordered 11th Armoured Division to seize the Antwerp docks – a huge area of 1,000 acres – before the Germans could carry out large-scale demolitions. No one realized that the river Scheldt was heavily mined and thus would render the port of Antwerp unusable for many months. During the four days needed to subdue the city's defenders and force a bridgehead over the key canal, General Schwabe, commanding the German 5th Army, managed to evacuate 65,000 men from eight battered divisions to the relative safety of the Siegfried line. Maps of the city were poor. General 'Pip' Roberts ordered 4 KSLI plus 'C' Squadron 2nd Fife and Forfar tanks to capture the Central Park garrison HQ with its network of bunkers, while 3 RTR plus 'G' Company 8 RB would seize the main dock area, with the 3rd Monmouths following up. These accounts by members of the famous Black Bull Division show some of the difficulties of storming a large defended city.

Everyone had gone Mad

'4th September. As we arrived at the city itself [Major Noel Bell and 8 RB] shots rang out, Germans began throwing grenades on to us from a window of a high building near us, 20 mm guns opened up and we knew we should have to fight for it. The main streets were densely packed with crowds awaiting us. Our vehicles were unable to move and were smothered with people; we were overwhelmed by flowers, bottles and kisses. Everyone had gone mad. We had to get to the docks at all costs to save them from being destroyed by the Germans who might now be getting organized. [But the riflemen in their carriers were separated from the tanks by the immense crowds.] We then came under fire from the far bank of the Scheldt at the same time as we were engaged in two different street battles on the near side. I began to wonder whether we should ever see the tanks again. It was difficult to describe over the wireless exactly where we were.'

Snipers Everywhere

Eventually 3 RTR arrived, running a gauntlet of German bazooka fire. There were snipers everywhere, as Bill Close, 3 RTR, wrote: 'I found myself crouching in the turret looking for the source of the bullets pinging about, while pretty girls waved madly from blocks of flats pointing out the enemy positions.' John

Dunlop's 'C' Squadron went for the docks with 8 RB and Bill Close took his squadron to Antwerp-South railway station. The White Brigade resistance fighters conducted their own private wars, often vendettas, settling old scores with the Germans or collaborators. The Shermans were pelted with fruit and flowers and every head exposed was offered a glass of cognac or champagne, plus cigars. John Dunlop led 3 RTR to the docks. He had stayed in Antwerp before and spoke French and enough Flemish to get by:

> We never closed the lids of our turrets, because we then became so blind and so deaf that we felt too vulnerable. We felt a lot safer with them open. But that afternoon I remember seriously considering closing them down. Sporadic firing from above [from Germans at the upper windows of houses] was confined to the outskirts of the town and later rather more kept on meeting bursts of small arms fire and an occasional grenade and there were civilian casualties.

Lieutenant Gibson Stubbs' troop sank a small steamer full of Germans in the River Scheldt. He fired AP at 1,000 yards and the boat went aground enveloped in steam.

A Difficult 'O' Group

Colonel Ivor Rees, CO 4 KSLI, described part of his 'O' group given out at 1500 on the outskirts of Antwerp on the Boom road:

> The difficulties of collecting one's 'Order Group', thinking and giving out orders, making oneself heard, linking various sub-units together among this mass of the populace crowding round, still kissing you, asking you to post a letter to America, to give them some petrol, some more arms for the White Brigade, holding a baby under your nose to be kissed, trying to give you a drink, inviting you to their house, trying to carry you away, offering information about the enemy, had to be seen to be understood, and were the same, but about three times as great, as in Amiens. In addition Brigadier [Churcher] would say at intervals: 'I want you to be as quick as possible.'

4 KSLI next marched 2 miles in a straight line from the Boomse–Meenweg roundabout towards the Central Park, cheered on by hordes of well-wishers thronging the tightly packed pavements. The large triangular park, each side about ¹/₂ mile long, was covered with bushes and tall trees and was overlooked by high buildings. Three substantial bunkers screened by thick shrubs sheltered the main German HQ. A large lake was another obstacle and snipers on the rooftops a distinct menace. A very professional little battle followed with 4 KSLI and 3 RTR combining well. General Stolberg and 2,000 prisoners were captured by the end of the first

day. 'It was unrestrained joy – mad and crazy. No war can have been more crazy,' Captain Spence, Ayrshire Yeomanry FOO, wrote. 'That night was chaotic. Café parties went on until dawn. Snipers fired and were hunted down by the Resistance.'

The Fair Ladies of Antwerp

Major Joe How, 3rd Monmouths, noted on 5 September: 'Even at this early hour [0600] the people of Antwerp thronged into the roadway to greet the advancing troops as they made their way in long files on either side of the road. Fair ladies of Antwerp showing signs of having been hurriedly disturbed from their slumbers, pressed bunches of flowers on the soldiers who, not wishing to appear ungrateful by throwing them into the gutter, continued on their way with bouquets in one hand and their firearms in the other.'

At 0900 on 5 September General 'Pip' received an unpleasant shock. The main bridge over the Albert Canal had been blown up. 'This was a blow to me and I realized that I had made a great error in not going into the city the evening before. I had thought that the canal went through the centre of the city.'

The Albert Canal Bridgehead

Colonel Ivor Reeves, CO 4 KSLI, described his bridgehead at dawn on 6 September:

> We found ourselves in the most ghastly factory area, one mass of small streets, passages, walls, walls within walls, piles of iron and waste of every description. We soon discovered some machine-gun posts and started to clear them. That started two days and a night's street fighting, the most tiring and trying type of fighting even under the best conditions. The Boche found us and soon [1100] had five tanks among us. We knocked out two and then ran out of all PIAT anti-tank arms. They shot us up with machine guns, AP shot and HE, knowing we couldn't touch them, stalking round and round day and night, blasting us out of houses as they discovered us.

The three companies were trapped without food in a factory area, 150 yds square. A section of 'C' Company was forced out of a burning building into the gardens and thirteen of the KSLI were taken prisoner. Colonel Reeves noted: 'We were surrounded by snipers and counter-attacks by up to two battalions of SS infantry. The Boche put down mortars, 88s and 155s, his heaviest field gun.' Eventually, the next day the KSLI was withdrawn across the canal, having suffered 150 casualties. But the proud city of Antwerp had been captured.

'German Medics in Uniform' – The Sapper's Story

Lieutenant Jim Kuipers was a Sapper officer with 612 Field Squadron RE (11th Armoured Division). He recounts:

In the early morning of 5th September 44 I was in a narrow street in Antwerp returning to my halftrack. Jerry stonking started and was very close to the truck in which my wireless-ops Hibbert and Harris were operating. In manoeuvring the vehicle out of range, a mortar landed too close and my left arm was riddled with small fragments – I fainted and must have been taken to RAP whereupon my CRE and OC arrived – I couldn't move my arm. Field hospitals had not caught up with the advance and I was shipped to a Brussels hospital and lay next to an American who had lost a leg at Mortain – he was in a bad way poor chap. The hospital was still manned by German medics in uniform: I was flown out to a civil hospital at Leicester and recovered fully in three weeks with the help of a pretty nurse! After home leave I was posted to a training camp near Maidstone – I hated it and wrote to 11 AD CRE – Colonel Galloway – to get me back – it worked and I rejoined the unit in Horst, Holland in December – never was I so glad to see my troop. Later wounded in the hand at Stolzenau in a Luftwaffe ground strafe. Having learned my lesson I kept a low profile from there on.

CHAPTER SEVEN

Operation Garden

Monty had persuaded General Eisenhower, the Supreme Commander, to allow him a daring grand-slam operation to seize crossings over the river Maas, the Waal and the Neder Rijn. The 1st Airborne Division had had sixteen possible dropping operations called off, and were raring to go under their new commander, Major General R.E. Urquhart. His Corps Commander, Lieutenant General 'Boy' Browning, had told him that the opposition in the Arnhem area would not be more than a brigade group with a few tanks. An intelligence officer at SHAEF reported that 9th and 10th SS Panzer divisions were re-equipping in the area. However, an earlier plan, 'Comet', had planned the identical operation that is in the history books as 'Market Garden'. This chapter deals with some incidents in Operation Market Garden in which practically the whole of the British 2nd Army were involved in a series of armour/infantry dashes to cross the Meuse–Escaut canal held by General Reinhard's 88th Corps and General Lieutenant Sievers 719th Infantry Division. XXX Corps in the centre (Guards Armoured, 50th Tyne/Tees and 43rd Wessex plus 8th Armoured Brigade) would advance due north to Valkenswaard, on to Eindhoven, then link up with the dropping zone of 101st US Airborne Division. The last two key laps were still due north to Zon and Uden, to the bridge at Grave, then link up with the dropping zone of 82nd US Airborne Division and jointly take and hold Nijmegen and its vital bridge. The last and most difficult task was to head due north to link up with the 1st Airborne Division drop at Arnhem bridge and town. The main problems were that 10th SS Panzer Division *was* concentrated on the so-called 'island' around Nijmegen and that 9th SS Panzer Division *was* concentrated north of Arnhem. The next major problem was that XXX Corps had to cover 64 miles to get to Arnhem on a very narrow front the width of Club Route highway. In the event this narrow centre line was frequently cut by General Chill's 85th Division retreating eastwards from the Antwerp area.

Guarding the left flank was XII Corps with 7th Armoured Division, 15th Scottish Division and 53rd Welsh Division. On the right flank, open to the substantial German forces gathered along the Siegfried line, was VIII Corps with the 11th Armoured Division and 3rd Iron Sides Division. On 17 September Lieutenant General Horrocks unleashed the Guards Armoured Division with the usual huge barrage and excellent Typhoon support and by evening Valkenswaard had been taken. During the day the air armada with its 30,000 Airborne troops were seen in the skies by the ground troops. On the next day contact was made with some of the 101st US Airborne troops and by 1000 hours on the 19th the Grenadier Guards group made contact with 82nd US Airborne who had captured the large bridge at Grave. Savage fighting took place in Nijmegen by the Guards and American Airborne troops. Nijmegen was taken with its bridges intact by the evening of the 21st. Monty had optimistically told General 'Boy' Browning that XXX Corps would be at the vital Arnhem bridge, 'Two days, they'll be up with you then.' On the morning of the 22nd, Household Cavalry armoured cars joined up with the Polish 1st Parachute Brigade, south of the Neder Rijn near Driel. Fighting for every inch, the 43rd Wessex Wyverns fought their way north of Nijmegen and put a doomed battalion over the river to join the Airborne troops, but could do no more. Operation Berlin on 25 September was the end of the battle for Arnhem as 2,163 Airborne, 160 Poles and 75 Dorsets were rescued.

Centre-line Battles

One account of the many desperate little actions to keep the centre lines open between Eindhoven and the river Maas to the north was given by Rex Wingfield, 1/6th Queen's Regiment, 7th Armoured Division:

> Next morning one Regt of tanks and an Inf Bn was left to hold our gains. The rest of us mounted on Cromwells turned back to clear the roads. We soon found the targets of last night's firing – ten gutted RASC lorries, one blasted to fragments. That had been the ammo truck. Two hundred yards further down the road was a roadblock of logs. By it lay another burnt lorry and four blackened bodies. A clatter of tracer bounced and sang off the tank as a Spandau opened fire from the roadblock. Cordite fumes blasted from our tank gun into our faces. A sixpounder shell hit right in the middle of the logs. The beams sailed upwards. A field grey rag doll jerked high into the air. We burst through, firing Stens and heaving grenades into the back of the smoking roadblock. The performance was repeated three times in four miles and then we pulled into the relief column. Each morning we had to clear the roads in front and behind before we could move on. Guards Armoured tried to smash through beyond Nijmegen to Arnhem to reach the poor devils. Only one road could be used as the surrounding land was either too soft or under water. One road they had. That road was zeroed exactly by 88s. As soon as a tank poked its snout beyond a building, it was hit. We tried to use the ground on the lee side of the embanked road. The tanks bogged down and churned themselves into a hopeless mess.

The Rifleman's Journal

'Our task as [11th Armoured] Division was to protect the right flank of Guards Division throughout the expected advance to Arnhem. On Sept 8th we [Roland Jefferson and 'E' Company 8 RB] followed the Guards centre line through Mechelen, Haecht, Rotsleer, Aarschot, Montaine and Diest. Our company stayed the night two miles from Beringen where we met up with Princess Irene's Netherlands Regt. We branched right through Helchteren and Sonnis. Stunned and cringing Germans gave themselves up having taken their toll of us with casualties. One RB section took up position near a haystack, after ejecting two Germans. During the night groans could be heard from a concealed trench. A most indignant pig emerged!'

1st Suffolk Liberate Weert

On the morning of the 21st 8th Brigade of 3rd Division crossed over the Dutch frontier and occupied Weert with the 1st Suffolk leading, followed by the East Yorks and 76th Field Regiment RA. Major Claxton led 'D' Company across the Dutch border at 1230; it was a desolate area of sand, scrub and fir plantations and they were met by heavy Spandau fire as they approached the railway from the dune. Shielded by smoke from their own 3 in mortars they pressed on, but at 2200 heard explosions east and southeast as the canal bridges and ammo dumps were blown. Lieutenant Colonel Craddock kept going across the sandy wastes of Boshover Heide and by 0315 on the 22nd had reached the Weert canal. In Weert itself the streets were soon decked with orange flags and be-ribboned portraits of Queen Wilhelmina, Princess Juliana and Prince Bernhard. They sang a shrill nursery song rather like 'Aye, aye, ippy, ippy aye'. The Dutch newspapers rebuked the kids for asking 'Tommy' for cigarettes and chocolates: 'Remember your manners, Dutch children don't scrounge,' and schoolmasters taught children how to sing a well-rehearsed 'God Save the King'. Windmills received new coats of paint in honour of the liberation, with red, white and blue sails and a strong splash of orange on the base of the mill. Little girls wore orange frocks or pinafores, and little boys wore orange shirts. Even the monks and nuns wore orange 'favours' to show loyalty to the royal family. The embarrassed Jocks danced on the village green.

The Belgian and Dutch resistance movements were invaluable. Besides beating up and arresting suspected collaborators, they telephoned around the countryside, finding out and reporting back the local German troop dispositions. And they rounded up German stragglers. Their courage over the last few years was indisputable; the underground movement had sheltered Allied airmen shot down over their country and devised intricate escape systems.

Harry's Ambush

The 5th Battalion Duke of Cornwalls had just made contact with the Polish Airborne Brigade. Major Harry Parker was leading 'A' Company's group of vehicles in his jeep, reached the De Hoof crossroads and suddenly encountered a tank column coming from Elst. He had passed the first tank before he saw their black cross and realized they were Germans. He drove flat out to Driel to organize an ambush. CSM Philp DCM said: 'We could not stop but charged on hoping to get through. The first two tanks pulled over to the right of the road. I was sitting on the top of the carrier with a Sten so I immediately gave the tank commander in his turret a burst and he slithered inside. The German tank opened up with two MGs. One fired too low, the other too high, so we baled out in a ditch containing mud and reeds and observed five Tiger Tanks on the road above us and a dozen infantry a 100 yards away.' Meanwhile, Major Harry Parker borrowed a number of PIATs and 75 type anti-tank mines and returned to lay his ambush.

I gave orders for complete silence. PIATs to be fired in a volley of three when given the order. No firing to take place until the leading tank had hit the mines laid across the road. We now heard the Tiger tanks shooting up 'B' Coy. We heard the tanks returning headed by a DR. He blew up. The leading tank was firing Verey lights to light the way every 30 seconds. It was fairly obvious that they were windy. There were five tanks. As the first tank reached the 75 mines, I gave orders for groups two and three to fire. There was a tremendous explosion and six PIAT bombs hit the tank. This put him completely out of action. The next tank hit the mines and received the same treatment. The third tank tried to back out but hit a string of mines behind it and came to a halt and was knocked out by Private Brown with his PIAT. The remaining two tanks ditched themselves in panic. The crews fled and CSM Philp dropped grenades down their turrets.

The Forlorn Hope – 'Chucked Away'

There is little doubt that the 4th Battalion Dorsets were sacrificed in order to make a token beachhead over the Neder Rijn. What the remnants of 1st Airborne Division needed was a complete relief armoured division across the river to do battle with 9th and 10th SS Panzer. An infantry battalion was indeed useless – a forlorn hope. Major James Grafton, 2 i/c 4th Dorsets, was told, 'I'm afraid we're being chucked away.' Captain 'Henry' Hall was 2 i/c of 'C' Company: 'My job was to supervise the loading of our company boats [for the crossing]. By the time when I should have crossed, there were no boats at all left for our Bn. They had all been sunk or swept away by the current. The enemy were firing mortars and 88 mm guns into the river as well as on the banks and machine guns everywhere.' On the night of the 24/25th at 2130 the Dorsets were under murderous fire. Major Mike Whittle of 'B' Company was with 'A' Company to lead the first flight of assault boats.

Two of the ten boats in my Coy group were holed badly before reaching the far bank. A strong current swept my two leading boats rapidly westwards where the factory 400 yds downstream was ablaze. We were beautifully silhouetted. By using spades as well as inadequate paddles we eventually landed near the factory, but only two more boatloads joined us. Two had sunk, three were holed and one swept away. On-the-spot strength was two officers [Whittle and Macdermott] and less than 30 ORs. We started an assault up a steep bank. The enemy were well dug in, rolled grenades down on us. We occupied the top with 15 men and were joined by the CO [Lieutenant Colonel Tilley] and Major Roper with about 20 men of 'C' Coy. They set out to the right to try to contact 'A' Coy and ran into opposition immediately. The CO's party advanced up wooded slopes, were soon surrounded and forced to surrender.

The Dorsets had 200 casualties killed, wounded or taken prisoners. In Operation Berlin, the rescue plan, another seventy-five Dorsets returned. It was a disaster.

'Blundered on through Shit, Shot and Shell'

The 4th Battalion Dorsets were ordered to make a bridgehead across the Neder Rijn. Private N.L. Francis of 'C' Company recalled:

We came under shell fire from Jerry SP (large gun on tank chassis). We abandoned our vehicles, dived into ditches at road side. Shell fire was frightening. Like express trains coming at you. We sheltered behind tufts of grass. When it slackened off, amusing to see Cooper, a big lad, with his not inconsiderable arse stuck in the air. Proceeded in DUKWs at full alert. We blacked up, issued extra ammo. Sergeant Abberley arrived with whisky and rum. Davies and I had a sip of whisky. He asked me to go and see his mother if anything happened to him, promised to do the same for me. Prepared ourselves in battle order, pack, pouches, gas mask, gas cape, entrenching tool, water bottle, bayonet, steel helmet, rifle, 2 bandoliers of 100 rounds of .303 ammo. Spare Bren gun mags, grenades and pick or shovel down the back of your pack. I got a pick as No. 2 on 2 in mortars and had two containers of bombs to carry, not much compared to WW1 lads but enough to stop record attempts on 4 minute mile. NCOs like mother hens. 'Keep up lads, close up, lads.' Original fear of going into action was subsiding, very cold and cheesed off. At start point allocated canvas boats. Follow white tapes down to the river, all hell let loose. First our guns to the rear of us, then heavy MG firing tracer, parachute flares which illuminated the scene. Jerry joined in and we just blundered on through shit, shot and shell while both sides attempted to outdo each other. Took what cover we could behind canvas boat until urged on; came to river, launched the boat, balanced flat bottomed craft as best we could, paddled with rifles, spades and hands. If we had gone into the river we would have had no chance with all the impedimenta we carried.

'God! Those Eyes!'

A few days later, Rex Wingfield, 1/6th Queen's, met the Dorsets of 43rd Wessex retreating from the Arnhem pocket. 'A shuffling column of men came down the road. We rushed to greet them. We shook their hands. They were dirty faces, grimy, unshaven. God! Those eyes! Glazed, ever moving, twitching, not seeing, staring south, ever south. We lit cigarettes and passed them out.'

CHAPTER EIGHT

Long Hard Winter – the Maas and Peel Country

The Island – 'Water, Water Everywhere'

Rex Flower of 1/4th KOYLI describes the winter battlefield between Arnhem and Nijmegen which the British Army garrisoned for the winter of 1944/5.

We passed over the Grave bridge, a long one over the river Maas captured by American 'Paras' of 82 US Airborne Div. We arrived at Nijmegen and went over the famous bridge captured by the Guards Armoured Division and American Paras. We veered to the right at the other side passing the wrecked 88 mm gun to the straggling village of Ressen. Just up the river a few miles, the mighty Rhine splits into two. One branch, the Waal, flows past Nijmegen then joins the Maas at Hollandsch Diep near Klundert. The other branch flows past Arnhem to the sea. It was water, water everywhere and it got worse before it got better. We shared the 'Island' with the enemy. I expect he hated it as much as we did. It was going to be a wet, cold and later icy and snowy winter. The river was in flood: it has huge banks and the water was well above the level of the surrounding countryside. A fearsome sight!

The 49th Polar Bear Division were later christened the 'Nijmegen Home Guard'.

'Danger of Leadership'

'We were fortunate to have so many men with the stuff of leadership in them. They were like rafts to which all the rest clung for support. It was these men, the pre-war territorial nucleus of our Bn – the Hallamshires – who provided the Warrant and Non-Commissioned Officers with the exception of course of the officers. It was they who suffered the most casualties. [CSM McKay of 'B' Company had just been wounded in the foot and had to have it amputated.] It was now getting most difficult to find men to accept the added responsibility and danger of leadership. There was little to offer in return for what one asked of them. Rank and money meant little these days. A dozen times they had escaped improbably. Long ago the few surviving men in the rifle companies had been bound to realize the odds against their remaining unharmed. But the honour and good name of the battalion meant much to them. After our reception in France and Belgium [Holland was still to come] it was no longer necessary to point out that ours was a crusade to free Europe from the yoke of tyranny. We only received young, inexperienced men as reinforcements and it took some time before they absorbed the spirit of the battalion. To make matters more difficult the reinforcement camps seemed to take a delight in holding up the return of our sick and wounded to us, often posting them to other units and sending us men from any Regiment in the army.

'More than one old Hallamshire absented himself [from the RHU] and jumped a lorry in order to get back to his old battalion. However, after six months of campaigning this was getting righted and it gave one a thrill to see the smiling faces of the old brigade among each batch of reinforcements. Towards the end of the campaign they became almost our sole source of supply of leaders.' [Lieutenant Colonel Hart Dyke, Hallamshires, 49th Division].

'Looking for a Fight. He Got One'

The 2nd Fife and Forfar Yeomanry Sherman tanks had an extraordinary action between Helchteren and Hechtel on 10 September as Lieutenant Steel Brownlie related:

My troop in a sort of side-show fought a most unorthodox action. 'C' Sqn was fired on from the area of the railway right of the road. We deployed and dropped the infantry ['C' Company 1st Herefords, 11th Armoured Division] who took cover. The fire was coming from hummocks half right. I fired at a Spandau position and some Germans got up and ran for it. It was sandy heath with heathery dunes, except for some low-lying bits where we might get bogged. There were a dozen Germans running, 800 yards away. I halted and was leaning out of the turret giving orders to the gunner, Buchanan, when suddenly the tank was spattered with bullets. I ducked down sharpish. We were in the middle of a large area of dug-in Germans firing at us from all sides with small arms and Panzerfausts. What to do? I had two other tanks with me. My Corporal Vallance having had a new idler fitted was just coming up. I was told [on the radio] that Major David Voller was on his way. Maybe he was just looking for a fight. He got one. I gave the order that we should keep moving among the enemy positions, never halt, run over trenches, fire at all possible targets. It seemed to work. Soon there were some 40 Germans out of their holes with their hands up. Easy! I got out to disarm them. David Voller and I were herding them when he was hit in the neck. I hurriedly remounted and resumed the previous tactics. There were far more enemy than we had supposed in a honeycomb of dugouts. They kept appearing and disappearing as we drove round and round flat out. We shot them, crushed them, blew them out of their holes. As soon as we passed, others popped up and let fly at us. They seemed to be everywhere. Voller was taken away in his tank. Corporal Vallance's tank was hit in the track by a Panzerfaust and had to limp away. I took one on the side which blew off the pick and shovel. Corporal Croney was shot and wounded. The tank withdrew. A grenade was lobbed into Corporal Barlow's turret. He and all his crew were badly wounded. I kept cruising about on my own, targets appearing all the time. The heather was burning. When the Herefords arrived and cleared the area, 400 German paratroopers were disarmed and herded by the railway line.

Education – 'One Bullet equals One Life'

When Rex Wingfield joined the 1/6th Queen's, an old sweat called Joe gave him practical advice.

After breakfast I sat cleaning my rifle. Joe brought my webbing equipment over and emptied my pouches. A Bren magazine, grenades and cartridge clips poured out. 'That's the Drillbook way. Now look at mine.' His pouches were further from the buckle than mine. 'You can crawl more comfortably without them sticking in your guts. Not too far round, or they'll interfere with your arm movements. Ammo is in the right pouch as I'm right-handed. Fags are essential but not a matter of life and death so they go in the left-hand pouch. The Bren mag goes in a box with the gun so they are not scattered about in a hot spot.' He took the two 36 grenades, safety pins firmly splayed out and clipped them by the safety lever to his belt by his right buttock. 'If I'm lying down or standing up, I can get at them easily.' The corner of his pocket was stitched to the back of his leg, drawing the whole leg round to the rear. The pocket contained more ammo clips. The map pocket on his left thigh was full of letters. The field dressing pocket was empty. The dressing was tucked inside his blouse. In the blouse pockets were his 'eating irons', cigarette-case and more ammo clips. 'May stop a bullet and easy to get at.' Joe kept his rifle loaded with the full clips of five, plus one up the spout with the safety catch on. 'You've now got one more in there than a sniper may think you have, and one bullet equals one life. When recharging you're the perfect target.' Joe took me outside to a TCV [Troop Carrying Vehicle], showed me how to use the side and top bars to swing over the side and back. We practised from all the seats in the truck. 'Then tank riding. Sit between the turret and the exhaust on the Cromwell. Too close to the turret and radio static would blot out the noise of shell or mortar bombs "incoming". Shells burst up and out, so be low down in the middle of the tank.'

The Fife and Forfars' Battle at Asten – 'A Bold, Desperate Plan'

The Willems canal was a formidable water obstacle. 'A' Company of the 1st Herefords had got across on 21 September to make a bridgehead while 11th Armoured Division sappers started to build a Bailey bridge. The opposition guarding the Zomeren/Asten area were Assault Engineers, good fighters. A bold plan was hatched, as Lieutenant Steel Brownlie relates:

Assuming that the bridge was ready in the morning, our Squadron was to charge across through the enemy positions, *on a one-tank front* and make for Asten a mile or so beyond. There we would fan out by troops, cover the approaches to prevent more enemy coming through and hindering the second wave of the attack, i.e. the rest of the regiment and our infantry [4 KSLI]. It was a bold, desperate plan. If anything halted us beyond the bridge, the entire Squadron would be sitting immobile in line ahead among the enemy defences. We would have been finished off at leisure. Don Bulley would lead with his three tanks then my 4 Troop with my three infantry carriers, then Pinkie's [Hutchison] Squadron HQ, plus three more carriers, then Jimmy Samson's Troop. Whilst still dark, we lined up on the road and waited. A stream of wounded infantry and stretcher bearers slowly passed back to safety. The Herefords had had a rough night and the sappers building the bridge had lost half their number. Under a barrage of medium and 25-pdr guns, we motored over the bridge, through the cluster of houses. Don had got 50 yards beyond the last house when his tank disappeared in a cloud of smoke and flames. His second tank swerved and stuck fast in the ditch. His third tank went to the left, also stuck. All I could see ahead was smoke and dust. There was a tremendous crash but the tank kept moving. There were enemy infantry all over the place, so I kept the guns firing and threw grenades out of the turret at random. Half-way up the road to Asten, I looked over my shoulder. Nobody was following so we went into Asten flat out, hard left at the church to the edge of the village looking north . . . the rest of my troop came up fast with two of the infantry carriers [Don Bulley was bleeding to death in his tank. His crew kept the Germans at bay with pistols]. Suddenly on my left front a company of German infantry emerged in open order, across the fields parallel to the canal. Corporal Vallance and I opened fire with all we had – two 75 mm guns and four Browning MGs. After five minutes, white flags were seen. Stop firing. There were 60 dead in the fields and 37 prisoners.

Retribution

The Jewish New Year in 1944 fell on 23 September. Trooper Tony Matza, 2 Troop 'A' Squadron of the dashing 23rd Hussars, was, much to his surprise, summoned by his CO, who told him he would be LOB that day. Being left out of battle meant, Tony thought, a quiet cushy day back at RHQ, making his peace with his Maker, etc. It did not quite turn out like that. For a start it rained heavily and Tony stayed in his Sherman tank contemplating. When it stopped raining he started to get out of the tank turret when a sudden enemy mortar stonk landed on RHQ. Tony fell off the tank in his eagerness to seek salvation and fell into a large manure heap. As he surfaced, a mortar fragment hit him in the back. Quite soon afterwards he arrived back in England with his 'Blighty' wound to be greeted by his sister. She told him his wound was 'God's Judgement for *working* on the Jewish New Year'!

'Play Cricket and Football'

The 1/4th KOYLI were in the outskirts of Ryckevorsel on 24 September, as Private Geoffrey Steer recounts: 'Our platoon took shelter behind the first house on the main street. It rained but the Dutch occupier brought out a large stone bottle of rum, so out came the mess tins.' His platoon was then ordered to the centre of town and into the church grounds by a five-road crossroads. On the way, Geoffrey, the Brengunner, was shot in the leg 'like an electric shock'.

> The seams of my trousers were severed. The Sergeant put a field dressing on me and told me to go back to the FDS 'as it was over for me'. I said I would take bandoliers of ammo across the road and then come back. The Germans found out where we were and surrounded us. We fought till 3 p.m. We used up our grenades, throwing them through the windows. By now we had run out of ammo. Another comrade was wounded in the back. We went down into the cellar with the Dutch owners and waited. The Germans threw grenades into the house, came in, took away the owners and lined us up in the back garden. We all thought 'this was it' and it would have been but a German corporal said that he had been a POW of the English in WW1 and had been treated all right. We had already smashed up the Bren gun, bending the piston and hiding the firing pin up the chimney on a ledge. The Germans took us back up the road where we had been firing. There were German dead and wounded all over the place. They made us carry them on stretchers until our own 25-pdrs pounded the town. We were taken back about 4 miles to a cottage in a wood where we were interrogated by a German officer. He said the war was over for us. All we would have to do is to play cricket and football. We were told that if we tried to escape we would be shot. We

were taken back to Breda hospital where the corridors were swimming in blood from Germans, English, Canadians and French wounded soldiers.

John Harper's VC with The Polar Bears

The Polish Armoured Division and 49th (WR) Division were advancing towards Merxplas on 29 September. 146th Brigade led with the Hallamshire Battalion of the York and Lancaster Regiment who were protecting the left flank of the main assault. Unaware of the strength of the enemy, the company was advancing with one platoon forward, it in turn being led by a section of six men commanded by Corporal John Harper of 'C' Company.

The Dépôt de Mendicité was a natural defensive position surrounded by an earth wall about 12 ft high and backed by a wide road and a moat about 30 ft wide. Before it there was not a vestige of cover for more than 300 yds on the dead flat ground.

There was no sign of life from the enemy until the leading section came within 50 yds of the wall. Suddenly a hail of mortar bombs and small arms fire burst upon the advancing troops. Harper's section rushed the enemy on the near side of the wall and were pinned down by fire from both flanks and by grenades thrown over the wall. His Platoon Commander, attempting to get forward, was badly wounded and Harper took charge of the platoon. Looking back, he could see the rest of his company pinned to the ground. The attack was on the point of failure. Looking up the steep slope of the wall, he could see spurts of dust where a machine gun was raking the top. A stick grenade flew across and exploded a few yards away. He could at least reply to that.

Angrily he pulled the pin from a 36 grenade, tossed it over the wall, then followed it with two more. By the time the third one had burst, he had scrambled up the wall and was firing at the enemy on the far side. Three of them dropped, four threw up their hands in surrender, while several ran and dived into the moat and began swimming to the far side. Harper dropped his rifle, picked up an enemy light machine gun and shot them as they swam.

He brought his prisoners over the wall, which was still under heavy fire, then returned to look for a way to cross the moat. Not finding one, in spite of bullets ricocheting from it, he crossed the wall again, gave orders to his section, climbed back on to the wall and covered them across with fire from a Bren gun, then occupied the abandoned enemy position.

Corporal Harper then left the comparative safety of a German weapon pit and once more walked alone along the moat for about 200 yds in full view of the enemy to find a crossing place. Eventually he made contact with the battalion attacking on his right and found that they had located a ford. Back he came over the open ground and on the way to report to his Company Commander he was hit by a rifle bullet and died on the bank of the moat. Later it became obvious that the battalion on the right were only able to cross the ford with the help of fire from Harper's platoon.

His citation for the Victoria Cross acknowledged that the success of his brigade's attack on the Dépôt de Mendicité 'can thus fairly be attributed to the outstanding bravery of Corporal Harper'.

A Tiny New Life

The Suffolk Yeomanry anti-tank guns spent a week in Aerle supporting the Gloucesters. Most of the time was spent under mortar fire.

While the stonk swelled and subsided and swelled again with increased fury, we played cards until George, ever resourceful, used the enforced spare time at our disposal to teach us to play 'cab'. While the stretcher bearers collected their grim burdens and trudged back along the road with them to the waiting ambulances, while men lay gazing in wonder at an arm or leg that wasn't there any longer, and while their mates lay, black-faced and still warm in death – at indeed the very moment that gallant lives were being taken away, across the sea a tiny new life was being born [to Dot, wife of Sergeant Bob Sheldrake] and was given into our care. It was October 8th, 1944, the day our daughter Kitty was born.

During one mortar stonk, Sheldrake found himself in a slit trench with 'General' Lee and Doug Brown.

I can remember their faces in the half-dark of the covered end of the trench, lit by the glowing ends of their cigarettes looking at nothing, seeing nothing, except the smoke and rubbish that tumbled into my end. Thus so many men spent so many long hours, crouching and waiting – here was no glory, no firing of the blood, no mad rush of men, shoulder to shoulder, yelling in the heat of battle – just the two of them alone watching the enemy, turning over a pack of cards, knowing that sooner or later he must turn over the Ace of Spades.

Watch on the Maas

It was customary for a wide range of different units to take their turn – usually a week at a time – guarding a patch in the long thin British 'red line' to the west of the River Maas: Dismounted Inns of Court, fiery Canadian marine commandoes, paratroopers and even distinguished Guards units. A company of the Scots Guards recently cut up in the Anzio bridgehead in Italy were now attached temporarily to 53rd Welsh Division. Between Ijsselstein and Veulen in October 1944 the front-line slit trenches were manned by the Scots Guardsmen, much too aggressive for the normally peace-loving Ayrshire Yeomanry gunners. At night they continually stirred things up and the Yeomen would crouch in their cellar and listen to such talk as: 'Aye, ah think we will. They're bound tae be hauf sleepin' by this time,

Jock.' The Brengun would open up, promptly to be answered by a Spandau 300 yd in front. The tracer from this gun would come right into the kitchen window of the Yeomen's billet and hum through the rooms, the OP party lying on the cellar stairs watching them fly over and wishing that some unknown power in the army would move those Scots Guards to some other destination!

Operation Aintree

German battle groups still held considerable pockets west of the river Maas. Their 180th Infantry Division plus groups called after their commanders, Paul, Hoffman, Kerutt and Walter, held the three key towns/villages of Overloon, Venraij and Oploo. Operation Aintree – no cavalry gallop this – was entrusted to 3rd British Division, while 11th Armoured and 15th Scottish cleared the remainder of the pocket. The US 7th Armoured Division (known as the 'Lucky Seven') had ventured into the Peel country with the same objectives. In the first week of October they took 452 casualties and lost seventy-eight AFVs in the dark woods, muddy tracks and minefields. Aintree was going to be a difficult, bloody operation and so it proved to be. 8th Brigade was to lead with Overloon as the objective, then to exploit south-west down the road to Venraij and then cross Laag Heide woods 2 miles north-west of Venraij and then cross over the Molen Beek.

South Lancashires advance on Venraij during Operation Aintree. (Imperial War Museum, London)

185th Brigade, initially in reserve, would reinforce the final attack and 8th AGRA, plus the divisional artillery of the three divisions involved, would bring down huge barrages. AVREs from 42nd ARE, Flails of the Westminster Dragoons and most of the 6th Guards Armoured Brigade were in support. The attack started on 12 October, helped by Typhoon sorties. Overloon was captured that day, but the woods, minefields and the Molen Beek – and the constant rain – meant that the Iron Sides finally took Venraij *seven days later* on 18 October, at a cost of 1,400 casualties, including three battalion COs and no fewer than sixteen company commanders. It was a brutal, soldiers' battle fought in appalling conditions – a foretaste of what was to come in the breaking of the Siegfried line.

1st Leicesters in Trouble at 'Stone Bridge', 21 October

Sergeant George Upton, 7 Platoon, 1st Leicesters recalls how the 'Tigers' suffered casualties and prisoners at this nasty little battle near Wuerstwezel. During the day they had 111 casualties, including twenty-five KIA.

> Corporal Marks and Private Ashcroft were with us and seriously wounded. We decided to lie up in the ditch which was well covered. The Platoon Commander was at one end and I was at the other. I was holding Corporal Mark's head and back on my chest. There were two or three chaps between us, some with minor wounds. We must have been there for hours. . . . We felt the heat from a gun firing above our heads. The tank had only just moved down the road from Stone Bridge when the next thing we heard was 'Oi! Tommie! Kom! Kom!' At least that's what it sounded like and there they were: four German soldiers with rifles pointed down at us. They took us back to the building and offered us civilian clothes because ours were wet through after lying in the wet ditch. We were later marched back 10 kms under escorts to German HQ where we met the other members of 'A' Coy, including Sergeant Johnny Goodlad and Sergeant 'Bunny' Austin.

Die Happy?

Sergeant Bob Sheldrake's troop of anti-tank guns (55 A/Tk Regiment) was ambushed in the centre of Loenhout on 21 October, so they baled out of their jeep, carrier and quads and sought comparative safety in a nearby barn.

> Great gaps were torn in the roof and the air was filled with dust and mortar which rained down as the building shook and crumbled. Occasionally the roof itself would be caved in by the slamming crash of a direct hit, the falling debris sending up a fresh cloud of dust. Through all the confusion, a few yards from me on a pile of straw, an infantryman was

making love to a girl, with her blouse open and her head thrown back. Both were grinning and chuckling, the bursting shells had no meaning for them. Had we been unlucky, two of us in that barn that day would have died happy.

On Being Wounded – 'Dicing Against the Odds'

Battalion HQ of 1/5th Gordons on the approach to the river Maas near Loon-op-Zand was in a convent school, a one-storey affair with acres of glass. The ceiling consisted of an inch or two of laths and plaster under a tile roof. During the night shells hit the roof, causing thirteen casualties. Martin Lindsay, the 2 i/c, describes what happened.

> There was an even louder crash and a shower of plaster came down from the ceiling. I saw David Martin [the IO] stagger and fall saying 'I've been hit.' John Frary [the Signal Officer, called the 'Dormouse'] and I pulled him practically unconscious on to his safari bed which made a good stretcher. Both the others in the room, John Inglis, the Battery Commander and Waters of the Intelligence Section, were sitting down, very green about the face and obviously wounded. There were half a dozen more in the room next door. John Inglis had a piece in the chest, David Martin a hole high up in his spine. The command post was indescribable, plaster on top of everything, blood all over the floor. [David Martin subsequently died of his wounds in Eindhoven CCS].

Bruce Rae, a company commander had a few days before been shot twice in the chest and also in the jaw.

> Such an attractive chap, gay, handsome and brave – he nearly always led his company himself and rarely deigned to take cover. This was the third time that he had been wounded since El Alamein. He was the *last* remaining of the twenty rifle company officers who came out with the Bn on D-Day. This is what was so superlatively gallant about these chaps. They would go into battle time after time knowing perfectly well that they were dicing against the mathematical odds. For an officer to go into a dozen actions without being killed or badly wounded was like a coin coming down heads six times running. He knew his luck could not possibly last, yet he would die of shame were someone to take his place.

Sergeant Wally Caines' Journal – Autumn

'Oct 1: 4 Dorsets take over from US Airborne at Groesbeek. Their Brigade HQ ninety percent chewing gum, their personalities were unchanged. The "Hiya bud" stuff, it was all very amusing. Oct 10: Our Bn front 1800 yards, twice usual Bn frontage. Oct 15: Private Paddy O'Leary chirping away on his mouth organ. Lads spent most of their spare time playing cards for money or writing letters to the folks at home. At night [telephone] line maintenance always carried out. Oct 16: Charly Bolton and I chased, shot and roasted, a pig. Oct 18–23: To village of Mook out of line. All officers and NCOs attended demos on the use of tanks, mostly for ready joined reinforcements. Infantry with tank support. Free rides *in* tanks were given to us but after travelling a mile or so across rough country I felt I would be an infantryman any day rather than fight in a tank. ENSA show. Oct 23: Took over from 4 Somersets. Oct 24: Artillery fired 25 shells for every 5 fired at us near Reichwald Forest. Nov 1: Rum became the daily tonic to keep out the cold. No one in Bn had dry feet after heavy rain bogged the area. Nov 5: To Groesbeek to take over from Wiltshires. Nov 11: Moved 120 miles to Brunssum, coal mining town in lower Holland. Nov 14: Bayonet training for all, assault training, grenade throwing, rifle and MG firing practice. [Major General 'Butch' Thomas, a thoroughly professional commander, insisted on top quality training whenever out of the line.] Signals carried out radio telephone practice, Morse sending and receiving, practical wireless fault finding. Nov 16: ENSA. This cheered everyone. The boys were always delighted to see a good show with English actors, enjoyed joining in during the chorus songs. Staff at ENSA did a jolly good job of work to keep standard of morale high. Nov 17: Recce to view Wiltshire's position, north of German line between Hatterath and Sittard overlooking villages of Scherwaldenrath, Straaten and Putt.'

'Savagely Beaten'

During the battle for Roosendaal by the 49th Polar Bear Division on 25 October, Private George Marsden, 'A' Company, 7th Battalion, Duke of Wellingtons, and his platoon of about forty men were ordered to cross the main anti-tank ditch outside the town. 'After crawling along a muddy field, we slid down one side of the ditch, climbed the other. After a short battle we captured the Germans guarding the nearby farmhouse. But at dawn next day fresh Germans [counter-attacked]. A close quarter battle took place and our Officer and several others were killed or wounded. The survivors were told to make our own way back to our Company lines.' George got entangled on a barbed-wire fence, ripped his trousers from top to bottom, but under fire managed to escape. But the Dukes were ordered back that night to retake ditch and farmhouse.

We again captured our objective, sending the Germans back as prisoners with our wounded. The next morning we were again counter-attacked in great force with armoured vehicles. The farmhouse roof was burning – lads were killed in the slit trenches they'd dug outside. My sergeant had his eye shot out. Then I was blasted through the shoulder at point-blank range with several bullets from a Spandau MG. I was left for dead and lay unconscious for several hours through loss of blood. When I regained consciousness, a German soldier picked me up, carried me into the cellar of the first house in the street – upstairs were some of my friends who'd been taken prisoner. I was repeatedly attacked and savagely beaten by two wounded German soldiers as I lay on the store floor.

Eventually George was operated on and taken by ambulance and hospital train to Stalag XIB at Fallingbostel.

St Crispin's Day

'In the third week of October another push was in the offing. This time the 53rd (Welsh) Division were to attack the key city of 's-Hertogenbosch. The nine battalions streamed westward from Nijmegen by roads, lanes and railway tracks. Many of the fields had been deliberately flooded. It was difficult to find a suitable position for the batteries of guns [25-pdrs of 81st Welsh Field Regiment]. Like many Dutch cities, 's-Hertogenbosch was criss-crossed with waterways and there was much hard fighting. Our guns were firing continually and when I wasn't manning a radio or telephone, I [Gunner 'Wally' Brereton] was unloading shells from the tailboards of trucks. We had more than the usual response from the enemy artillery. Their guns were mainly SPs and it was difficult to knock them out. Our own guns did a lot of damage to the posh southern suburbs, but the centre of the city with its magnificent Gothic cathedral was almost untouched. As the street fighting was rather confused, there would have been the danger of hitting our own troops. Also the Dutch resistance was very active in the city. On St Crispin's Day, 26th October, the German troops were pushed beyond the river Maas. Most of Holland north of the city had to endure another seven months of starvation and occupation.'

The Capture of Tilburg

On the evening of 27 October the services of 16th Assault Squadron RE were badly needed. From the 's-Hertogenbosch sector they moved rapidly to the outskirts of Tilburg where their AVREs carrying fascines and bombards were needed. The following afternoon they bridged a stream a mile outside the town after clearing with crowbars and sledges the wreckage of a former bridge. Beyond the stream was a large crater between houses: the bulldozers could not fill it so another 'SBG' was dropped. Bulldozers then crossed, demolished a long roadblock and yet a third assault bridge was laid. The AVRE crossed its own bridge and was the first vehicle to enter Tilburg.

About 100 tanks and Kangaroos followed and the town surrendered without more ado. The Tilburgers, who had enjoyed a reputation for

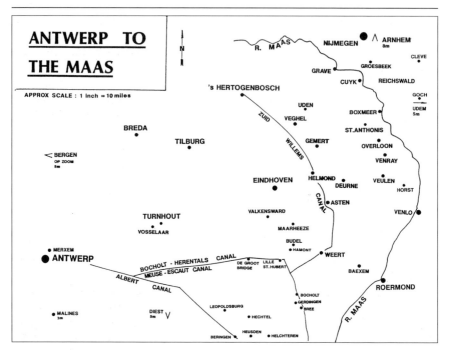

Battlefields of the long, hard winter

collaboration with the Germans, were anxious now to celebrate the liberation of their city. During the festivities which followed, the senior Assault RE Officer felt it his duty to propose the health of Queen Wilhelmina. This he did amid cheers which shook the rafters. Quick as a flash a Dutchman rose to reply. His glass held high and voice charged with emotion, he cried in English, 'Ladies and Gentlemen – Lloyd George'! [Raymond Ellis]

Ask for Typhoons – And You Get Them!

There was an interesting battle on 28–29 October in the sandhills of Loon-op-Zand far from the sea, as Major John Evans DSO recalls:

We [1/5th Queen's] liberated Dongen, did recces into Waalwijk and then into position before the river Maas near Heusden and Haarsteg. From Bree to Ittervoort and took up a ghastly position on flat ground overlooked by a flat-roofed factory. We couldn't move in daylight, staying in slit trenches all day. We were grateful for them because we asked for Typhoons to take out the factory with their terrifying rockets. We cheered as they arrived but the radio operator sharing my trench said, 'You'd think they were diving straight at us, sir, wouldn't you?' I said, 'They bloody well are!' Five minutes of explosions, columns of dust, noise and the smell of cordite. Check around the platoons. No casualties. Some of the lads were half buried by near misses. The CO told me later that the RAF had reported they had wiped out a party of Germans.

We waited for the REs to repair the bridge over canal at Zandfort. We kept the enemy busy by sending over patrols. One enemy concrete pillbox was brought under artillery fire. We could see it being hit. When we eventually took it, we found inside a kettle boiling on the stove. On the table was a hurriedly written note reading, 'Well done boys. The way to Berlin is long and strong. Lieut Kessenich L62282 G Lgp Minster.'

The End of the 50th Tyne/Tees Division

Montgomery never would fight with weak divisions: he always insisted on their being at full strength, although that meant fewer divisions [the 59th had been disbanded in Normandy]. So now the 50th, which had fought in North Africa, Sicily, Italy and North-west Europe, was disbanded. Its most experienced people would return to England to take charge of the army's training and its less experienced soldiers would reinforce divisions in Europe. As far as the 1st Hampshires were concerned, twelve officers and 100 men would go to England as instructors. Between 6 June and 17 November the 1st Hampshires, whose fighting strength was usually between 500 and 600, lost 231 killed, which was nearly twice what most battalions suffered, and about 1050 wounded. Effectively the battalion was twice wiped out. At the end it was still a superbly efficient fighting machine. [Geoffrey Picot]

'Big Fleas Have Little Fleas'

Michael Wilford took part in the 82nd Assault Squadron RE amphibious attack on the island of Walcheren to support 52nd Lowland Division in Operation Infatuate.

The clearance of both sides of the Scheldt was a major priority of 21 Army Group. The attack would be in two parts. 4th Special Service Brigade consisting of 3 RM Commandos and 4 (Army) Commandos was entrusted with the assault, the former to make a seaborne attack on Westkapelle and the latter with a Brigade of 52 Division to make the shorter trip across the Scheldt from Breskens in RN LCAs with RTR Buffaloes in support. The troop-carrying LCTs to beach and deposit their load of Buffaloes which were carrying Royal Marines, their vehicles (Weasels) and light supporting arms (mortars). It reminded me of the old rhyme, 'Big fleas have little fleas upon their backs to bite 'em; little fleas have smaller fleas, and so *ad infinitum*' (LCT, Buffaloes, Weasels). Hallowe'en (31 October) the convoy sailed, but 284 Assault Sqn had been

Night assault on Savojaard Plaat Scheldt from Terneuzen, 8 October 1944. (Birkin Haward)

RE Terrapins, each carrying 800 tons of ammo, petrol and supplies, at Amber Beach, Savojaard Plaat, 10 October 1944. (Birkin Haward)

destroyed three days before when jerri-cans of liquid explosive were dropped from a lorry onto a Schü-mine. The first wave of 82 Sqn consisted of 3 LCTs, with Paul Bennett's 3 Buffaloes with a commando troop aboard; the next myself with 4 Buffaloes and another commando troop plus their mortars. And in the third LCT was the OC, Tony Poynder, with 4 Buffaloes and Commando HQ. In the second wave were Jim Skelly with 5 Buffaloes and Bill Green with 4. Dawn came about 0730 and an hour later in the grey and still misty light the bombardment force, including HMS *Warspite*, opened up on the island. There must have been 25 to 30 LCTs carrying troops with the Support Sqn on both flanks. Once beached and the ramp was down, all hell was let loose with a mixture of shells, mortar bombs and small ammo. Soon some of the Flails and AVREs became hopelessly bogged and then drowned by the rising tide. We set off through the huge gap in the dyke created by the RAF, to the dry inner slopes from which 48 Commando set off southward to link up with 4 Commando and the Scots who had landed at Flushing.

The enemy were all prepared. The assault on the island began on 1 November and the result hung in the balance for 36 hours. It took five more days to clear the island completely. Antwerp was opened for shipping at the end of November. 82nd Assault Squadron RE had started with a strength of 102. During the assault they suffered two officers and seventeen ORs killed or wounded. Michael Wilford was hit by a shell burst which badly damaged

82nd Assault Squadron RE LVT park, Terneuzen, loading for assault on S. Beveland, 25 October 1944. (Birkin Haward)

Night assault on S. Beveland (Operation Vitality), 25 October 1944. (Birkin Haward)

a leg and foot. He was brought to a dressing station manned by Canadian doctors, then back by LCT to Ostend, by hospital ship to Tilbury and train to hospital at Stoke-on-Trent.

Operation Clipper – 'Eight to Five Day'

Before the main offensive aimed at Cologne could get under way, the town of Geilenkirchen with its key road junctions had to be taken. It was on the river Wurm 4 miles into Germany. On the high ground to its east ran the Siegfried line. Lieutenant General Horrocks planned to encircle the town starting on 18 November with the 84th US Division (the Railsplitters) advancing north-east from the south and Major General 'Butch' Thomas' 43rd Wessex Division attacking the town from the west and north. Thomas had a small army under his command, with not only the American 'Greenhorn' Division, but also the 8th Armoured Brigade, 113rd US Cavalry group (i.e. armoured brigade) and four specialized 'Funny' Squadrons of 79th Armoured Division.

Eric Codling, 8th Middlesex, wrote:

18 Nov barrage throughout day. *Picture Post* photographer took photos of our mortars in action. Nightmare chore carrying 80 lbs of bombs two/three hundred yards from the road, thousands of rounds, then transfer mortars into prepared pits, with several inches of rainwater in them. Target Bauchem, 3 mortar platoons fired 10,000 bombs in 3¼

Assault on Westkapelle, Walcheren, launched from Ostende with 48th RM Commando, 1 November 1944. (Birkin Haward)

hours plus Div artillery fire. Little resistance when infantry moved into shattered town. It was quite awe-inspiring to observe such devastation even though it was in Germany. Daily passwords were Tooth, reply Brush. On the boundary with US Division who moved out at night leaving flank open. They worked an eight to five day. Mud, our boots became sodden, feet permanently cold and damp.

Rainsoaked, Green-faced Bodies

The Wessex Wyverns were ordered to clear Hoven woods 3 miles north of Geilenkirchen on 10–12 November. They were described by Lieutenant Jary, 4th Somerset Light Infantry.

Hoven woods were cold, stark, torn and mutilated by shell and mortar fire, the ground low lying and waterlogged. 5th Duke of Cornwalls Light Infantry had attempted to attack Hoven village through these ghastly woods and had taken heavy casualties. Their rainsoaked bodies littered the paths and clearings. While carrying out a recce I came across one of their sections lying along a small path facing the enemy. At first I thought them alive until I saw that the studs on their boots were rusty and their webbing equipment was bleached with rain. Their battledress was starched with mud and their hands and faces were green. German booby traps were on or near many of the tracks. I was told by the CO of the 4th

Bn Wiltshires, from whom we took over the position, that some of the bodies were also booby trapped. 'Don't try to bury them,' he said. It was without doubt the most grisly and horrifying position that we ever held.

Breaching the Siegfried Line – 'Discussing Poetry'

Brigadier Prior Palmer, CO 8th Armoured Brigade, spelt out the difficulties that lay ahead [16 November] in seeking to breach the Siegfried line at one of its strongest points. The capture of the town of Geilenkirchen was entrusted to the 'green' US 84th Infantry Division and the 43rd Wessex Wyverns, backed by the Sherman tanks of SRY, 4/7th RDG and 13/18th Hussars.

The Line itself was extensive and several thousand yards wide with huge minefields and the most massive and complicated concrete fortresses that dwarfed any pillboxes hitherto encountered. In some cases underground communication between strongpoints had to be dealt with. Air recce had shown that hills had been levelled, and created in other places in order to increase the line of fire. Under artificial moonlight 0500 hrs on Nov 18th the breaching party of Lothian and Border Horse Flails plus Churchill AVREs made a gap in the first minefield, supported by flame-throwing Crocodiles. 'A' and 'B' Sqns of SRY took Prummern, knocked out four pillboxes, took 350 POW. Major John Sempken CO 'A' Sqn had three tanks destroyed by mines under him on that day, without any of the crews being killed or wounded. Padre Leslie Skinner went forward to try and find him, found him in a small captured pillbox, back to the wall, reading poetry. He was very 'bomb happy', almost as though high on drugs. We sat together for half an hour or more discussing poetry until we decided to walk out.

The following day the padre – by mistake – buried eight members of his regiment in a *minefield*. He had also become the first British padre to take a service in Germany. The SRY lost nineteen KIA and ten tanks destroyed in the battle for Geilenkirchen.

Cornwall Wood – 'Our Only Defeat'

'Oh grim wood of Hoven, now mined and silent lying. Here men of Cornwall fought and died,' was Lieutenant Colonel George Taylor's epitaph to the many casualties his battalion, 5th Duke of Cornwall's Light Infantry, suffered here. Immediately after the taking of Geilenkirchen the Wessex Wyverns had to hold and dominate Hoven, Hochheid wood and Kraudorf, held by 10th Panzer Division. The area north of Geilenkirchen was under fire from the guns of the Siegfried line. During a shattering battle which started on 21 November, the Cornwalls suffered some 200 casualties and had to be withdrawn. Their CO, Lieutenant Colonel George Taylor, wrote:

Except for Hill 112 in Normandy, this was our only defeat in the whole campaign, due to the general fatigue of the men and Bn before the action. We had already been engaged for over 96 hours. The heavy rain turned the ground into a quagmire. Our tanks – the Sherwood Rangers – could not support us in either attack or defence. The Germans had a lateral road for movement and could operate with their wider tracks. No anti-tank guns could be moved up to resist the German counter-attack. The wireless set at Hoven was put out of action and the telephone line cut by fire – and finally our Start Line was not secure at the beginning of the operation.

Lieutenant Colonel Taylor had told Brigadier Essame his reservations beforehand. Ironically, Taylor was awarded his second DSO for operations of three months back. After Cornwall Wood he said, 'Morale of the Bn remained high. What marvellous soldiers our men can be.'

Dante's Inferno

In mid-November Lieutenant Sydney Jary, 4th Battalion Somerset Light Infantry inspected near Geilenkirchen three abandoned Mk III German SP 75 mm guns painted in a desert sand camouflage. They were 400 yds in front of a brickworks. At dawn he went out by himself.

Climbing up above the tracks, I put my head into the cupola which was open. A familiar and terrible stench hit me. Inside was a charnel house. Six inches away a set of bared teeth, set in an unrecognizable black and incinerated lump, grinned at me. Beside it a charred and bony arm reached up in agony. Spread on the floor, like a pool of tar, lay the melted remains of the driver. I had entered Dante's inferno.

Operation Guildford – 'Wet, Cold and Miserable'

'B' Squadron 22nd Dragoons took part in this operation in mid-November from Weert, Nederweert and Panningen to clear the way to Blerick and Venlo for the infantry. 'The weather was wet,' wrote Lieutenant Ian Hammerton, 'it barely stopped raining for weeks on end so we were wet, cold and miserable.' The first issue of the new winter tank suits, with zips everywhere, helped a bit.

Mines of several different kinds were everywhere. A half dozen would be hidden across every sandy track, or at a corner of each of the many little copses, hedgerows or woods. Anti-tank Teller mines, anti-personnel Schü-mines and some new non-metallic mines which could not be detected by a mine detector. The streams of Dutch refugees were at risk. Casualties were heart-rendingly inevitable! All five Crabs [Flails] of 1 Troop succumbed to mines owing to the soft going, usually with broken tracks from the detonation of a mine. Sergeant McGuffie's tank was blown up by a group of linked Teller mines that had exploded altogether.

Dorset Wood in the Siegfried Line

Most of the winter battles in Holland, before the German pockets west of the River Maas were pinched out, were fought in truly appalling conditions. The Wessex Wyverns had a terrible time, as Sergeant Wally Caines recounts:

20 Nov: 4 Dorsets take over 'Dorset Wood' from 5 Dorsets. They had suffered badly, lot of casualties as had our 'D' Coy, two newly joined officers, brothers, one was killed, other badly wounded. We noticed the dead of the 5 Dorsets. Jerry had allowed the attacking infantry to get within a few yards of his MG nests, opened up. Many met their death almost instantly. Situated right into the Siegfried line, subjected to heavy artillery fire. Many members of the rifle Coys became lost making their way through wooded country – pitch black night, only lit up by gun flashes. 'A' Coy under Major Hall completely lost and 'D' Coy missing altogether. It was a hell of a night, everything seemed to go wrong. Transport failed to turn up, most of it had got stuck in the mud along the main route, all ammo had to be manhandled by carrying parties to the companies well forward. This operation took hours and hours to complete, while all of Bn area under very heavy fire. Rain also fell heavily, all of us soaked to the skin. Trenches of 5 Dorsets half full of water. Signals carrier lost: no communications for Bn apart from runners. It was bloody miserable, only remedy – a swig of the bottle. Nov 21: 'D' Coy made contact, numerous casualties, reinforcements needed badly. All transport bogged down in the mud. Line laying was a difficult task, men were cursing as they went out, the lines completely vanished in the mud bed. Stonks were coming down every few minutes. Nov 22: Weasels brought up rations including baked beans, tinned foods and tea. Charlie Bolton brewed up tea every 2 hours. A mug worth pounds in English money! The HQ shelled every few minutes. Many times we clutched the sides of our trenches quietly kneeling and saying our prayers. Morale still high, though we were all wet through, cold and filthy, hardly a man failed to produce a smile. Casualties were piling up, plus sick with trench feet and severe influenza. Sergeant Manning and I gave the signals office boys a good stiff drink, mugs of whisky, gin and lemon warmed up. Some men had to be evacuated with battle exhaustion. Worn out with dodging shells, bullets. Sitting in a trench is no good for morale.

The Padre's Diary – November: 'Broken through Siegfried Line'

Thurs Nov 23rd: The Americans [after Operation Clipper] have given glowing reports of our support. Our casualties have been high, theirs even worse but together we have broken through the Siegfried line. Our casualties for this five-day battle were 64, including 19 KIA [Sherwood Rangers Yeomanry]. We had lost 10 tanks destroyed, 15 damaged but recoverable and 12 so hopelessly bogged down as to be irrecoverable for further use. Conditions in the British sector immediately to our left similarly difficult and costly. The 13/18th Hussars and 4/7th Dragoon Guards supporting 214 Infantry Brigade of 43rd Div have widened the breach in the Siegfried line to capture Bauchem, Niederheide and Tripsrath alongside Wurm to the north of Geilenkirchen. Tues Nov 28th: Python leave scheme to start for all with five years' overseas service and less than six months in England. Splendid but CO estimates this Regt has over 100 men who qualify, all experienced and key men.

Padre Leslie Skinner, a front-line 'soldier' if ever there was one, pondered his role.

It all boils down to what one considers a padre's job to be. Those who see the role in what they call 'spiritual' terms want padres further back, caring for the wounded and working in areas where 'services' could be seen to be more suitably done. They often describe what I have called 'front line' padres as 'playing at being soldiers' or as being 'ecclesiastical undertakers'. To a certain extent they have a point. Once a tank has been hit and the wounded, if any, got away, other tanks of the troop know that one or more of their comrades remained in that knocked-out tank. They draw comfort from me – or anyone else – just going to look – even if the actual removal for burial had to wait until later. The morale and 'spiritualness' of the men actually doing the fighting seems to me to be paramount and trying to do the things I did and do, is the best that I can do. . . . I would sooner clear the tank *on my own* than accept tank crews as helpers.

Happy Birthday

'In November 1944 patrolling continued in the "Watch on the Maas" campaign. As FOO for Fox troop 13 RHA my Sherman was tucked away into the courtyard of a large tannery overlooking the river. The tank gun faced down river but there was no risk of daytime patrolling. About the 24/25th, to my surprise a hearty Canadian unit of Airborne Division paratroopers arrived on my doorstep. They were having a peaceful busman's holiday after the Arnhem trauma but they could not resist a challenge, and on the night of the 27th we sent a patrol, faces blacked, across the river in black rubber rafts. I went with them plus a 38 radioset. There were five farmhouses which we wanted to bounce as noisily as possible so I had arranged a couple of minor troop targets to help things along. All went according to plan and we rudely disturbed a number of dormant PZ. Our boats were carried about half a mile down river in the fast current. But on our return the Canadians plied me (and themselves) with glasses of piping hot rum laced with a little orange juice. Three of these and you slept till doomsday. On the morning of the 28th I arrived at the tannery from our safe house inland with the Inns of Court, got out of the Sherman, checked for booby traps, and after "cha" and bangers, resumed a rather tedious watch across the river. Every two hours on the hour Spandau fire raked the OP quite thoroughly but once I knew the schedule I nipped down from the first floor to the tank in the courtyard. But that day the ground rules had been changed. The PZ were obviously furious at the Canadian raids. From 9 a.m. onwards mortar bombs and one horrifyingly accurate 88 mm airburst rocked the tannery. For four hours we were stonked, not Normandy style, but enough to be very unpleasant. At lunchtime I called it a day, there was no point in counter battery fire on the vast woodlands on the other bank. Needles in haystacks. "Right," I said, "we will sit this out in the tank." The 88 mm was bursting right on top of the courtyard, right on top of the tank. I closed the hatches down. The strong, leatherbound hip flask which my father (gunner WWI, SHAEF WWII) had given me when I went to war was always filled with Scotch and I passed it around my OP crew. "Have a drink on me," I said, "it's my 21st birthday." The PZ kept up their stonk until closing time. The Canadian paratroopers, who thought it was funny, again plied me with hot rum and sympathy.' [Lieutenant Patrick Delaforce, 13 RHA]

The Island – 'Man Management Became Supreme'

Lieutenant Colonel C.D. Hamilton, CO 7th Duke of Wellington's Regiment, kept a journal which describes life on the Island, the salient of the bridgehead between Nijmegen and Arnhem.

It was across this narrow strip of fertile low-lying dyke country with orchards of every fruit that General Horrocks' XXX Corps dashed to link up with the 1st Airborne Div. Every field had its scars of graves, smashed vehicles and signs of such divisions as 43 (Wessex), 53 (Welsh), 51 (Highland), Guards Armoured [and, of course, 49th Polar Bears, known as the 'Nijmegen Home Guard'], 101 US Airborne and the great 50 Tyne Tees Division. The apple and cherry picking of the autumn had given way to smashed ruins, 1914–1918 mud and the slashing rain of the winter when our recce parties arrived on 31st November. Slit trenches were flooded and there was hardly one brick standing on another anywhere.

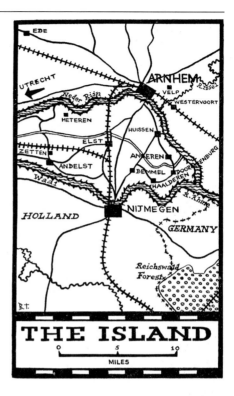

The 'Nijmegen Home Guard' battlegrounds

There was talk of spending the winter there. The CO of the Dorsets talked of sinking obsolete tanks in the mud to make strongpoints. For two days we watched the waters rise in the Rhine over the towering winter bund or dyke, on our right over the sides of our slit trenches. We formed strongpoints amid the ruins and in the cellars – man management became supreme. The German was aggressive with his artillery only and our mortar platoon suffered heavily.

On 3 December the evacuation scheme 'Noah' came into action as the Germans blew several gaps in the bund and the rushing Rhine floodwater overwhelmed several posts on the north-west of the Island without any warning. Then the 7th Dukes were suddenly attacked by three companies of a Para regiment and furious fighting took place in and around Haalderen, once a pretty village on the Rhine, in a desperate venture to seize the vital Nijmegen bridge.

The complete assaulting force was wiped out: 110 men were taken prisoner and 50 Boche, three officers and two CSMs killed inside the Bn area. More were drowned in a pond avoiding our Bren fire. Great slaughter was inflicted on the remaining enemy companies by the firing of DFs [Artillery Defensive Fire stonks]. The booty included 25 Spandaus, nine bazookas, a tremendous amount of small arms and two dogs. The DWR suffered 31 casualties.

A fine victory.

Reluctant Warriors

Rifleman G.H. Kingsmill of 8 RB eventually got his well-deserved leave in Brussels.

Most of the men stationed in Brussels are only too anxious to leave the pleasures of this delightful city for rather sterner duties elsewhere. This desire 'to get up and at 'em' was pointed out to me by various members of the Brussels garrison at different times during my short stay. They assured me, with the tears practically streaming down their cheeks, that time and time again they had applied for permission to 'get up there' with the infantry and the tanks. But it was not to be. Not for them the fun and frolics of the front line. All that they could look forward to was the hard work and daily grind, the filling up of form after form. My heart bled for them as I shook them sympathetically by the hand. I know how they felt, the same way myself, only in the reverse order. Such is life.

Home Comforts

Every front-line soldier in that long cold winter of 1944/45 at one time or another was temporarily made at home by a Dutch family. Lionel Roebuck, 2nd Battalion East Yorkshires, and his section took part in the capture of Venraij.

For Jack and myself, Sam Rigby, Edwin Barkwell, Bill 'Pedler' Palmer, Jim Pilkington, Hill and Preston, the house at No. 30 Stationweg became our home for the next few days. The Janssen family, despite all their own hardships, made us most welcome. Pieter, the father of four small children, was headmaster of a local school and he could speak good English. His youngish-looking wife was small in stature but with a big warm heart as she fussed around us, intent on looking after her suddenly enlarged family. The Janssen family all slept safely in the cellar and the eight of us, by then all rather scruffy, made do as best we could on the ground floor. The children were very good and never seemed to fret. Army rations of sweets and chocolate were shared out and Pieter was given cigarettes from the 14 man ration packs. On most evenings we played card games. Pieter spoke seriously of his concern for the rebuilding of Venraij. The ruined churches and school in particular before civilized normality could return to the town. From her larder store, Mrs Janssen occasionally gave us some bottled fruit to supplement our ample, but plain, Army compo rations.

Jary's Men

'Infantry warfare is a wretched business. It makes physical and emotional demands on participants that run contrary to all human instinct. The strong minority must quietly help the weak majority. The jewel in the crown of the British Army is the regimental system, the strong foundation on which we all relied.

A certain amount of dementia is required of the junior infantry commander trapped in his mad world. Our gunner officers brought not only extraordinary competent artillery support but also stability – a lifeline to sanity.

The British infantry soldier is an extraordinary man. Put him in physical conditions which will reduce most foreign armies to gloom and sometimes mutiny and he will respond with a defiant cheerfulness. Repartee flows and derisive stories, usually about officers and NCOs, are remembered with malicious accuracy.

Troops lose personal aggression after about two months in battle. After three months they acquire a mature compassion which in no way detracts from their offensive capability. They simply know a lot more about war.' [Lieutenant Sydney Jary, 4th Battalion Somerset Light Infantry]

The Peel Country – 'Utter Misery'

The 2nd Battalion East Yorkshires held the line at Griendtsveen. Lionel Roebuck describes their winter battleground.

Section positions, pushed way out into the open heath, were anything but comfortable. They were near to the tracks in the peat-bogs and marshland made by the peat diggers and without doubt the most depressing situation ever experienced. Close to open ditches and low banks, adjacent to the soft track, an attempt was made to dig our defence line of trenches. At two feet down they filled up with water which soaked in through the sides. Any attempts to build them up were a failure, so, in the damp misty and muddy spot, with water over our boot tops, the long day and night vigil continued. All the ingenuity of experienced soldiers could not improve matters nor provide any relief from our feelings of despair. The scenery was just as depressing as the ground conditions. Bare individual trees stood out starkly on the flat marshland as in the distance the rumble of battle continued. The odd game bird flew over, mallard in their ideal habitat quacked, but nothing more. What enemy in his right mind would

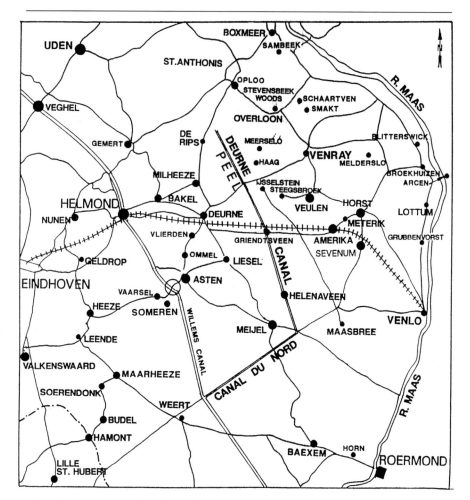

The Peel country of south-east Holland

have ventured out to fight over such appalling ground? The Yorkshire Tykes were presented with a large container of evil-smelling whale oil to prevent WW1 trench feet! The miserable wet, dreary days and nights on 'De Peel' at Griendtsveen left us all with a lasting impression of utter misery.

On the Island – The Old Story

On 10 December the Germans opened the river wall – the bund – and the water from the Neder Rijn and Waal poured through the trenches and flooded most of the island. The village of Elst was almost completely surrounded by water and the only way to reach it was by boat. Sergeant Bob Sheldrake made a nightly pilgrimage with rations and drinking water. The Boche sometimes sent out boats with outboard motors fitted. All civilians were evacuated but chickens, geese and pigs roamed more or less freely. 'We ate anything that was eatable on that Island. One detachment killed a pig, but we stuck to the birds. I remember 'General' Lee in one particularly gruesome killing of a goose. Should we have left the livestock alone, did we deprive some farmer of his livelihood? It was the old story, if *you* didn't, somebody else did.' On one dry farm British and German patrols clashed – to secure the pig herd!

The Mortarman's Journal – 'Wartime Tunes and Songs'

'8 Dec: Relieved by Hallams, back into Nijmegen, billeted with Mrs Klaason who made us welcome. We slept on the floor upstairs. I played my harmonica, a small Bandmaster, and they would ask us for wartime tunes and songs. It was nice and homely and that of course was what we were missing. I used to go to Café Eindos and dance the evening away. 13 Dec: Tracked down a pig in a deserted farm. Shot it, put it in the carrier, covered it with sacks. I sat on it as we passed the MPs. We let the "civvies" have it? Well it was better than the poor thing starving to death, wasn't it? 14 Dec: To the Winter Gardens to hear the band of the Coldstream Guards. I love to hear a military band. 19 Dec: My 26th birthday, sixth in the army. 20 Dec: Xmas dinner in Winter Gardens, in two sittings. A band played the whole time. A great dinner and the officers waited on us, as is the tradition. 22 Dec: Over the bridge took over from 1 Leicesters at Halderen. No mortar pits or slits. Breastworks or sangers had been built up with sods, sand bags, anything handy. We were issued with leather jerkins and "wellies" which were a godsend in the cold and wet. Plenty of buzz-bombs coming over. No means of heating; used "Benghazi" burners in the day for cooking. 24 Dec: Xmas Eve and the frost really clamped down. What a nasty place to be in at Xmas. We were better off in Iceland. The sleeping arrangements were that we all put our blankets together on the floor of the ruined cottage to make a large bed. Jacket and boots off only and into bed when we came off duty in the night. The only time we were warm. At the simple shout of "Action" we would be out in a crack, which happened many times that winter. The mail came up, to my surprise, I received a parcel from Mother. I thought "Good old Mum". Jerry had a lot of machine guns, they were all around here. We got used to their rapid rate of fire. One was the Machinegewehr MG 42, box-fed with a rate of 1,200 rounds per minute!' [Rex Flower, 1/4th KOYLI]

Uncle

'When 11th Armoured Division occupied tracts of Peel country west of the Maas, GOCs on both sides of the river ordered heavy patrol activity. One winter's afternoon in mid-December I was ordered to join the Inns of Court near Oploo, preparatory to setting up an OP on the river some 500 m to the east of them. So with Bren gun carrier and driver/signaller, I arrived at dusk at a large Dutch farmhouse with outbuildings, which housed the Inns of Court and their nippy little Daimler scout cars. All very cosy and peaceful, as I got on radio set, reported in and started thinking about supper. There were about 25 of us with a couple of sentries posted outside.

About 9 p.m. the first shots came in from the woods about 100 m away from our little stone fortress. Next came Spandau fire from several sectors. Then a lot of tracer which tore through our windows and set the attics on fire. Finally a spray of PZ grenades prompted me to call in for a troop target. It must have been about 11 p.m. when to my surprise and horror a familiar, fruity, *avuncular* voice came across the air. "Sunray here, what's going on? Over." My CO, Lieutenant Colonel Bob Daniell, was probably enjoying a convivial evening out with the CO of the Inns of Court. At least he sounded convivial. I told Sunray rather tersely that I was ordering a troop target to deal with our little local problem. We were taking casualties and the roof was now on fire. The avuncular voice then said, "Sunray speaking. Oh I think we can do *much* better than that, give me a map reference." In a flash I gave him the farmhouse map reference, plus 50 m east. And then I told my "fast little friends" of the Inns of Court. "Sorry chaps, we're in real trouble now, for God's sake keep your heads right down – and pray." I prayed that it would be a regimental target and not an *UNCLE* target. We might survive the first. No way would we survive the latter. Within a minute a tornado of shells fell down on top of us, around us, and very probably on top of the marauding Panzer Grenadiers. (I estimated a mere platoon of them). The stonk went on and on. At least a dozen shells hit the farmhouse and outbuildings.

Some time later we ventured out through the acrid smell and smoke and cautiously searched the woods. The PZ had scarpered. Or some of them had. Many of them were not likely to be of much martial use again. We put out the fires, posted more sentries, patched up our wounded and I put in one final radio message. "Fox One to Sunray. Many thanks, noisy, has done the trick. Out." As my "fast little friends" said in the morning. 'We were between the Devil and the deep blue sea." On the whole they seemed quite grateful.

One doesn't mind being killed by one's own regimental target, but being finished off by a divisional *UNCLE* target would have been rather ignominious!' [Lieutenant Patrick Delaforce, 13 RHA]

Christmas Day

The Sherwood Rangers spent their Christmas Day at Schinnen.

We had a carol service on Christmas Eve and on Christmas Day we served the men's dinners which were excellent and had our own in the evening. It was preceded by a cocktail party for all the SRY officers with presents (designed to cause a laugh) issued off a Christmas tree. We then had our UK leave draw. I [Lieutenant Stuart Hills, now with a MC] came 6th and received the first vacancy in February. The dinner was magnificent. There was any amount to eat and drink. We felt rather sorry for all those at home in England. On Boxing Day we gave a party for the village children. Neville Fearn dressed up as Father Christmas and George as a clown. They were towed through the streets of the village on a sleigh by a 'Honey' light tank, finishing up at Schinnen village hall where they gave a present to each of the village children (mostly chocolate which we had saved up).

Realities of War

'Boxing Day brought a return of hostilities and the adjacent village of Gebroek was captured by the Germans. They took the 11th Hussars by surprise and brewed up a number of their vehicles. After a splendid artillery bombardment [by 3 and 5 RHA] Frank Saxby's troop [8th King's Royal Irish Hussars] went in and cleared the village again. It was a sharp but punishing engagement and it brought us back to the realities of war. We stayed in Gebroek with our friends in the 1st Battalion Rifle Brigade for two weeks, celebrated the New Year well and then woke up to witness the tremendous air effort which the Germans mounted at that time. We watched dogfights going on above us and were thankful that the bombing and machine-gunning was not directed at us. We were astonished to see large numbers of V–1 bombs going extremely low over our positions on their way to the port of Antwerp. One of the most remarkable things about the winter of 1944 in the south of Limburg was the sheer, almost unbelievable, harshness of the weather. We were not accustomed to the fierce biting winds which blew consistently for weeks, freezing still further a land already thickly covered with snow and ice.' [Lieutenant Bill Bellamy MC, Troop Leader of 3 Troop]

CHAPTER NINE

The Ardennes

Longstop

Adolf Hitler took one enormous gamble that for a week or so looked as though it would come off. By a masterpiece of secrecy he had re-equipped with new Tiger tanks his 5th, 6th and 7th Panzer armies and unleashed them on four unsuspecting American divisions in the Ardennes. On 16 December Lieutenant General Horrocks' XXX Corps were on standby as longstop back-up. The 29th Armoured Brigade (of 11th Armoured Division), busy swapping beat-up Shermans for brand-new Comets, had to nip back into the vehicle parks around Brussels, reclaim their Shermans and, en route to guard the river Meuse between Dinant–Namur–Liège, paint them a winter white. A few days later 6th Airborne Division was flown out from the UK and arrived in the Dinant and Givet area. General Manteuffel, the German commander during a week of thick fog which prevented air interdiction, had made a huge triangle of advance 60 miles deep. 1st US Army were trying to contain the northern flank and 3rd US Army the south. Although the total credit for holding, then repulsing, this audacious counter-attack must go to the Americans, plus the two air forces, the British troops were in action on a 40 mile front. By the end of January the German Panzers, with huge losses, were back behind their Siegfried line, but the American casualties, many captured, were 60,000.

Welcome?

The 2nd Fife and Forfarshire Yeomanry, with the rest of 29th Armoured Brigade of 11th Armoured Division, were on the way to the crisis battle in the Ardennes. Lieutenant Steel Brownlie records:

> By midday, with a miracle of organization the whole brigade were armed, rationed and fuelled [in their old Sherman tanks]. We moved at 2 p.m., Pinkie leading in a scout car, me following in his tank. There were cheering crowds in Brussels, worried that the Germans would come back, and maybe we could stop them. The roads from there to Namur were deserted except for a few road blocks manned by local volunteers. Not much to stop the Germans, if they got across the Meuse. I was sent ahead in a scout car to arrange a harbour in Belgrade, a suburb of Namur, and

picked a street of brick-built houses where the tanks parked. We were most welcome and my own billet was with a delightful damsel (but naturally) who was serving me a four-course meal when her large policeman husband came in off late shift and she produced a baby daughter from the back room. You can't win them all.

Later the Fife's Shermans were in action on 1,000 ft Chapel Hill near Bure in heavy snow. On 4 January four of their tanks were knocked out with casualties. They withdrew to Tellin where nuns gave food and wine to the tired and shivering tank crews. The next day 23rd Hussars took over and the Fifes moved back to Wellin. The Airborne troops acting as infantry also suffered casualties from tremendous stonks by enemy medium guns in the Chapel Hill area.

'The Most Exciting Christmas Day of One's Life'

3 RTR, commanded by Lieutenant Colonel A.W. Brown, the third tank regiment in 29th Armoured Brigade, arrived in Dinant via Namur and were in action on 24 December. 2nd Panzer Division had arrived in Celles, Sorrines and Boisselles a few miles east of Dinant.

'C' Sqn brewed up a Mk IV at 0900. Full marks for the Sherman 17-pdr Firefly gunner who was relieving nature at the time! German infantry cut the road between Achene and Sorrine but 'A' Sqn knocked out a halftrack and another vehicle in Boisselles. Then two Panthers moving up to Sorrines were knocked out. But the Black Bull tankies now had two medium gunner regiments on call and on Christmas Day went on the offensive. The Germans were running short of petrol and the objectives were the recapture of Sorrines, Foy-Notre-Dame and Boisselles. Sorrines was easy but the bag in Boisselles was substantial. Then a squadron of US Lightning fighter-bombers ground strafed 3 RTR and again an hour later. Foy-Notre-Dame was ablaze and together with the US 2nd Armoured Recce Squadron, an allied combined operation, many Germans, vehicles and halftracks were captured. In all the three villages at the 'end of play', an immediate search was made for wines and spirits. The Chateau cellar at Boisselle was productive and at 0130 the Americans were terrific, they produced wine, K rations and stories equally quickly. An American Captain carried round gin, brandy and rum. It had been one of the most exciting Christmas Days of one's life. The next two days saw devastating attacks by RAF Typhoons as the German Panzers withdrew, leaving scores of petrol-less tanks and AFVs behind them.

Hogmanay 44/45

The Fife and Forfars were still in the Ardennes, at Falmignoul, with everyone feeling a little low. The NAAFI spirit ration appeared. Lieutenants

Tony Porter and Steel Brownlie were sitting quietly by the stove when at 10.30 p.m. there was a loud knocking at the door. In came Corporal Dave Finlay and Troopers Armit and Ballantine, well 'on' already. Dave kept reciting:

> Ma feet's cauld
> Ma shin's thin.
> Gie's ma cakes
> And let me rin.

Armit insisted that this referred to Hallowe'en, not Hogmanay. Dave kept shaking an empty cigarette packet and hinting, 'Nae reiks, nae reiks.' We played along for a bit, then produced our cigarettes. Unfortunately, we had put our treasured NAAFI bottles on a shelf behind the bar, more as ornaments than anything else – now they were spotted and had to be opened. Dave now insisted on getting our Squadron Leader, Pinkie Hutchinson, out of bed and downstairs. 'Whour's Punk?' We [Lt Steel Brownlie and Co.] went to Jimmy's billet and found him much recovered, singing to the music of Trooper Grieve's guitar. On the way back we came upon the half frozen body of Philip Noakes, the Intelligence Officer, lying in the road. He had been on the way to visit us but didn't quite make it.

Thus the Fifes saw in the New Year in the Ardennes.

Ardennes – The Rifleman's Journal

Late in December, 8 RB were out of the line in Poperinghe in civilian billets refitting their tracked vehicles and preparing for Christmas.

We got two hours' notice to move out again. Reluctantly, we moved off under command of 2nd Fife and Forfar tanks and travelled by night through Brussels down to Namur. The weather worsened. It was so bitterly cold that there was ice everywhere. We moved to the river Meuse and were told the bridge must be held at all costs. By Christmas Eve we [Trooper Roland Jefferson et al.] had continued alongside the river to Dinant where there was a lot of frantic American activity. Lots of Germans dressed as Americans using US transport and tanks made things rather uneasy. The bridge at Dinant was wired ready for blowing up. Most of the traffic across it was retreating Americans. We then went further south to Givet. The German advance had been halted at last. We were now to cross the river and throw them back. We moved into a village called Heer and spent New Year's Day (my 20th birthday) there. We experienced trouble with frozen engines, frozen guns and frozen carrier tracks, so much that they wouldn't steer. We did get our teeth into the enemy. We took our revenge and shot at anything that moved. At least this kept the guns warm enough to use. In one defensive position a dead

German was lying a few yards away. We tried to bury him in a nearby shell hole. It was too small so one of my colleagues simply hacked off his legs with a machette. Then we covered him with snow to bury him.

Communications

'In the battle of the Ardennes 8 RB found themselves guarding Dinant. They were issued with ten carrier pigeons which, when released, would fly back with messages to 21st Army Group at Brussels. They were lovely birds and with them arrived their rations and a pamphlet couched in the best Army "Q" language on their maintenance. Their arrival provided us with a very welcome light interlude and after much animated discussion, a caretaker, in the person of the faithful and versatile Hodgson, was found. We were very tempted to dispatch one bearing Christmas greetings from us all to "Monty".' [Major Noel Bell, 8 RB]

The Horseback Patrol

61st Recce Regiment were about to be disbanded when 50th Tyne Tees Division was broken up but were granted a temporary reprieve when the Germans launched their savage counter-attack in the Ardennes in mid-December. Colonel Brownrigg, their CO wrote:

> We joined the armoured brigade of 11th Armoured Div first sitting along the length of the Meuse from Namur to Givet then gradually patrolling further forward until towards the end of the campaign, we had a battlefield of our own with a front of 20 miles between the British and the Americans. Day after day our armoured cars set out to find and kill as many enemy as they could. And daily they met anti-tank guns and tanks. And when the armoured cars could not get on, the assault troops penetrated deep into enemy territory.

Lieutenant Spreag, on his first operation towards St Hubert, had his carrier blown up on a mine. Undeterred he commandeered a horse (first-ever ride) and with two Belgians rode to and through St Hubert. The enemy had just left. That night the RBC reported that British *armoured cars* had entered St Hubert. The following day the intrepid Spreag, with Lieutenant Abercrombie, walked/marched 20 miles through mine-infested country to meet the British 6th Airborne Division hastily sent south to help out. In two days in icy conditions they covered 50 miles on foot!

CHAPTER TEN

Breaking the Siegfried Line: the Reichwald Battles

A Cosy Little Nest

There were certain well-known 'Bomb Alleys' on the Dutch/German borders which were notorious for their casualty rate. Desolate, mainly destroyed, villages such as Leunen, Veulen and Ijsselstein had to be defended come what may. Major W.N. Mitchell with the Ayrshire Yeomanry had established himself with the infantry battalion HQ in a farm.

> In the large farmstead we constructed the only bomb-proof pigsty I have ever seen, with ammo boxes filled with earth to reinforce the walls, and four feet of wood and earth on top of the walls. It was an eye-sore but a safe place for the wireless sets. Each infantry unit which came into the area used to scoff when they saw our den, but after a week in Veulen they became rather jealous of it. One day we were very heavily shelled and there were dozens of casualties in the village but we were still at full strength at the end of the day so all our labours were justified. What was most important was that we were at all times fully operational. On one occasion two strangers in trench coats came into the famous bomb-proof pigsty enquiring politely whether there was any tea and a brew was put on for them. Major General 'Pip' Roberts GOC 11th Armoured Division was seldom far from the front line – at any time.

Portrait of a General

The GOC of 3rd British Division was Major General 'Bolo' Whistler, who earned his curious nickname in the fighting in Russia after the First World War. In the 7th Armoured Division he was known by his Queen's Brigade as 'Private Bolo' due to his penchant for going out on patrols in the desert dressed like the rest. He was a big man, a chainsmoker, a great leg-puller and owned three cars at Divisional HQ, known as 'Bolo Major', 'Bolo Minor' and 'Bolo Minimus' (his jeep). His CRE, Brigadier Tony Evill, described him as 'a tall scornful General with a twinkle in his eye who knew more about fighting in this war than anyone I had previously met. In 1940

Monty talks to GOC 'Bolo' Whistler, May 1945. (Imperial War Museum, London)

one of his nicknames was "The Man who went back to Dunkirk" after he returned to collect a missing 4 Royal Sussex company from the beaches. I saw an infantry Bn on its way into battle. They were resting on both sides of the road when "Bolo" came back from the sharp end. He was driving himself, flag flying and his hat as usual on the back of his head. Every man stood up and waved to him as he went past, laughing and waving in reply.'

Operation Blackcock

XII Corps were given the task of clearing the triangle formed by the rivers Roer, Wurm and Maas, defended by 176th and 183rd German Infantry divisions with many dug-in SP guns and 88 mm. Operation Blackcock started on 13 January with the Desert Rats on the left flank and 52nd Lowland Division plus 8th Armoured Brigade in the centre. Starting from Gebroek, the main towns and villages were Susteren, Heide, Slek, Echt, St Joost and Montfort. For fifteen days and nights, savage fighting took place among minefields and in the intense cold. The 'Funnies' of Hobart's 79th Armoured Division did great work, with Flails, vicious Crocodile flame-throwers, and AVREs with fascines for bridging anti-tank ditches and large bomb/shell craters. The success of Blackcock did much to restore the reputation of 7th Armoured Division.

The Songbirds

Major Derrick Watson, 1/5th Queen's, recalls:

Rather apologetically my CO [Lieutenant Colonel Freeland] told me that my first orders as a company commander would come from the 9th DLI to whom I was detached under command. We were to advance across two water obstacles [over the Vloed Beek] carrying sections of Kapok bridging, then towards a main road [Sittard to Roermond]. I was given a map and an incomprehensible aerial photograph. So we set off at last light – in the distance there was continual mortar fire, Very lights, Spandaus firing on fixed lines.

They reached their first objective, the derelict buildings of a concrete works, safely. Derrick Watson was next ordered by Lieutenant Colonel Freeland to take his company to join up with 'C' Company under Major Lilley, who had been supporting the tanks and the Rifle Brigade near Millerode. 'Contact had been lost. With a heavy heart I ordered the Sgt Major to fall the men in on the road – they had spent a cold night – no sleep, no food or drink for more than 12 hours. Was it too much to ask? I had a dreadful thought – suppose they refused to follow me? As we marched off the men behind me spontaneously burst into song!' After a mile or so they reached the next village, 'a scene of devastation which silenced the singing'. The houses in the main street had been shelled to ruins. Some wounded 'C' Company told him where to find Major Lilley and 'he greeted me with a broad grin and said, "This rum has kept me going for the last 36 hours."'

'Rushed in Screaming and Shouting'

At 0200 on 17 January 1/5th Queen's attacked Susteren from the west in the pitch dark and in thick mud. It was impossible to get the 6-pdr anti-tank guns across the dykes. A counter-attack was driven off by Brens and 3rd RHA stonks just after a foggy dawn. 'B' Company under Major John Evans DSO moved forward at 0400 and got within 30 yds of the outskirts of Susteren, 2 miles from the German border. Evans wrote:

We heard a guttural shout and a single shot was fired. We then adopted our usual tactic of rushing in screaming and shouting, firing from the hip. We ran through the forward part of the town taking about 37 prisoners and not suffering a single casualty. At dawn we discovered three enemy tanks in the town. There were no 6-pdr A/Tank guns. Our own tanks had failed to reach us because of the dykes, drainage ditches and soft ground. There followed some desperate fighting with the tanks demolishing corner street properties on top of our men. Corporal Dolly knocked the track off one tank with a PIAT for which he later received the Military Medal. I fired my captured Schmeisser – two short bursts at two tank commanders in their open turrets. It was obvious we were in for a long day and would suffer many casualties.

The acting CO, Major Jack Nangle, arranged that the Corps Artillery would shell the village to try to knock out the tanks. During the shelling and counter-shelling Evans was badly wounded and Lieutenant Stone was killed. It was a shambles but the company held its position in spite of thirty-nine casualties, including all the officers, but twenty-nine Queen's were taken prisoner. Against that forty enemy prisoners were taken and at least that amount killed. 'Less than 40 men survived that day. Captain John Franklyn and all the platoon commanders were killed.' John Evans was the only officer to survive, although with two sets of wounds, including the eventual amputation of his left arm. The war artist Bryan de Guingeau had two pages of illustrations of the Susteren battle in the *Illustrated London News* of 17 February 1945.

Battle for St Joost

The Desert Rats grimly fought their way northwards, as Lieutenant Bill Bellamy of the 8th Hussars reported:

Meanwhile the battle in St Joost itself became fiercer and fiercer. It was a desperate struggle between first-class British troops and one of the toughest of the German Parachute Regiments – Hübners. Early on the morning of the 21st another attack was mounted on St Joost. Once again 'B' Squadron under Wingate Charlton fought with great gallantry in support of the infantry. Thick fog reduced visibility to less than 100 yd. Richard Anstey and Douglas Ramf were ordered to take their two troops, retrace the route of the previous day and find a way round St Joost to outflank it from the east. I was sent to the bridge in Hingen to act as a forward wireless link if needed. The tanks clattered off into the dense fog and all went well for some minutes. Then I heard Richard shout over the wireless, 'Two SPs to our front – engaging', and at the same time I heard the crack of three shots from tank guns, followed by a series of shots, then silence. [Two of Richard's and one of Douglas's tanks had been knocked out by three Mk IV 75 mm SP guns.] I had an extraordinary view of St Joost and could see and hear the noise of the battle. It sounded and looked to be terrifying, flames, smoke, continuous machine-gun and rifle fire, the crack of tank guns and the whistle and crump of artillery shells.

'The Usual SNAFU Followed'

Sapper Lance Corporal Les Baynton, 757th Field Company RE, wrote:

We were holding the area known as the Island. The retreating enemy had released floodwaters to inundate the whole of the low-lying land, so that only roads built on bunds and villages on the higher ground could be seen. Intelligence reports knew that German paratroops would make a diversionary attack in early January in the direction of Zetten. There was a vital bridge over a canal which the enemy would use so sappers would prepare the bridge for demolition by explosives protected by infantry in front. At least that was the plan. The usual SNAFU followed. Our RE platoon arrived in the ice and snow to find that the Gloucesters [49th Polar Bear Division] had not crossed the canal. We waited until dusk shivering in the freezing air, without rations all day. Nothing to see but the leaden sky, frozen acres of water, twisted enemy corpses covered by a fresh fall of snow, the distant crump of mortar bursts, the torn-silk rapidity of German 42 MG and the slower rhythm of return fire from Bren guns.

Everything went wrong. The bridge was a flat concrete structure. The flooded canal level was up to the underside of the bridge. Baynton and his platoon were shelled by *their own* 4.2 in mortars. The infantry were lying half-way across the bridge, under Spandau fire. The RE dinghy party went the wrong way and were seized as possible saboteurs. So Baynton inserted the detonators, set off the igniter and made a dash for safety. The bridge was not shattered. The RE Adjutant got a MC for the job!

Player's Please – the Padre's Story

'Jan 31 1945. Cigarettes were things I was never short of. After Colonel Kellett had been killed in the North African Desert he was succeeded by his 2 i/c Donny Player, the MP for Newark and a member of the famous cigarette manufacturers in Nottingham. The Sherwood Rangers being a Nottinghamshire Yeomanry Regiment had a number of men in the regiment who worked for Player's. Following the death of Donny Player, killed in action, the family wrote asking if there was anything they could do for the Regiment. A reply was sent saying the men much preferred Nottingham-made cigarettes to anything that was being made elsewhere! From then on the Regiment received 15,000 cigarettes in packets of ten each month and the padre distributed them how and whenever he liked. This continued in North-west Europe. In the regimental Aid Post, when the wounded were sent on, ten or twelve packets would be stuffed under the blankets or put in his small pack. When I went back down the line following up the casualties, similar handouts were made and of course one was giving them away when visiting forward areas, etc. How these monthly deliveries continued to arrive mostly on time remained a mystery! But I have often wondered just how many Woodbines Studdert Kennedy gave away to earn his nickname in the First World War!' [Padre Leslie Skinner, Sherwood Rangers Yeomanry]

The Dead Village

The Cherry Pickers had spent many dreary, cold, wet weeks in and around Dutch and Belgian farmhouses and hamlets. This is Lieutenant Brett-Smith's description of Moerdijk in early February 1945. It had a world-famous bridge, road and railway side by side, a mile long, a great engineering feat, which had been blown up by the retreating Germans at the end of 1944:

> Moerdijk was an exception even here, for it was nothing more than a shambles, with not one house untouched by fire, shot or bomb. The only signs of life were the cats – rangy, furtive animals who would suddenly streak across the street from one ruin to another. Of the German occupation there was little enough sign – a destroyed SP on the main street, an AA gun near the convent, and one grave – a rough affair with four empty shell-cases to mark the corners and the usual scrap of paper in a bottle, the cross made by nailing two bits of packing case together. From the tower of the convent you could see as far as the fine church of Dordrecht on a clear day, and all the village spires and windmills and red-roofed hamlets in between stood out in a vivid and colourful landscape when the sun was shining. On the far bank there were a number of white pillboxes manned by the enemy who sometimes got over-confident and sunned themselves on the grass nearby or watched their rations and ammunition coming up in little carts. Occasionally we registered a direct hit on these pillboxes but they were too strongly built to yield to our small mortar-bombs. Still it no doubt shook all the occupants and may have done some harm to the careless ones. But the chief memory of Moerdijk remains the dead village itself – the upturned piano in a front garden, riddled with bullet holes, the grave grey statue of St Francis of Assisi behind the convent gazing unseeingly at a pile of empty bully-tins, an old Ford car lurching on its rims in a charred garage, its tyres nothing but grey ashes. Moerdijk was strangely reminiscent of the villages in Normandy; there was the same smell of death, the same incongruous but terrible destruction.

The Battle of the Rhineland – Operation Veritable

Now that the scare about the Ardennes incursion had been settled, Field Marshal Montgomery and his planners laid out a new, truly massive operation. The holding of the line of the river Maas was now mainly entrusted to the Belgian and Dutch brigades and the Poles. 'Veritable' was to be the responsibility of 1st Canadian Army, which included under XXX Corps control, most of the British Army. The plan was to destroy the enemy holding the heavily fortified Siegfried line between the Maas and the Rhine. In order to avoid a costly head-on attack, 1st Canadian Army would roll up

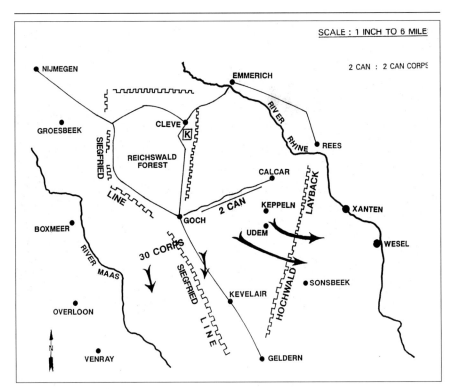

The battle of the Rhineland

the enemy defences from the north and meet the 9th American Army coming up from the south. From north to south the assault started on 8 February, led by 2nd and 3rd Canadian Divisions, the 15th Scottish along the north edge of the Reichswald forest to Cleve, the 53rd Welsh Division into the Reichswald itself and the 51st Highland Division on the right. The 43rd Wessex Wyverns and the Guards Armoured Division were in reserve. The Desert Rats had just, painfully but successfully, closed out the Venlo–Roermond triangle and 11th Armoured, after the Ardennes, were exchanging Shermans for the new Comets. Laboriously, the enlarged XXX Corps arrived east of Nijmegen to start the massive thrust south-east. The Rhineland towns of Cleve and Goch were now all-round defensive fortresses. The immediate front around Nutterden was held by the German 84th Division with five divisions in reserve.

A Wessex Wyvern Attack during Veritable

The 7th Battalion Somerset Light Infantry left Geldrop mounted on tanks and started out from Nijmegen. Private Len Stokes of 'B' Company recalled:

Operation Veritable: entry into Reichswald with the 53rd Welsh Division, 9 February 1945. (Birkin Haward)

We spent the whole night [of 9 February] on the tanks. It was bitterly cold, icy rain and driving sleet. I could not find any footholds and could only just manage to hold on with my fingers. We could not sleep for fear of falling under the following tank. The sky was full of tracer shells floating up. In the morning I shared breakfast – one tin of self-brewing soup with the CSM, but my hands and arms were useless – last stages before frostbite. [The SLI covered the 10 miles to Kranenburg and at 1600 on the 11th had to capture the village of Hau along the Goch road.] During the rest of the night and all the next day, 12th Feb, we were heavily shelled and mortared. At 1448 hrs 'B' Coy were counter-attacked by two companies of infantry supported by three Panther tanks. We had spotted them forming up but could not get through on the radio to Bn HQ for artillery support.

Len Stokes was detailed to run 60 yd back along the road to get a verbal message to the CO, Lieutenant Colonel Ivor Reeves. But the CO came up in his Bren gun carrier to check the accurate map references for the artillery. 'The mortaring and the small arms fire was now very heavy. To me this seemed a very brave act. The bombardment slaughtered the Germans.'

'Failure was Unthinkable'

The Siegfried Line battle was probably one of the most important in the long proud history of the Gordon Highlanders. The 1st Battalion took 350 prisoners for the loss of twenty-five casualties. Their FOO, Major Frank Philip, had brought down 850 rounds per gun in support of the Gordons. During the action on the west of the Reichswald near Del Hel, 'A' Company under Dennis Aldridge had failed to take their objective, a strongpoint astride the main road to Mook-Gennep. The Gordons' acting CO Major Martin Lindsay wrote, 'I knew that both the Divisional and Corps Commanders were waiting for the news that 1st Gordons had opened up the road. Failure was unthinkable.' So Lindsay personally took command of 'D' Company and told its CO, Alex Lumsden, to act as Battalion CO.

> We climbed up the face of a steep ridge and the four platoons deployed, two in front, two behind facing west. But the wood was jungle, so many branches and trees having been felled by our shelling. We might well have been in darkest Africa. Every hundred yards took us about 15 minutes. The confusion was indescribable. All we could do was to push on slowly, climbing over tree trunks and branches or crawling under them. What an awful balls-up I've made having lost all control. It's all going to be a ghastly failure.

The Gordons were ambushed and mortared but captured seventy-one of a column of Huns all shouting 'Kamerad!' Lindsay ordered his pipers to play the regimental march 'Cock o' the North' and then ended up in a minefield. By the end of the day all four of 'D' Company officers were dead or wounded. But the vital Mook-Gennep road had been cleared.

A Truly Gruesome Sight

On the outskirts of Cleve, the 43rd Wessex Wyverns Division, was involved in house clearance and street fighting. Lance Corporal Miller and Privates Skilton and Hewett of the Wiltshire Regiment dashed into their Platoon HQ during a pause in the battle. Skilton decided to run across the street to his section billet. He had just left when three shells burst all around them in rapid succession.

> We were sure that he must at least be wounded so Sergeant Stacey, Lance Corporal Miller and I [Pte R. Gladman] went to look for him calling his name. We found no trace of Skilton until we reached the doorway of his house billet and saw what was left of him after a direct hit from an 88 mm shell. His scalp was stuck on the wall two feet over the door. His head was hanging by the skin of the back of his neck. One leg and one arm were missing and the remaining leg was shattered. His wrist was hanging by a bit of skin. His intestines were in a heap covered by his body. All we could do was to scrape the pieces into a blanket and carry it away, leaving a pool of blood in front of the door and drops spattered all over the front of the house. A truly gruesome sight.

Leaning on the Barrage

When 50th Tyne Tees Division was disbanded, Lieutenant Geoffrey Picot became a Platoon Commander with the 7th Battalion Hampshires in the 43rd Wessex Wyverns. He led an attack during 'Veritable'.

To help us on our way we are to have a rolling barrage of artillery fire, moving forward at a predetermined speed, about 100 yds every minute. The barrage will make the enemy cower at the bottom of their slit trenches or in the cellars of their buildings. If we arrive at these positions the *instant* the barrage lifts we can kill or capture them all. But if the enemy spring to their firing positions before we can get there they will be able to mow us down mercilessly.

All depends on our keeping up with the shell-fire. 'Lean on the barrage,' we have been taught in training. 'It is better to risk casualties from the occasional shell from your own side falling short than to allow the enemy a few seconds to recover.'

I place a section of ten men in front, in line abreast. I follow immediately behind, with the other twenty-five members of my platoon strung out behind me. The barrage starts and we move with it. For ten minutes I do not stop shouting.

'Keep up the pace. Don't slacken. Keep up the pace. Keep up. Don't stop. Keep up.'

A soldier complains. 'But there's a Spandau firing at us from over there on the right. I had better take it on.'

'No,' I yell. 'Don't stop for anything. Fire the Bren back at him from the hip if you like, but keep moving. Throw a smoke grenade if you like, but keep up, keep moving, keep up, don't stop.'

Another soldier reports. 'Two wounded enemy here, sir, we can't leave them.'

I reply, 'Yes, you can. Leave them. Leave everything. Just keep up with the barrage, that's all we've got to do. Keep up. Keep up. Don't lose the barrage.'

'It might be dangerous to leave them,' the soldier persists.

'Shut up,' I bellow. 'Don't stop. Keep up. Keep up.' There's plenty of shells landing everywhere. I'm not surprised there's some wounded.

One of my men reports, 'There's movement on our left, sir.'

'Fire as you go with anything you've got,' I reply. 'But don't stop. Keep up. Keep up. Faster, faster, keep up.'

Lack of Leaders – Fun while it Lasted

1/5th Gordons were ordered to take Thomashof, just south of Goch, on 19 February 1945. Major Martin Lindsay, their acting CO, wrote a detailed account of the action.

It was a lovely clear night with visibility a good 200 yds – pleasant to be in open country after the dirt, dust and shelling in ruined Goch. . . . Unfortunately for one reason or another it took about two hours to get 'B' Company off with some tanks. Just before they started, one or two men from 'A' Company came in to say that the company had been overwhelmed and they were the sole survivors. The enemy was very strong and shortly afterwards put in several attacks and the company was overwhelmed through lack of leaders. Our experience was that once the leaders were hit, an attack petered out. We found eight or ten dead but forty-three men were missing. 'B' Company had 10 men killed in capturing Thomashof but took 80 prisoners. George Morrison was exceedingly brave in a very nasty attack and later received the DSO. A new officer, Ventris, also did well, being wounded five times in the course of the battle. He had been with us for only four days. 'It was fun while it lasted,' he said as they took him away on a stretcher.

Operation Heather, and Stokes' VC

On 1 March, 3rd British Division (the Iron Sides), crossed the Udem–Weeze road, the 2 KSLI and Warwicks leading, across very difficult country – woods, water-logged fields, no roads and scattered houses. The Warwicks only repulsed an enemy counter-attack after very heavy fighting, but on their right the battle for Kervenheim continued. 185th Brigade, now commanded by Brigadier F.R.C. Matthews DSO, bore the brunt of the subsequent fighting and their advance was bitterly contested. Here, Private J. Stokes of 2 KSLI 17th Platoon 'Z' Company, won a posthumous Victoria Cross. The citation for the award ran:

During the advance the platoon came under intense rifle and medium machine-gun fire from a farm building and was pinned down. The Platoon Commander began to reorganize the platoon when Private Stokes, without waiting for any orders, got up and, firing from the hip, dashed through the enemy fire and was seen to disappear inside the farm building. The enemy fire stopped and Private Stokes reappeared with twelve prisoners. During this operation he was wounded in the neck. This action enabled the platoon to advance to the next objective and Private Stokes was ordered back to the Regimental Aid Post. He refused to go and continued to advance with his platoon.

On approaching the second objective the platoon came under heavy fire from a house on the left. Again, without waiting for orders, Private Stokes rushed the house by himself, firing from the hip. He was seen to drop his rifle and fall to the ground wounded. However, a moment later, he got to his feet again, picked up his rifle and continued to advance, despite the most intense fire. He entered the house and all firing from it ceased. He subsequently rejoined his platoon who, due to his gallantry, had been able to advance – bringing five more prisoners.

At this stage the company was forming up for its final assault on the objective, which was a group of buildings, forming an enemy strongpoint. Again, without waiting for orders, Private Stokes, although now severely wounded and suffering from loss of blood, dashed on the remaining 60 yds to the objective, firing from the hip as he struggled through intense fire. He finally fell 20 yds from the enemy position, firing his rifle to the last, and as the company passed him in the final charge he raised his hand and shouted goodbye.

Another Cat and Mouse Game

Near Weeze in early March, 13th Platoon, 2nd Battalion East Yorkshires were in action in the woods. After 'Tabby' Barker had been wounded, Lionel Roebuck decided that 'a more vigilant lookout was then kept'.

I fired at every movement where it was obvious that the Germans were preparing to make a counter-attack. Artillery fire called for to shell the enemy position, dropped shells just clear of the defence line. The evening came without our position being rushed. Whenever a move started from the trees, a volley of rifle fire and grenades stopped it. My Mills .36 grenades had been used and a lot of my rifle .303 ammo. I even resorted to using the Luger pistol. It became a cat and mouse game with the Germans just waiting to make their move. [At nightfall the East Yorkshire platoon moved back into the Schaddenhuf farm where Company HQ was situated, while shells rained down on their shelter.] A direct hit on the dugout sent shrapnel crashing through my steel helmet and into my head with such a bang! Taking off my helmet, I saw a big hole through it. One of my mates pushed it back on, then I knew nothing more until coming round in a Military Hospital after an operation to remove the bone and splinters! My first recollections after at least two days of unconsciousness were of brightness and of voices asking questions about sensitivity to touch on my legs and the right side of my body.

Lionel was flown back to hospital in Oxford and eventually recovered. During twenty-four hours of intense fighting the East Yorkshires suffered 160 casualties. The enemy lost forty-five dead counted on the battlefield, 150 POW and several hundred wounded.

Operation Veritable

Appalling weather had slowed down the impetus and tank and AFV support was very limited. The Germans breached the banks of the Rhine upstream and floods started to rise; they rushed up reinforcements and eventually had some ten divisions, 1,000 guns and 700 mortars with very well prepared Siegfried line bunkers, registered DF targets, Dragon's Teeth concrete obstacles and the advantage that defenders usually have. Lieutenant General Horrocks had XXX Corps increased to 200,000 men and 1,400 guns supporting his five leading divisions. The real stumbling block was the huge, dense Reichwald forest which had to be laboriously cleared by 53rd Welsh Division and 51st Highland Division. The River Roer had been so flooded by the Germans blowing dams, that the US 9th Army coming up from the south could make little progress, so the German forces were able to concentrate on XXX Corps. The 'Funnies' of 79th Armoured Division were magnificent, with Flails beating through minefields, Crocodiles breathing flame into the mouths of pillboxes, AVREs with fascines for blocking up anti-tank ditches, and bridging tanks for larger crossing places. But General Mud nearly won. The 15th Scottish and 43rd Wessex met in the middle of Cleve – bombed and shattered by the RAF – in the largest traffic jam of the campaign. And on 16 February the fortified town of Goch, also destroyed but heavily defended, fell to the 43rd Wessex Wyverns and 51st Highland Division. The 52nd Lowland Division were now on the extreme right flank, and in Operation Heather 3rd British took Kervenheim and Winnenkendonk between Weeze and Xanten. On 23 February the 9th US Army finally managed to cross the swollen river Roer. The battle continued until 10 March, when all German resistance west of the Rhine had ceased. 'Veritable' was over, with 10,000 British casualties.

Monty's moonlight RE assault bridges and fascines support the 51st Highland Division near Goch, 28 February 1945. (Birkin Haward)

The Reichwald Battle – 'Damn Difficult Country'

The GOC of 3rd British Division, 'Bolo' Whistler, wrote on 4 March after returning from leave on 24 February:

> It seems the hell of a long time since February 24th. I would say we have had our most successful battle. Damn difficult country – centre line nonexistent, or on a mud track – yet we have done everything asked. We have captured 1,200 prisoners, nearly all paratroopers. We must have killed and wounded many more. The scenes of devastation in Germany are quite remarkable. There is nothing that has not been damaged or destroyed. The civilians are mostly old and have genuinely had enough. They are responsible after all and I do not think they will want another war. We have captured Kervenheim, Winnenkendonk, and Kapellen of the largest places. I would say that 9 Brigade under Renny have done best; 185 next under Mark Matthews. 8 Brigade have not had so much luck, though E Yorks had a terrific night holding a bridgehead against repeated counter-attacks. The 7.2 in Howitzer Mk VI which was only 50 ft from my caravan fired all night and the harassing fire of the field guns firing just over my Tactical HQ was really a bit much.
>
> Where all have done well it is difficult to single out any, but the Gunners have been first-class as usual under Gerald [Mears] – the sappers ditto under

Night attack on Weeze: 82nd Assault Squadron bridge A/TK ditch, supporting the 53rd Welsh Division, 28 February 1945. (Birkin Haward)

AVRE Skid Bailey bridge being launched in attack on Weeze, 28 February – 1 March 1945. (Birkin Haward)

Tom Evill. The RASC, under the most trying conditions have kept us topped up with ammunition (and we have certainly shot off a bit!). The Staff have been fine, too.

Comparisons

'I am sure that every infantryman has compared himself with his opposite number. No other front-line man in the world can be compared to a German. He must be born with militaristic tendencies. He obeys his commands without question. I have seen a German company form up in a long line and at one word of command move forward into a hail of fire without flinching. It always seemed to me a reckless, mindless stubborn attention to duty. I know I could not recommend it to myself or my comrades. The Americans when we fought alongside were slap-happy in their approach. They had a heavy reliance upon superior armour and used ten times as much material as they need have done to accomplish their targets. There was spasmodic bravery among their members but on the whole their hearts were not in the war game, although the British cause would have been lost without them. The British soldier was dogged in approach and in my own Division [43rd Wessex Wyverns] he excelled himself in defensive tactics. In attack he was often brave but ineffective. He was a civilian in uniform doing the best as far as he knew it and was willing to persevere to the end. The Germans fought bravely to the end when all hope was gone. The British fought as a duty and begrudged the

Action on the road to Weeze: a Petard 'dustbin' is on the right, 1 March 1945. (Birkin Haward)

sacrifices made, but in all decency they fought well, knowing that in the end, the outcome was assured.' [Corporal William Gould, 1st Battalion Worcestershire Regiment]

Next of Kin

'Regarding the "Casualty" letters – it was the [Sherwood Rangers Yeomanry] Regiment's invariable custom for letters to be sent to the next of kin of all those Killed in Action and those who had been with the Regiment for some time, before being seriously wounded, or posted Missing. The Colonel would write regarding all Officers, senior NCOs and any other rank of whom he had personal knowledge, and this meant a great many indeed. Each Squadron Leader would write regarding all ranks of his own Squadron. I [Revd Leslie Skinner] also wrote regarding *all* casualties throughout the Regiment in addition to those already mentioned. If, as usually happened, the family wrote back then it fell to me to reply. Finding time to write these letters at the end of a long day or at odd moments in the midst of battle, writing in adverse conditions, was a continuing problem to us all. My Pocket Casualty book and personal diary provided invaluable reference material. Hardest of all was the impossibility of giving complete detail. Having dealt with the remains of a body blown to pieces either in the tank or on a minefield, it was impossible to say their boy had died instantly without suffering.'

Showbusiness

'On 10 March "Monty" came to pin on medals in the theatre in Peerbohm Platz in Ypres. Outside there was a guard of honour but he gave most attention to the huge crowd of civilians who were roped off some way away. Inside there were banks of lights on the stage and "Monty"s photographer in the orchestra, ready to record each presentation. Enter the great man and his first action was to adjust one of the banks of lights. Only then, to the packed audience, "Sit down, please." Centre-stage was a chalk circle into which each recipient marched, halted, exchanged a few words, had his ribbon pinned on and marched off again. Comparing notes later, we found that he had six stock questions, of which he would ask each man three. Mine [Lieutenant Steel Brownlie, Fife and Forfars] were "What were you in civvy street?" (music-hall reply, "Happy"', but I restrained myself), "When did I come over?" (D+10, same day as the King), "What did I intend to do after the war?" (no idea).

A group photograph was taken outside and later each man decorated was sent two copies, one signed by "Monty" and two copies of the pinning-on, one signed by "Monty". He was a great showman, but why not? He was a morale-booster and I think a great general as well.'

Departure for the Front

On 12 March 1945 the Fife and Forfars loaded their brand-new Comet tanks on railway wagons or tank transporters en route for the Rhine crossing. They were leaving Ypres after ten weeks of tank-training and rest. Steel Brownlie recalls the departure:

> It was not an orderly scene in the military sense. Almost all the population at six in the morning were out on the pavements, waving. Some were weeping and one of the sergeants ran out of his billet (where there was a woman in a dressing-gown) and jumped on the nearest passing vehicle: fairly well dressed except that he was wearing one black shoe and one brown one. I then had to pack up the Squadron Mess assuring Madame de France that all bills would be paid by the Town Major. She was not too happy. We then had a sumptuous meal in the Vieille Barrière (roast duck, etc.) which cost me a week's pay. Alan Gardner, Bill Waller and I went round the cafés, where some of the girls did some extraordinary tricks. Like . . . Our fitters were billeted in a brothel and there was some trouble getting them out at the first morning parade.

CHAPTER ELEVEN

From the Rhine to the Baltic: 'Twilight of the Gods'

'The Black Watch has Landed Safely'

Within two weeks of the end of the battle for the Reichswald, immense and detailed plans had been made for the crossing of the river Rhine. A massive two Corps attack – Operation Plunder – was to take place on 23 March. Between the small towns of Wesel and Emmerich, Lieutenant General Horrocks' XXX Corps would be on the northern flank, and XII Corps to the south. In addition, two airborne divisions, 6th British (who had been part of the Ardennes 'Longstop' battles) and 17th US, would drop a few miles *only* into the heart of the German defences of 8th Parachute Division round Rees, and 6th and 7th Parachute Divisions on its flanks. In reserve were 15th Panzer Grenadier Division and 116th Panzer Division. Prime Minister Winston Churchill visited the British Forces and spoke to the 51st Highland Division. They played a Divisional Retreat with their massed pipes and drums – the Last Post, and 'Flowers of the Forest' and all the haunting Scottish airs. Field Marshal Montgomery was supposed to have said that the Scottish Divisions were best for assaulting, so 51st Highland and 15th Scottish made the initial assault crossings. The artillery fireplan was the biggest of the campaign. Along a 25 mile front 3,300 guns fired an intense hour-long barrage. The two artillery regiments of 11th Armoured Division fired 16,800 25-pdr shells in fifteen hours. The actual crossing of the Rhine – Operation Varsity – was backed by the amazing airdrop watched by almost 100,000 soldiers on the west bank. 250 Liberators were protected by 900 fighter planes. 6th Airborne were carried in 1,700 aircraft and 1,300 gliders but German AA defences still took their toll and downed seventy aircraft and fifty gliders. The Scotsmen crossed in Buffaloes and by 2100 the signal came back, 'The Black Watch has landed safely on the far bank.'

'The next morning dawned bright and clear; of all this stretch of brilliant days the most splendid. At about a quarter to ten, a few minutes before we expected them, the first aircraft carrying the parachutists came in, their blunt noses sparkling in the sun. They flew low, in parade-ground echelons, steadily and with irresistible purpose. From that first sighting the sky was as if paved above our heads with a ruler-straight road down which group after

Rhine crossing (Operation Plunder): scissors bridge and fascine at Haffen. REs support the 15th Scottish Division, 24 March 1945. (Birkin Haward)

group of these tubby, dark-green Dakotas serenely flowed. For more than an hour they rode in, close-packed, the 'road' in the blue sky stretching without gap into the haze to east and west. Soon the air held a fantastic jumble of traffic: the incoming echelons in perfect formation at the fixed, unwavering jumping height; the returning planes, their rigid patterns broken, returning fast – one by one, above and below, speeding home and away. Their jumping doors were open. They went by with their parachute ribbons trailing in the wind. Here a machine lurched past with a great tear in its tail-plane; another, with one engine shot away, slid crabwise and painfully home. And there were the few that tumbled down.' [Major Raymond Birt, 22nd Dragoons]

Death of a General

Major-General Thomas Renny, GOC 51st Highland Division, who had been wounded in Normandy, returned and was killed in his jeep by a mortar bomb during the Rhine crossing on his way to 152nd Brigade HQ. He was a brave man and took, for a very senior officer, almost foolhardy risks. He set great store by personal bravery and of officers setting an example. He refused to drive in an armoured car which most sensible senior commanders did on the battlefield. He watched many of his Scottish battalions going into the attack under mortar fire and on more than one occasion he was sniped

1st Leicesters on the Rhine banks *en route* to Arnhem, April 1944. (Charles Pell)

at on reconnaissance. He was one of the tallest men in the Division, and always wore a naval dufflecoat with the hood hanging down at the back and his hands in two large front pockets. He always wore a tam o' shanter with the Black Watch red hackle. No wonder his Jocks loved him. His death in action brought a ripple of shock through the British Army.

'Like Felix the Cat, They Kept on Walking'

On 29 March the Sherwood Rangers were supporting 152nd Brigade of 51st Highland Division near Dinxperloo after crossing the Rhine near Rees. Stuart Hills was now OC of the SRY Recce Troop and had to send a section of tanks down two roads while he and Sergeant Pothecary, Sergeant Hinett and the rest stayed put at a key junction. But soon Corporal Slater's tank was brewed by a bazooka and Trooper Southam was still inside it, now covered by enemy small arms and machine gun fire. Stuart asked Jack Holmes, his OC, for some infantry support to help rescue Southam in the 'dead' tank.

> The tanks and infantry duly arrived from 51st Highland Div. Their Coy CO as good as told me that I was a liar. He was sure there was no opposition on this road. The Bn 2nd i/c was with him. They made an impressive pair, the former with the DSO and MC, the latter an MC and bar. They were both armed with walking sticks only! 'Well, come on, show

RE Petard blasting a road block in support of the 53rd Welsh Division, Bocholt, 29 March 1945. (Birkin Haward)

us where this opposition is.' We started to walk up the road. I said to Jack, 'This is too bloody silly for words. As soon as we go round this next corner we're all going to be shot to pieces.' I warned the other two, but like Felix the cat they kept on walking. As we rounded the corner, we were met by withering fire and we all landed up in the ditch together.

Duly convinced, the Scots officers arranged an attack; Jack laid on artillery support and under fire the brewed-up SRY tank was towed back into safety. But Southam had had his head shot completely away.

Looting in Germany – the 'Unofficial Rules'

'We [51st Highland Division] were going to take *only* what was necessary to make ourselves more comfortable:

(a) such as bedding or furniture;
(b) necessities that the Germans could well get on without, e.g. eggs and fruit, but not food, such as meat or poultry;
(c) forbidden articles we wanted for our own personal use, such as cameras, field glasses, shotguns and cartridges;
(d) wine – usually looted from France already.

The Brigadier of 154 Bde was on his "throne" that morning and a Jock from his HQ passed his field of vision with a side of bacon, another with a wireless set and a third with a goose under his arm. Whereupon he rose in his wrath, sent for his Brigade Major and issued some very firm *new* edicts.'

After the Battle

On 7 April 1945 the Germans defended Loccum, a village north-east of the river Aller, where 12th SS Panzer Division fought almost to the last man. A combined attack, infantry and tanks of the Fife and Forfars, took the town, including the crews and covering infantry of seven 88 mm guns, amazingly overwhelmed by 'C' Squadron of the Fifes. Steel Brownlie wrote:

> At dusk I was withdrawn to harbour in the middle of Loccum. It is with relish that I recall the scene.
>
> Sqn HQ was in a café on the X-roads. There was a back room ready for the HQ officers where I put down my bed-roll, then went into the huge bar. Almost the whole squadron were crammed in there, in clouds of tobacco smoke and the aroma of suppers being cooked. The Comet tanks were parked outside with the usual guards and we were behind the infantry, who had dug in round the town. So, relax! There was a family of three or four Germans and half-a-dozen serving wenches, and they were ordered to keep steins of beer coming to all ranks. Within about an hour we had drunk the place dry. I liberated the entire stock of cigarettes, not for our use, but for distribution to any ex-POWs or Displaced Persons who might want them.

Spring

'As if to emphasize that the worst was done, the weather had dramatically changed. *Spring* burst upon us as decisively as if it had been ordered by a producer of a stage show changing his lighting between the acts. The sun burned hot, drying up the fields and bulldozed roads which now bred vast clouds of dust behind the lorries. Here and there in ruined gardens daffodil, crocus and primrose came suddenly into flower; or among the heaped bricks a cherry or a weeping willow was bright with blossom and new leaf. In their desolate setting these signals of renewal were, perhaps, the most moving of their kind that most of us will ever see. In the context of this stage of our journey they gave to the knowledge that it was nearly the end, an edge of joy. How moving, too, to see in fields so recently the setting for bitter fighting, and now edged with broken guns and tanks and new-made graves marked by a helmet or a down-thrust rifle, the footballers out in their shirts of canary yellow, Cambridge blue, and pillar-box red! It was impossible not to yield to the prevailing mood of optimism and happiness. One more effort, one more offensive, and it must be over, we told each other. There was a quality in these days before the last offensive of war in Europe that sets them

Wessex Wyverns on the march, April 1945. (Stan Procter)

apart in the memory. For we were at this time keenly aware of our unity, of the richness of the comradeship that now knit us close together. We had experienced much and shared many hardships. Having lost some of our best – whether by death, by wounds, or by transfer to other units – we had yet been fortunate beyond expectation that so many of us had come through. As one moved about, indeed, the regiment seemed hardly altered. The good, familiar faces were everywhere. And the very fact that so many friends of three and four years' standing were survivors bound us the more firmly. Latterly it had been very hard to bear the inevitable losses of battle. For the loss of any one of us was the loss to many men of a proved and trusted comrade whose virtues had been made clear in the trials of battle.' [Major W.R. Birt, 22nd Dragoons]

The End of the Gallant 3rd Monmouthshires

The Teutoburger Wald is a long, thin strip of dense woodland some 30 miles long and 2 or 3 miles wide running north-west/south-east a mile or so to the east of the Dortmund–Ems canal, 12 miles west of Osnabruck. It is a magnificent natural defensive position. Armour was useless on the tree-lined slopes, gunfire on top of the huge forest area was inadequate and the infantry as usual bore the brunt and were just sucked into its lethal maw. By the time 11th and 7th Armoured Divisions had forced a bridgehead over the Dortmund–Ems canal, no less than seven full companies of young, dedicated infantry cadets from a NCO training school in Hanover, leavened with middle-aged and experienced commanders, were dug in along the Ibbenburen Ridge. This was to prove one of the major defensive actions fought by the Germans in the closing months of the war.

The three key villages were Ibbenburen, Holthausen and Tecklenberg. The 159th Brigade of infantry, part of 11th Armoured Division, had the unenviable task of clearing the thick woods in the north-west sector. The 3rd Battalion Monmouthshires and 1st Herefords, backed up by the Shermans of the 2nd Fife and Forfarshire Yeomanry, blasted the outskirts of woods with HE and divisional artillery rained down stonks on the well dug-in Hanoverian cadets – all to little avail. The Mons made two gallant attempts to dislodge the enemy from the top of the crest. The thick undergrowth reduced visibility to a few feet. In the forest fighting 'C' and 'D' Companies were pushed back 400 yds by a sudden counter-attack. Fighting became confused, the companies were disorganized and with no information and many company and platoon leaders killed or wounded, sections lost touch in the undergrowth.

Roy Nash's Story – Chapman's VC

On 3 April there was torrential rain all night. At dawn an enemy counter-attack on Battalion HQ was only just beaten off by a troop of the Fifes. Corporal E.T. Chapman, a Brengunner from Rhymney Valley, won the VC for conspicuous gallantry and then took the mortally wounded Captain Mountford back to the RAP. Private Roy Nash was with 'D' Company at the time and wrote:

> Our radios were useless [in the thick woods], so the signallers were laying lines for field telephones. The wounded should find the wires and follow them back to the RAP. As we moved forward I said to Corporal Chapman that the wood was full of Germans. I could see footprints in the molehills and on the soil outside rabbit warrens, and a lot of dew had been knocked off the bracken. I spotted three Germans walking over to the right. I fired my rifle as fast as I could. I shot one, wounded the second but the other got away. We moved forward again up a hill down into an old slate quarry. As we neared the top of the far side, we were cut down by murderous machine-gun fire. It was the worst I had experienced in ten months of action. Many were killed and wounded and the terrible screams of the wounded and dying haunt me. I kept firing until I ran out of ammo. I lay down behind the wall, picked up thirteen empty bullet cases and pushed them into the ground in the shape of a cross. The German fire was still devastatingly accurate and many more of our lads were killed and wounded. [Nash was hit and the back of his right hand blown off.]

Suddenly I felt pain, terrible pain, wicked pain and I cried, broken-hearted for my Mum. Corporal Chapman told me to lay down and that the stretcher bearers were coming. He then picked up my Bren gun, put on a full magazine and said, 'I'll kill the bloody lot of them, Waas' (that was my nickname). I could see him firing hosepipe fashion from the hip.

One company was cut off on the top of the hill and when the Dorsets of 131st Infantry Brigade came to their rescue they trapped two companies of the German NCOs and killed them all. The Mons eventually took 100 prisoners, but by the time they were relieved at 1100 on 4 April, their casualties – forty-one killed, eighty wounded – were the heaviest in any action. That was the end of the magnificent Mons. Their casualties in the whole campaign were sixty-seven officers (twenty-five killed) and 1,000 ORs (242 killed). They had three commanding officers killed in action and 'C' Company had six consecutive COs killed. The battalion was taken out of the line. Corporal Chapman was awarded the Victoria Cross.

The Three-horse Race

By now 7th Armoured Division had advanced an astonishing 120 miles into the heartland of Germany within a week. On their right was 11th Armoured Division heading towards Osnabruck and this amazing three-horse race was completed by the 6th Airborne, recovered from their costly drop east of the Rhine with commandeered and makeshift transport (steam-rollers were popular), almost level-pegging. 'Snatch' Boardman, Skins (5 RDG), wrote:

Our centre line was to be Ahaus, Heek, Metelen, Wetteringen, Neuenkirchen and Rheine. There was plenty of resistance but the German population in general had suffered more than enough and most houses displayed white surrender flags from their windows. We had expected some form of resistance movement and sabotage attempts on our supply lines but there was nothing of the sort. Lack of sleep was becoming our main problem. [Later.] My troop was given the task of checking a road parallel to the main centre line, leading into Rheine. The leading tank struck a mine. The driver Bill Whitcombe was slumped in his seat desperately wounded, and was placed on a stretcher on a carrier to be taken back to the RAP. The carrier struck a mine and the crew became casualties and Bill was killed instantly. It was a gruesome business. He had been in the Recce Squadron for a long time.

The Cherry Pickers' 'Swan'

The advance was now going very quickly, as Lieutenant Brett-Smith wrote in his diary:

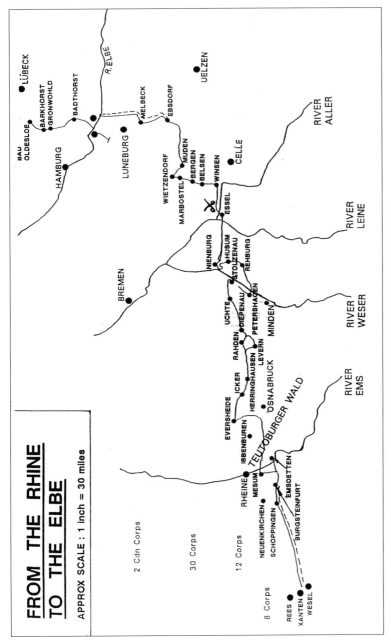

Operation Plunder: the race to the Baltic

On the 11th Hussars' first swan on a beautiful sunny day we streamed towards Rheine. On the faces of most of the civilians was a look of blank wonder and incredulity, for to them it did not seem possible that there were so many tanks, guns and cars in the world, for by this time the whole column was almost nose to tail. Scores of wounded Germans, some with an arm missing, some one-legged, others with bandages over their heads, limped and hopped to the roadside from the hospitals we passed, most of them silent and grim, a few excited and a few sneering. In the narrow streets of Neuenkirchen the rumble and rattle of the tanks and the explosive coughing and banging of their exhausts sounded unearthly and forbidding: a group of Luftwaffe pilots, with either no aircraft or no fuel left, stared sourly out of a café, and a stream of awed townspeople hurried down the steps of the church and back to their houses for it was Sunday and a service had just finished.

Easter Sunday in Enschede

3rd British Division Centreline in Operation Plunder after the Rhine crossing on their way to Bremen travelled along the German–Dutch border. The 22nd Dragoons, about to change their Flails for more traditional cavalry pursuits, received a marvellous welcome just inside Holland, as Major W.R. Birt recalls:

At dawn we were across the border once again and in Holland. On the one side empty windows, silence, and the white flags out on every house; on the other a delirium of joy and the orange and red-white-blue banners making the streets riotous with colour. It was Easter Sunday, and for the people along the road to Lichtenvoorde, Groenlo, and Enschede, a festival of rebirth and liberation indeed. They were out on the roads, a waving, cheering mass that surged over the tanks whenever they halted, shaking our hands or embracing our grubby faces, between tears and laughter. The colour of the House of Orange was everywhere: orange sashes, hats, hair ribbons, gloves; orange in the coat lapels and shoe buckles; orange festooned about the windows and on the doors; orange even on the collars of frenzied dogs and the tails of sober horses. And in Enschede (described to us with pride as the 'Manchester of Holland', but of a spotlessness that no man in Manchester would have owned to), which we reached next door, the welcome was even madder. Six hours earlier the Guards had driven straight through. On 185th Brigade fell the whole weight of the city's welcome. From the tank turrets one looked down into a pink blur of faces, of fluttering hands, of fingers raised in the V-sign, of flags and orange streamers waving. There was hardly room to drive the tanks between the crowds which pressed into the road and swarmed shouting about us whenever the tracks ceased to turn.

'They Never Stopped Fighting'

The names of Rees, Bienen, Millingen, Megchelen and Isselburg all represented a stiff tussle before they became ours. We were still battering our heads against the German paratroopers and they fought with a grim, hopeless bravery that no man could fail to admire. To defeat them was to kill the majority and then a few might surrender. In Megchelen they even continued to fight from houses that we [Major John Stirling, 4/7th RDG] had set on fire with the Crocodile flame-throwers. Fanatical and misguided, yes, but brave and well-disciplined also, yes. We never ceased fighting and we met some sticky patches. Progress was tremendously hindered by extensive demolitions and roadblocks. But it was no longer an army that was opposing us. Opposition was pushed steadily back, or overcome, or bypassed. Where before there had been tanks and anti-tank guns galore, they were now rarities. The ranks of men with bazookas who hid in ditches and hedges were prepared to blow themselves up, if they could blow up a tank at the same time. They never stopped fighting. Nor did they ever stop the steady, inexorable momentum of an army that knew it had won and was forcing its opponent into the corner of the ring and wondering whether the knockout or the towel would come first.

The 4/7th RDG drove through Enschede, Hengelo, Nordhorn, Lingen, Haselunne to Lindern. Then they were switched to attack Bremen from the south-east and pushed up towards Bremerhaven. 'To drive for miles through enemy territory and see the Germans standing outside their billets, standing and staring, a beaten foe, was the most marvellous finale to the show. Yes, he is beaten, thoroughly and absolutely trounced as never before.'

The End of the Luftwaffe – Silk Scarves

One of the last air battles of the war took place over the river Weser. An observer with the Ayrshire Yeomanry recalled:

The tactics of the air battle could be clearly observed. The Tempests patrolled up and down the line of the river trying to protect the 8 RB bridgehead and the near bridge being built by the sappers. When they were at the end of their 'beat', a German plane would appear from the clouds in which it had been waiting, dive on the bridge and drop the bomb. This went on for some time until the Tempest pilots realized what was happening and instead of continuing with their patrol, doubled back and caught the enemy just as they were poised to drop their bomb. In this way three Luftwaffe pilots were shot down in quick succession. One baled out and as he floated down crowds of khaki-clad men converged on him. He reached the ground, obviously thinking that Tommy's wrath would be the end of it and he would be torn to pieces. Not a bit of it. On the contrary, he was ignored! The troops descended on his parachute, cut it to pieces and each went off with a very small scarf of the type that was all the rage at that time. The German pilot limped away, relieved but slightly puzzled at his reception. Prisoners in those days unless they came by the score or the hundred were just a nuisance.

The Motley Collection

All over Germany, villages and hamlets were defended by scratch battle-groups hastily cobbled together – a handful of 'pros', the surviving SS and Panzer Grenadiers, plus a motley collection of AA gunners, anti-tank gunners (without their guns), cooks, administration staff, policemen, U-boat crews, Luftwaffe, fire brigade, and of course the veterans of the First World War – the 'Dad's Army of the Fatherland'. But blow a bridge, put the schoolboys with their bazookas in a wood or farmyard, and at point-blank range a new Comet tank, let alone Shermans, Cromwells and Churchills would be 'brewed up'. Just occasionally a brand-new Tiger, or even King Tiger tanks in penny pockets, would turn up hot from the Ruhr factories. On the outskirts of Bremen, Hitler's troops fought ferociously. At every canal or river, they did the same. Every little battle took its toll of the invaders. Like it or not, the German troops fought superbly and many of them seemed happy to die for the Fatherland and so they did.

A Bit of a Shambles

The Panzer Grenadiers were fighting tooth and nail to keep their centre lines open into Bremen, as 'Snatch' Boardman of the Skins (5 RDG) relates:

As we re-entered Wildeshausen [on the evening of the 10th] we were met by a relaxed Sergeant Ted Glynn who directed us to the local school which would be our billet for the night. 'Get yourselves cleaned up. We have captured some hooch and we are going to have a party.' We told him there were 17 German tanks just up the road, but he replied, 'Don't worry, the Norfolk Yeomanry [with 17-pdr SPs] are in position all around the town and we can stand down.' We were having a meal when we heard a sudden shot and a round went through the roof of the school. 'Bloody fools,' said Ted, 'Some stupid bastard has started on the booze and fired his main armament.' The shot was followed by another, and another and a lot of Spandau fire. 'Mount up' came the shout and we were back in our vehicles and hearing radio reports that German tanks and infantry had followed us in. The Norfolk Yeo had assumed that they were with us. The leading tank had a heyday and simply shot at unmanned tanks as he drove down the road. The only crewmen in a tank were the RHQ radio operator, maintaining a link to Brigade, and 'A' Sqn leader's gunner, who knocked the leading tank out at point-blank range. The German infantry were in among us and we could not distinguish friend from foe. The RHA guns were called down upon *our* own position. We were lucky to escape with the loss of two scout cars and one tank damaged.

The Durhams lost their RAP and six medical orderlies were taken prisoner. It was a bit of a shambles. One theory was that the SS troops were determined to get their gin back before the Skins had drunk it all!

Steimbke – House-to-House Fighting

'We crossed over the River Weser at Petershagen, into the Nurnberg Forest and harboured at Husum. At daybreak we carried on through Luisburg and Wenden until we met stiff opposition at Steimbke, defended by young SS troops. They were holding practically every house and a grenade was thrown from one upstairs window into one of our carriers. Here we practised house-to-house fighting as we had been taught in training. We would throw a grenade into the house. As soon as it had exploded, rush in after it, and so on from room to room, and house to house. Trouble was we soon ran short of our "36" grenades. The only thing was to ask our tanks to help out with HE and shot after shot was fired into the houses until the whole village was a mass of flames and debris. About 40 Germans gave themselves up. There were well over 150 German dead lying around. The next obstacle was the River Leine. The bridges were blown but tanks and infantry were ferried across to form a bridgehead. Then the REs got us a bridge at Helstorf. We crossed and went on to Schwarmstedte.' [Rifleman Roland Jefferson of 8 RB]

Volkssturm – 'Dad's Army'

Towards the end of the Third Reich the elderly Home Guard were – in theory – called to defend their 'Vaterland'. It did not always quite work out like that. The Ayrshire Yeomanry at Beckendorf, south of the river Elbe, surprised half a dozen aged members of the Volkssturm eating their breakfast in a village right in front of their gun positions. Far from putting up a fight, however, the elderly defenders of the Reich requested permission to finish their meal before being taken prisoner, and the request was granted. The Troop Commander of 125th Battery RA thought the party looked too much like the Seven Dwarfs (without Snow White unfortunately) to be treated harshly!

Sitting Target

'The Aller bridgehead battle had been a desperate business, coping with hundreds of 15-year-old Nazi SS officer training cadets who were doing a final Götterdämmerung. I was FOO with 13 RHA and used my Sten as much as my 38 set to bring down DFs on the verges of the pinewoods. We buried most of the young Siegfrieds, and the following morning at 0700 found me in my Sherman OP tank bustling along a lonely road to join up with 3 RTR. The vast, gloomy woods made excellent hiding places for Wehrmacht. Soon I spotted a dozen on the left-hand side and ordered my gunner to brass them up. "We are loaded with AP, Sir." Most tanks had AP up the spout, just in case. "Target 100 yards, left, fire, load with HE." That was enough and the would-be werewolves scuttled away. Half a mile further on was a firebreak ride and track across our road. "Halt. 10 minutes break for cha, don't switch off, brew up, but keep a look out." Armed with Sten gun and spade I set off to answer the early call of nature on the edge of a soggy clearing about 75 yards away from my tank crew. Having done what was needed, I used the spade and was about to pick up the Sten. Suddenly I heard (truly!) three loud, clear "plops", rather like a large cow in rural surroundings. Not unduly worried, I looked round. There, about 20 yards away, quivering in the muddy grass, were three small mortar bombs. I ran back to the tank and urged my startled crew to pack up and set off – smartly! I doubt if they believed my story that a Panzer Grenadier had enough sense of humour to try for a "Tommy" officer – literally a sitting target in the woods. But I missed my early-morning tea.' [Lieutenant Patrick Delaforce, 13 RHA]

Belsen

Early on the morning of 13 April two German officers, both Medical Corps, arrived at 1st Cheshire Regiment HQ of 11th Armoured Division in a large staff car with a white flag. They stated that they had been sent by the camp commandant of Belsen concentration camp, 10 miles north-east of Engenhausen, to warn the British troops not to approach within 3 miles of the camp as a serious typhus epidemic was killing many of its wretched inhabitants. The camp, they said, housed 500,000 people, mostly Poles and Hungarians [all totally untrue] of whom 5,000 were stricken with typhus. Dysentery was also rife. Lieutenant Colonel Kreyer, CO Cheshires, sent the two German doctors back to Brigadier Churcher, CO 29th Armoured Brigade, at Bucholz, then via Division to Corps HQ. Major General 'Pip' Roberts, GOC 11th Armoured Division, wrote: 'It was arranged that the Germans would withdraw their troops by 1000 on the 14th and a Corps medical team would follow our leading troops to investigate the camp. It all went according to plan and we went on with the war.' In fact this terrifying place between Hermanaugberg, Bonstorf and Bergen, north of Winsen, held 35,000 men and 25,000 women, mostly German political prisoners, in two large camps. On arrival there were found to be 13,000 unburied corpses. All the first-line troops on the evening of the 13th were sprayed with white DDT anti-typhus powder.

In order to get medical help quickly into this disaster area, 11th Armoured Division 'management' had agreed to an unofficial 24 hour truce which allowed the German troops a breather. The dreadful camp staff were lined up on the right-hand side of the road, watching almost with amusement as the armoured cars, tanks and carriers of the Black Bull Division came through – slowly – honouring the truce. Lieutenant Patrick Delaforce, 13 RHA FOO with 3 RTR, spent an hour in his Sherman on the road between the two camps, looking at (and smelling) the awful scene. That same evening a few miles further on, 'We bumped their rearguard who gave us a torrid time. Little did I know at the time that in a couple of months I would be in Flensburg hospital "dying" of a typhus derivative, nor that a few months after that, forming part of a War Crimes Tribunal in Hamburg and on Friday 13 December be an official witness at Hameln when Mr Pierrepoint hanged thirteen convicted Belsen staff – before lunch.'

Miracles Do Indeed Happen

On the outskirts of Bedburg a German parachutist fired his Schmeisser at Lieutenant Sydney Jary, 4 SLI, from about 10 yd. One bullet went through Jary's beret, another under the jacket epaulette grazing his right shoulder, and a third ricocheted off the road and lodged in the palm of Jary's right hand. The German looked at Jary in amazement, threw away his Schmeisser, shrugged his shoulders – and surrendered!

Overkill!

'All lead tank commanders worried about bazooka men: one well-concealed resolute German Grenadier with a cheap, expendable short-range, anti-tank projectile (Panzerfaust) against 30 tons of the best available tank technology and five crew members, and often the odds were in his favour. On the morning of 18 April 1945, I was lead tank nearing Luneburg clearing the brigade centre line; on the right the woods came close to the road and as we were passing a small glade, I just glimpsed a steel helmet and the tip of a Panzerfaust in a fox-hole barely 50 ft away. "Driver halt – Co-ax traverse right – steady – on – 50 ft – fox-hole – fire"; the .30 Browning jammed. I reached for a phosphorous smoke grenade and then had a better idea and a 17-pdr APCBC armour-piercing shot was despatched to his fox-hole from which an ill-aimed bazooka had been fired. We hurried on. Some Cheshires were off-loaded from the tank troops behind but they found no trace of a bazooka man in the woods which really didn't surprise me at all. Fear (Knowing War Will End in Two Weeks) Lieutenant Ted Deeming 15/19th King's Royal Hussars.'

Fraternization, or 'Frat' (1)

The powers that be issued strict instructions about fraternization with the enemy. Now that Operation Plunder had taken the British Army into the heart of the Fatherland:

(a) no talking (except on duty), laughing or eating with Germans;
(b) no playing games with them;
(c) no giving them food or chocolate, not even to children;
(d) no shaking hands with them;
(e) no allowing of children to climb on/into a car;
(f) no sharing a house with any Germans.

Frat (2) – A Lost Cause

But as the end of the war loomed, the ban on *personal* contact with the German population became more difficult. A Yeomanry officer with 11th Armoured Division (Ayrshires) wrote at the time, 'But how can anyone hope to persuade lusty young Scottish troops to pay NO attention to the well-filled sweaters of the Fräuleins who paraded outside our billet areas? It was a lost cause. I made the fatal error of saying so to our new Commander Royal Artillery (CRA) who reproved me for allowing my men to fraternize. I was posted to India for my pains!'

Belli's Circus

Just south of the river Elbe, the little village of Neetze harboured an unusual 'enemy' battle group. A German SP gun had opened up on the advance units of 11th Armoured Division so a section of Rifle Brigade carriers were sent to make a reconnaissance of the area. The first thing that met their eyes was a collection of vehicles hidden deep in the wood, which they assumed was German transport, so they fired a belt of Browning at these objects. The reply to this was noises which made them think they had been suddenly transported to the jungle – for these were caravans of artistes and animals belonging to Belli's Circus. As darkness was coming on, the Recce Troops withdrew to the next village for the night. On their return the next day a great reception had been prepared. The fat lady, the lion tamer, the midgets and countless others turned out to greet the 'liberators'. The 23rd Hussars were there too and found lions, bears, two elephants, many ponies, a monkey, several fat women and an overpowering smell. Unfortunately two lions had been killed by 'A' Squadron Comets (the Hussars mistook them for Tigers) and two bears and three lions had ambled off into the woods unscathed. Two elephants surrendered!

Iron Tonic

'Ahead of us now within sight lay the mighty river Elbe. There was a rumour that certain Corps Commanders had bet each other 20,000 cases of looted French champagne to go to the first corps who reached the Elbe. We were in with a chance. 4 KSLI were to clear the last 1½ miles of gentle grassy farmland on which were eight or ten farmhouses, each made into defensive strongpoints. There was then a bridge across the river to Lauenburg. On the morning of 19 April I was FOO on foot with my signaller to support 4 KSLI advance towards the river embankment. It was held by 200 dedicated SS with plenty of Spandaus and one Tiger tank, and supported by artillery fire from the other side of the river. It was a nasty little battle and I used my Sten, as well as my radio for close support. By late afternoon we had gained the river bank and with light-hearted humour, I fired several Sten bursts at grey-clad SS running down the embankment, just to see them off the premises. We had a final "O" group on the first floor of a farmhouse overlooking Lauenburg across the river. I had started a nice little battery stonk onto targets on the far bank and while I was on the 38 set to my BC, "Bunny" Davies, a large grenade or small mortar shell came into the window opening, exploded noisily and wounded all six of us in the loft. I said to Bunny, "Keep on Battery targets. We've all been clobbered by a mortar bomb. Wait out." Fortunately no one was seriously hurt. I had six small shrapnel fragments in my left arm, shoulder and forehead and later that evening RMO Cree laboriously prised out four of them with medicinal whisky as the anaesthetic. Two fragments remained embedded out of reach of his extracting weapons. He shook his head sadly. "Hey," I said. "Come on Doc, get it over." He replied, "I can't operate here, you will have to go to hospital . . . or else!" "Else what?" continued the silly dialogue. "Or else we could leave the fragments in." I liked the royal "we". "Anyway," he said after further thought, "iron is good for your blood. You look rather pale. *You need a good iron tonic.*" And I think he meant it. Perhaps it was Scots humour but I did get an immediate week of sick leave in Brussels, with instructions to go to hospital, if I felt like it. The fragments are still there.' [Lieutenant Patrick Delaforce, 13 RHA]

Hell Let Loose – Trust in the Lord

Wally Caines, now promoted to Lieutenant OC Signals, wrote:

23 April, 4 Dorsets were in Volkerston protecting 52 Lowland Div's right flank going into Bremen. 1000 attack on village of Hellwegge, near Bremen. Troops were carried on tanks. The battle was like hell let loose as 'A' Coy went into the assault. The tank Regt CO ran from tank to tank pointing out enemy guns. 'There they are – the Jerry guns – fire.' The village crossroads is in our hands. Only a few prisoners taken, the main body literally slaughtered. TAC HQ near X-roads. We had no cover whatsoever, nothing to offer than to trust in the Lord above. Shells rained down upon us for several seconds. Shells burst all about us. I thought it was all up. The Colonel lay wounded on the ground with his legs smashed. I lit a cigarette and stuffed it in his mouth. This left Major Joe Symonds in command.

Arnhem, Second Time Around

The 49th Polar Bear Division garrisoning the Island launched an attack northwards. Sergeant Bob Sheldrake (Suffolk Yeomanry) wrote:

> It was a dead city [the Germans had evacuated the Dutch population]. The civilians were gone. Seemingly every shop was looted to its very floors. The plate glass windows of a large store lay shattered over the rubble, a dummy figure of a nude woman lay in the gutter, its stand sticking incongruously up into the air. Smashed glassware, clothing display stands half out of the windows, fire and smoke, crumbling walls and battered furniture littered the streets in utter and hopeless confusion. As we drew into a side street, the inevitable mattress lying in the road was split open by one of the tracks and the wind scattered the straw down the length of the street. [Later] some of the chaps investigating an old mill had found a complete silver band, left behind by the Boche, a complete set of beautiful silver instruments. The men had dragged the whole lot away and were now parading them among the gravestones of a cemetery. 'Math' and Charley Hole could manage some kind of tune. The ornate baton was swinging out in front, a host of wind instruments of all kinds were roaring out in one note, in time with their marching. The kettle drums were rattling and behind them all came 'General' Lee with the big drum. By nightfall the band was in full swing. Fred Savage had taken on the big bassoon. Now the snorts and blares were in time with the cymbals and 'Math' and Charley had got together with 'Blaze Away'.

'The Pinch of War'

'It was fun being in Germany proper. After five negative years we were at last bringing the war into the country of the people who started it. If you shelled a house because there was a machine gunner in it it was a German house and no longer did some wretched French or Dutch family go homeless. For the first time the warmongers were feeling the pinch of war, the scenes they had forced on Europe were being enacted at home now, and they were the players. German families were pushing German prams and handcarts laden with their household goods as they fled to safety. It was the German towns and villages that were the piles of rubble now and wherever the battlefield was, whichever side shelled it, it was Germany that suffered, and the phrase that had followed us across Europe was in German now and about Germany. "Alles kaput."' [John Stirling, 4/7th Royal Dragoon Guards]

'Something Snapped'

On 5 May the 2 i/c of the Kensingtons (MMG and Mortar Battalion of 49th Polar Bear Division) was ordered to negotiate capitulation terms at the HQ of a SS battalion beyond Utrecht. Major S. Jacobson MC wrote:

> I went off in my jeep with Private Hall, my driver, with a Dutch Resistance interpreter (with a Sten gun) and a German SS officer as guide. We passed the Recce Regt near Utrecht and went through the area not yet occupied by Allied troops. It was a queer drive. The villages seemed deserted except for armed German sentries, but as we drove through, curtains were drawn aside, windows flung open, flags put out and we could hear the hum as the streets began to fill with Dutch civilians. The SS Colonel and Adjutant had obviously just bathed, shaved and put on their best uniforms. He gleamed all over. I was in rather tired battledress. When the capitulation paper was signed, we were faced with an amazing sight. Piled high with flowers, the jeep was hemmed in on every side by men, women and children, all perfectly quiet. But when I came out with the bit of paper in my hand, something snapped. They cheered, laughed and cried. Led by their Pastor they sang the Dutch National Anthem. They made speeches. The interpreter made a speech, I made a speech. It was funny, it was exciting and it was deeply moving. For, at that moment, we realized that the war in Europe was really over.

The Capture of Bremen

The XXX Corps battle plan was for 51st Highland Division to make a feint attack on Delmenhorst on the west side of the city. The 3rd British Division in Buffaloes would make a surprise night attack across the flooded south-west sector of Bremen while 52nd Lowland Division and 43rd Wessex Wyverns attacked the main part of the city from the south-east. Although General Becker had been ordered to fight to the last, many of his troops had already tamely surrendered – that is to say, under a nonstop deluge of RAF bombing and XXX Corps shelling. The Wyverns captured Flak gunners, civil police and firemen, merchant seamen and U-boat crews plus German ATS in uniform. Brigadier Essame noted, 'They were treated with utmost correctness. Besides they were very plain.' Brigadier J.O.E. Vandeleur, CO 129th Brigade, recalled: 'We had to capture Burgher Park, a stronghold on the east side of the city. Our opponents were German marines who were lusty fighters.'

'By God, We've Got It'

Brigadier W.F.H. Kempster's 9th Brigade of the 3rd British Division were

REs support the 52nd Lowland Division clearing roadblocks, Bremen, 26 April 1945. (Birkin Haward)

Blasted, ruined Bremen, 26 April 1945. (Birkin Haward)

given a key task to take the southern sector of Bremen on the night of 24/25 April. The capture of Kattenturm village and the bridge over the heavily flooded Ochtrum canal would allow 3rd British Division to clear the main aerodrome and Focke Wulfe Aircraft works and provide a first-class advance axis into Bremen. The vital bridge was known to be prepared for demolition with four 500 lb aerial bombs connected up and ready to blow. A daring plan was hatched. A noisy artillery barrage in the middle of the night would drown the noise as the 2nd Battalion Royal Ulster Regiment under Lieutenant Colonel J. Drummond was ferried in Buffaloes with a special RE party to tackle the bridge demolition preparations. The Brigadier and his Brigade Major plus Reuters and Associated Press journalists visited the Ulsters just before H-Hour (midnight), all fortified with tea and rum. About 0130 radio reports came in: 'Leading sub-unit now disembarked and on firm base.' Then, between 0200 and 0430 more messages: 'Build up of Buffaloes complete. All sub-units landed and Fox Group, wheels and tracks complete.' 'One 88 mm and crew captured, also two 40 mm.' Then at 0530 – a moment never to be forgotten – came an excited Ulster voice over the radio: 'By God, we've got it – I say again – bridge captured intact and demolitions disarmed, three officers and eighty ORs PW now on their way back.' The Ulsters, nicknamed by the enemy 'Der Schwim Panzers', had done magnificently but had lost ten KIA and forty-four wounded, but had accounted for over 200 of the opposition.

Mein Kampf

Captain John Meredith gave a vivid description of Bremen:

> A shambles of tangled tram wires, cratered gas mains and fallen buildings. Open sewers gaped and smelt. The devastation of the factories and docks was indescribable. Mountains of rubble later removed by armoured bulldozers. Emergency wells prevented a water famine. In a prosperous shipbuilder's house was a copy of *Mein Kampf* on a round coffee table. The Brigadier wrote on the flyleaf: 'This illuminating volume is left to you by courtesy of the British Liberation Army. If you can believe it, you can believe anything. It is left in the hope that you will study its follies in the years to come.'

'Heroic Twilight'

Major Raymond Burt, 22nd Dragoons, whose squadron had been supporting 2 RUR, 2 Lincolns and 1 KOSB, described the last days of Bremen:

> So this was how the city was falling – without fight, in rain, and betrayed by those who had brought it to its present squalor. For all their boasts and

AVREs on the road to Bremervorde, 1 May 1945. (Birkin Haward)

Assault bridge at Bremervorde, 2 May 1945. (Birkin Haward)

threats, the Nazi leaders had gone and the city was abandoned to a few thousand AA gunners and marines and the old men and women and children who waited our arrival in the air-raid shelters. The advances into the suburbs were something of a formality. But they were carried out, block by block, with care and precision – companies and supporting tanks leapfrogging through one another along the silent and mined streets. It looked formidable enough: the road blocks were defensible. Slit trenches and anti-tank ditches had been dug across street intersections: enormous land-mines had been laid and wired ready for explosion by the roadsides. The windows of the ruined houses provided the 'heroic twilight' of the Nazis of the city of Bremen. But no shot was fired.

Hitler's war was running down – it had collapsed into a dreary mopping up operation which went on because no one in authority had the desire to cry 'stop!' What was left of Bremen was formally surrendered by the Burgomaster in the evening of 26 April. In disbelief we saw ourselves surrounded by acre after acre of ruin that either fire or high explosive had created. It seemed to be a signal not only of the defeat of Germany but also the death of civilization.

The Surrender of Hamburg

Admiral Doenitz had ordered General Keitel to order General Woltz to surrender the city of Hamburg to the Desert Rats. That night (1 May) on the German radio could be heard Wagner's 'Death of Siegfried' and 'the end of Adolf Hitler fighting [sic] to the last against the Bolshevik hordes'. Next day it was 'Goebbels Kaput', or words to that effect. Hitler and Goebbels had committed suicide and Admiral Doenitz was now the Führer. Negotiations were continuing with Field Marshal Montgomery for unconditional surrender of all German forces facing 21st Army Group. 11th Armoured Division had reached Lübeck on 2 May, 30 miles away from the Russians at Rostock.

Just after 1600 on the 3rd, the Desert Rats set off through Harburg, flattened by the RAF, initially in pouring rain and later in the late-afternoon sun, to cover the 8 miles across the two remarkably ugly bridges over the Elbe into Hamburg. By 1715 Lieutenant Colonel Wainman had led the Cherry Pickers into the main square, followed by 1/5th Queen's and 5th RTR. The civilians were under strict curfew and stayed indoors. The roads through the rubble were lined with police, who presumably had just returned from the Harburg front line. The adjutant of the Queen's, Captain R.G. Newell, hoisted the regimental flag over the Rathaus (town hall), Brigadier Spurling accepted General Wolz's surrender and 9th DLI took over control of the two vital river bridges.

Hamburg had Ceased to Exist

Lieutenant Brett-Smith's (11 Hussars) diary is revealing:

The first thing that struck us was the incredible tidiness of the place. Everything that the RAF had claimed was true. Hamburg had ceased to exist. Yet the streets were absolutely clear, the telephone lines and tram wires were in perfect order and we drove down wide empty streets on either side of which were heaps of rubble which had once been houses. There was no broken glass, nothing lying about the streets: the German clearance organization must have been brilliant. But all the same the damage was terrific. Not single houses but whole streets were flat. Sometimes you would see a row of houses standing but on looking closer they were only empty shells. In Adolf Hitler Platz the garrison commander – a rather fat man with spectacles – stood outside the Town hall which was curiously intact. A water-bug of the 1/5th Queen's flashed through the square, obviously miles adrift. Colonel Wainman arrived in his Dingo dressed in an American combat jacket, a pair of corduroy trousers and an 11th Hussars cap. He produced a packet of Army biscuits and proceeded to feed the pigeons walking sedately round the square.

The Final Round-up

On the outskirts of Lübeck the 23rd Hussars encountered, according to their historian:

A wild delirious crowd of Allied POW who surged forward, many of them British. They swarmed round the tanks, white, emaciated, hungry, footsore but riotously happy. Down the road came crowds, more German soldiers, a hopeless, defeated mob, caring nothing but that they should be able to surrender, lie down and sleep and not worry about fighting any more. They came in large cars, small cars, dusty yellow lorries, in carts, bicycles and on their weary legs. They came in hordes – Marines, Panzers, Gunners, even the once redoubtable SS.

Generals arrived in twos and threes, politely or arrogantly, but all to surrender. Simon Frazer, 15/19th Hussars, reported that every visible roof in Lübeck was painted with huge red crosses, or white crosses on red roofs.

There they were, literally hundreds of them, tired, cold and wet and hungry German soldiers. They had been lying down so thick on the ground that little grass was visible. They were dragging themselves to their feet. We were literally surrounded by thousands of exhausted men. They posed absolutely no threat. They had not eaten for three days, many were ill or wounded. There was no room for them in Lübeck, which had been converted into a vast hospital.

Battles on the Baltic Coast

23rd Hussars/8 RB pressed on towards Travemunde and Neustadt, north of Lübeck on the Baltic coast. The great bay was full of shipping and the ships and U-boats were attacked by RAF Typhoons and the Comets of the 23rd Hussars. The Fifes also sank a ship in Lübeck harbour. The U-boats had AA guns but the Typhoons destroyed two large ships which blazed from end to end and capsized. Unfortunately the SS had imprisoned their own political prisoners on board one of them. The majority had had no food for eight days. On the appearance of the RAF the SS guards had opened fire, run up the Nazi flag and made off, leaving the exhausted prisoners to burn alive. The Inns of Court, ever in the lead, had assembled a great many prisoners in front of the Hussars, and they were passed back down the line. Watches, cameras, useless Marks and trinkets of all kinds were acquired by 'searchers'. Everyone waited for orders to head for Copenhagen, perhaps to meet up with the Russian armies. Rumours spread. David Swiney with 'Todforce', who had appeared after the Kankelau battle and arrived at Niendorf, wrote: 'We looked after some of the 20,000 prisoners at Lübeck and prepared for the assault on Kiel.'

Altogether 11th Armoured Division took 70,000 POW in the period 2–4 May, including twenty-five generals and admirals.

Major David Swiney's 'Todforce' troop occupied a camp at Eckenforde:

82nd Assault Squadron RE celebrate the ceasefire at Grossenhain, 4 May 1945. (Birkin Haward)

'My troop escorted several U-boat crews to Kiel. They were arrogant, defiant and sang most of the way, including the song (translated) "We're marching against England".'

Everyone went Crazy with Joy

'The last few hours of 4 May will remain clear in our memories for ever. We were sitting in our headquarters [in Strukdorf], with the wireless booming out dance music. Suddenly a little before nine o'clock the music stopped and all was quiet. Then the voice of the announcer rang out – you could have heard a pin drop in the room. "The German armies facing the 21st Army Group have surrendered to Field Marshal Montgomery." Everyone went crazy with joy. Very lights and tracer bullets were soon making a crazy pattern in the sky and people were madly rushing about shaking hands with each other and slapping each other on the back. Fantastic rejoicing went on till the early hours and every drop of liquor accumulated during the past months was soon exhausted.' [Major Noel Bell, 8 RB]

Envoi

'We were young men. We had trained – lived – fought and died together. There was a bond between us that cannot be defined. When the chips are down, the only help available is the man next to you. We knew we could rely on one another. Thank you Joe – Stan – Bert – Ken – Johnny – Sid – Bill – Percy and oh so many more of my friends. Thank you for my life. I hope I am worthy of your sacrifice. I feel great sadness in losing so many dear friends, and immense pride in having had the privilege to have served with them. I would not have missed it for the world.' [Private Albert Kings, 1st Worcesters]

'Sadness in losing so many dear friends'

Index